Praise for **Biblical Principles for Becoming Debt Free!**

"There is a message of deliverance as well as a mandate to disciplined living here—a balance I pray will bless multitudes."

—Dr. Jack W. Hayford, Chancellor
The King's College & Seminary

"Do you want freedom to pursue all of God's destiny for your life? A crucial step toward realizing this is to break financial bondage. *Biblical Principles for Becoming Debt Free!* is your practical and exciting guidebook for making this happen!"

—Dr. C. Peter Wagner, Chancellor
Wagner Leadership Institute

"It is a privilege for me to highly recommend the book, *Biblical Principles for Becoming Debt Free!* One of the absolutely most devastating consequences of our economy is the debt load that so many people carry. I have counseled with thousands over the years, and can state unequivocally that being debt-free is better than having any debt whatsoever. I want to encourage you to take to heart what God has to say about living your life with the financial freedom that comes from being debt-free."

—Ron Blue, President
Christian Financial Professionals Network

"Frank Damazio and Rich Brott's work, *Biblical Principles for Becoming Debt Free!* equips you to do exactly what it promises: 'rescue your life and liberate your future!' This book provides you with a key, explains the required attitude, assigns the responsibility, clarifies the biblical principle, then gives you the practical application. The Key section will open the door of opportunity and informed action. The 'I Can' attitudes of the second section enable and encourage you to realize you can be debt free—break bad spending habits—choose to pay cash—and ultimately change your attitude and change your life! The third section assigns responsibility to you—for acknowledgment, productivity, diligence, generous giving, seeking financial wisdom. The Biblical Principle section covers in-depth insight into the scriptural perspective of finances—dealing with things like 'First Things First' and 'Tomorrow Thinking' and 'The Biblical Principle of A Good Name.' Then finally—there are 35 practical applications to put these biblical principles to work in your life—and your finances. You'll find yourself ultimately making financial decisions based on sound scriptural principles. Your life is rescued; your future is liberated!"

—Tom F. Tenney

"Frank Damazio and Rich Brott have developed an outstanding resource for getting our financial houses in order. This resource is not only practical; it is solidly biblical. It provides a great framework for any Sunday school, small group or personal study."

—BILL GREIG III, PRESIDENT
Gospel Light Publishing

"Teaching us how to avoid the debt trap with sound biblical teachings, this exceptional helpful manual gets right to the point. I highly recommend it to you!"

—CHEN HUI LIN, DIRECTOR OF MASS MEDIA
Campus Crusade Asia, Singapore

"Within the Church are wonderful people who genuinely love the Lord. They love the message of being used by the Lord for Kingdom purposes. However, there is a problem these people face. Personal debts hang over them like a dark cloud. Their debts keep them from being involved with the dreams God has placed within their hearts."

"Rich Brott and Frank Damazio in their book, *Biblical Principles for Becoming Debt Free!* have answers. Guidelines for building wealth also are provided. Every believer will greatly benefit from this incredibly timely and practical guidebook. I highly recommend it for individuals and for small groups. Your life and your finances will never be the same!"

—DR. BARBARA WENTROBLE, FOUNDER AND PRESIDENT
Wentroble Christian Ministries

"I just finished *Biblical Principles for Becoming Debt Free!*. I found it to contain profound truth in a way that was easy to understand with great practical application strategies. I know that one will do what the book suggests their lives and finances will be revolutionized. This is a much needed message in this millennium."

—CHRISTINE CAINE, HILLSONG NETWORK COORDINATOR
Hillsong Church, Sydney, Australia

"In their book, *Biblical Principles for Becoming Debt Free!*, Frank Damazio and Rich Brott have touched the pulse of society and offered biblical answers for a 21st century scourge—debt. Step by step, this teaching will lead you beyond a world of bondage and worry into the freedom and joy of debt-free living. Chock full of wisdom and practical applications, this book will help you break bad habits, adjust flawed attitudes, and change your financial life forever!"

—MARILYN HICKEY, FOUNDER AND PRESIDENT
Marilyn Hickey Ministries

"What a two-man team! This is an extremely talented team of great men. Frank Damazio and Rich Brott are to be applauded again. Now they have added a great book to stand along their recently released book, *Family Finance Handbook*. This two-book set will greatly enhance your life and your financial future."

—JIM ROAM, FOUNDER
Christ Life Church, Tempe, Arizona

"In an age of surging materialism, financial freedom alludes most people, including, unfortunately, many Christians. This should not be so, as God's will for us is that we live with our own needs met and with enough to give away. The book you hold in your hand is packed with outstanding practical keys for becoming debt free—all based on biblical principles. I enthusiastically recommend it!"

—MARK CONNER, SENIOR MINISTER
Waverley Christian Fellowship, Melbourne, Australia

"This new book by Frank Damazio and Rich Brott will give you the desire, vision and practical know-how to achieve financial progress and freedom from debt!"

—KAREN MINNIS, SPEAKER OF THE HOUSE
Oregon House of Representatives

"One writer said, 'When your outgo exceeds your income, then your upkeep will be your downfall.' Each year, millions fall into debt traps, which impact virtually every area of their lives. *Biblical Principles for Becoming Debt Free!* is an easy read filled with wisdom that can emancipate those who apply its tenets.

—TED HAGGARD, SENIOR PASTOR
New Life Church, Colorado Springs, Colorado

"Debt has emerged as one the great limiters of our day, for individuals and families alike. Many desire the freedom and peace of mind of debt-free living, but don't know how to achieve it. This new resource from Frank Damazio and Rich Brott will show you how! Read it with an expectation for a brighter future."

—DICK IVERSON, FOUNDER AND CHAIRMAN
Ministers Fellowship International

Biblical Principles for becoming
Debt Free!

RESCUE YOUR LIFE & LIBERATE YOUR FUTURE

CITYCHRISTIAN
PUBLISHING

Published by City Christian Publishing
9200 NE Fremont
Portland, Oregon 97220

Printed in U.S.A.

City Christian Publishing is a ministry of City Bible Church, and is dedicated to serving the local church and its leaders through the production and distribution of quality materials. It is our prayer that these materials, proven in the context of the local church, will equip leaders in exalting the Lord and extending His kingdom.

For a free catalog of additional resources from City Christian Publishing please call 1-800-777-6057.

Biblical Principles for Becoming Debt Free!
© Copyright 2005 by Richard A. Brott

ISBN: 1-886849-85-4

Cover Design by DesignPoint, Inc.
Interior design and typeset by Katherine Lloyd, Bend, Oregon

All Scripture quotations, unless otherwise indicated, are taken from the *Holy Bible, New International Version*® NIV®. Copyright © 1973, 1978, 1984 by International Bible Society. Used by permission of Zondervan Publishing House. All rights reserved.

Other Versions used are:
American Standard Version, 1901.
KJV-King James Version. Authorized King James Version.
NASB-Scripture taken from the New American Standard Bible, ©1960, 1962, 1963, 1968, 1971, 1972, 1973, 1975, 1977 by The Lockman Foundation. Used by permission.
NKJV-Scripture taken from the New King James Version. Copyright © 1979, 1980, 1982 by Thomas Nelson, Inc. Publishers. Used by permission. All rights reserved.
TLB-Verses marked (*TLB*) are taken from The Living Bible © 1971.
Used by permission of Tyndale House Publishers, Inc., Wheaton, IL 60189. All rights reserved.

Every effort has been made to supply complete and accurate information. However, neither the publisher nor the authors assume any responsibility for its use, nor for any infringements of patents or other rights of third parties that would result.

First Edition, January 2005

This publication is designed to provide interesting reading material and general information with regard to the subject matter covered. It is printed, distributed and sold with the understanding that neither the publisher nor the author is engaged in rendering legal, accounting, investing, financial or other professional advice. If any such advice is required, the services of a competent professional person should be sought.

About the Authors

RICHARD A. BROTT

Rich Brott holds a Bachelor of Science degree in Business and Economics and a Master of Business Administration.

Rich has served as CEO of some very successful businesses. He has functioned on the board of directors for churches, businesses, charities and served on advisory boards for colleges. Formerly the Family Life pastor at City Bible Church, Rich currently serves as the director of City Bible Publishing.

He has authored four books, including his most recent CBP bestseller titled the *Family Finance Handbook*. He and his wife, Karen, have been married for 33 years. The Rich Brott family has three children: Julie, Jana and Nathaniel and son-in-law Ollie White.

FRANK DAMAZIO

Frank Damazio and his Australian-born wife, Sharon, have four children and live in Portland, Oregon. After graduating from Portland Bible College in 1976, he taught full-time at PBC until 1981. He then pioneered a successful church in Eugene, Oregon, until 1992. Returning to Portland, he succeeded Pastor Dick Iverson as senior pastor of City Bible Church in October of 1995.

City Bible Church is a large and influential 4000 member church in the city of Portland. Pastor Frank Damazio leads the City Pastor's Network in city prayer and intercession, citywide racial reconciliation and city leadership.

Along with his Bachelor of Theology degree, Pastor Frank also holds a Master of Divinity degree from Oral Roberts University. He is currently president of Portland Bible College and vice-chairman of Ministers Fellowship International, a fellowship of several hundred ministers and missionaries. He has authored several books: *The Making of a Leader, Developing the Prophetic Ministry, Effective Keys to Successful Leadership, The Vanguard Leader, Seasons of Revival, Seasons of Intercession, From Barrenness to Fruitfulness, Crossing Rivers and Taking Cities, The Gate Church, The Power of Spiritual Alignment*, and his most recent work, *Miracles: Receiving the Miracles Prepared for You*.

A DEDICATION TO ALL

This book is dedicated to all the people who have a deep desire to rescue their life and liberate their future. In the process they will become debt free, stay debt free and become financially independent. Consequently, they will become free to bless the purpose of God and His kingdom, having entered into prosperity with a purpose.

TO MY FRIEND & MENTOR

I dedicate this book to **Jim and Sharon Roam** of Tempe, Arizona. Jim and Sharon were my first pastors after I left home for college. Jim quickly became my spiritual leader and personal mentor; believing in me when I didn't believe in myself. Over the years, he made it possible for me to learn in many ways. At his personal urging, I have walked successfully through many open doors.

The Roams have been senior pastors for the past 39 years. Exceptionally strong leaders and builders, they have excelled in taking small congregations and building them into very successful churches; large in numbers with great facilities; leading hungry people into significant spiritual growth. The entire Roam family have shepherds' hearts; warm, friendly, always caring about the well being of others. Their deep, sincere love and humility radiates to each person they touch, making each one feel like a part of their extended family. They are persons of excellence; people builders, rare and precious! Just a few short years ago the Roams founded Christ Life Church in their living room. God has once again blessed the work of their hands. Just a week before Jim was taken home to be with the Lord, Christ Life's regular attendance was near 1000 people.

A few days ago, God decided that Jim had suffered long enough from a very rare bone disease and invited him home to his eternal reward. My wife Karen and I will miss him greatly! Jim was a man of God, a man of purpose, a man of vision. He had a unique ability to see the dream as if it was already a reality. He lived his life with great passion and zeal, balanced with patience, organization and hard work.

Both Jim and Sharon exhibit all of the Christ-like characteristics that I have always desired. They have been people of impeccable character and integrity, modeling the very persona of Christ. They have always been especially encouraging; believing that all people can become better when given a chance to respond to biblical teaching and personal encouragement.

Thank you, Jim and Sharon, for believing in us. It has been a privilege to have been mentored and loved by both of you. It is with great thanksgiving and enthusiasm that we dedicate this book to you Sharon and to the memory of Jim Roam. You have profoundly impacted our lives; thank you for being such a blessing to us!

Rich Brott

Section Contents

Contents

Section IV: The Biblical Principle

Section V: The Practical Application

Foreword

*D*ebt is a "cancer" that cripples the lives of many. Not only does it affect individuals, it also often leads to the breakdown of families, relationships and businesses, tearing up the very fabric of otherwise successful and affluent societies. With the proliferation of hard-sell marketing tactics coupled with the increasing ease of obtaining credit, it is truly not easy for one to live a debt-free life.

The message of debt-free living has always been a key biblical principle in the kingdom of God. Jesus Christ Himself came to set us free from the debt of sin. Debt is never a normal part of Christian life and it must be avoided at all cost!

I commend the timely release of this book by Frank Damazio and Rich Brott. It provides clear and timeless biblical principles that guide every believer towards taking the practical steps necessary for a life of effective stewardship and financial liberty.

—REVEREND DR. KONG HEE
Senior Pastor
City Harvest Church
Singapore

Preface

*T*his book is all about refusing to live a lifestyle of debt. If you are not ready to commit to that, this book is not for you. If you are happy with your lifestyle and debt is not a burden or concern to you or anyone you care about, then don't read this book. However, if you need real help in the area of finances and want to rescue your life and liberate your future, then you have come to the right place.

What does it mean to become debt free? Is this an achievable reality? Can one truly become free from all debt? If so achieved, is it then possible to remain without debt?

To be debt free means to owe nothing: no auto debt, no credit card debt, no education debt and no mortgage debt. Any person can become debt free, no matter what their current load of debt.

In this book you will be shown how that is achievable. First the bigger picture is written about and then it is narrowed down to the little steps, the minor tweaks and the daily decisions that must be made to continue on the debt free path.

To become debt free for life, certain areas of your life must be confronted in an honest, open and accurate manner. You must confront the following areas:

- spiritual
- attitudinal
- habitual
- practical
- personal

Addressing only selective areas of your financial life will not get you to a place of becoming debt free. You must be willing to tackle each area and come face to face with the glaring reality of your past decisions. This means a new determination to change past spiritual decisions and a change of attitude toward money.

It means that old habits have to be reversed and new practical steps taken, not only to repay existing debt, but to avoid new debt. It means a new lifestyle change and the acceptance of personal responsibility for every financial decision.

No more excuses can be tolerated. No longer can you blame circumstance, your employer, your parents or your spouse. It is time for personal accountability and the acceptance that only you can help or hurt yourself. No longer can you blame someone or something else.

What is debt? Debt is nothing more than borrowing from your future income to buy now what you cannot afford to purchase with current income. The only problem with borrowing money is that you have to pay it back. No pressure on a household is quite like the burden of debt. The pressure to repay debt can feel like the powerful tentacles of a giant sea monster pulling you down into the suffocating deep.

A much spoken axiom is "live within your means." While that is very good beginning advice for those who dive into heavy debt by "living beyond their means," it hardly provides for one financially over the long haul. Getting out of debt is an attitude before it is an action. To live a life that is debt free, bondage free and heading happily towards a comfortable retirement requires a different pattern of living.

Financially, you must "live below your means." If you have been living above your means, you are already in serious debt with no hope of becoming debt free unless you quickly change your financial habits. If you have been living within your means, you may be debt free, but you have little or no savings or investments to carry you through your retirement. What you must begin to do is live below your means. The book will show you how to do just that.

Introduction

When considering a lifestyle free from debt, secular financial understanding is not enough and it becomes woefully insufficient in the long-term perspective. If you only choose the practical aspects of this book and don't first understand God's principles, it will only leave you with holes in your pocket.

Spiritual principles cannot be ignored. Faith, obedience, giving God His due, giving to the poor, giving to the church through offerings, living a principled life and on and on will help you ultimately become debt free.

Haggai 1:6

"You plant much but harvest little. You have scarcely enough to eat or drink and not enough clothes to keep you warm. Your income disappears, as though you were putting it into pockets filled with holes!" (*TLB*).

Malachi 3:10-11

"'Bring all the tithes into the storehouse so that there will be food enough in my Temple; if you do, I will open up the windows of heaven for you and pour out a blessing so great you won't have room enough to take it in! Try it! Let me prove it to you! Your crops will be large, for I will guard them from insects and plagues. Your grapes won't shrivel away before they ripen,' says the Lord Almighty" (*TLB*).

In *Biblical Principles for Becoming Debt Free!* five essential areas are addressed: The Key, The Attitude, The Responsibility, The Biblical Principle, and The Practical Application. While separated by section titles, these important areas overlap, interweave and have connectivity throughout.

It is my conviction that you could sum up the entire book with five simple values. They are listed as keys in the first section. Here they are: Stop spending on yourself, start giving to others, discipline your cash attitude, begin to live below your means and start saving for your future. Learn these basics effectively and you will be well on your way to living a debt-free life.

Next, the all-important attitudes are listed. A proper attitude and approach to your financial affairs is not only exemplary, but also necessary. They are the *I Can* attitudes. Not only are they life changing, but also very attainable. With the right guidance, you can become debt free. With the proper attitude, you can break bad spending habits. With enough self-discipline, you can pay cash instead of using credit. You can renew your thinking, change your flawed value system and rise above your burden of debt. If you are financially accountable, you can enjoy life without spending massive amounts of money. If you will let us help you to discover financial solutions and change your improper attitudes, you can change your life!

You have some personal responsibilities to fulfill as well. Some are very basic, such as simply acknowledging that God owns it all. Others have to do with productivity, time management and learning how to plan ahead. If you are to lead a prosperous and successful life, you must apply biblical instruction to work hard and lead a disciplined live. Then there is the responsibility of diligence, not being wasteful and knowing how to be good stewards in the handling of our possessions. We are to be accountable in caring for our resources, give generously to God and seek wisdom in matters of finances.

While the Bible is full of principles, just a few are mentioned in this book. Of course partnering with God in every area is basic, seeking His will and way first, focusing on giving rather than getting and understanding the principle of open heavens. Resisting the views of the world in handling our personal finances means we do not trust in riches, money or possessions. These things will pass. But we do trust in God as our sole provider and the controller of our life.

Millions of people today are on a quest to accumulate possessions and wealth. It is hard to be content with what we have when the world's entire system is geared toward making us unhappy with everything we have and wanting everything we don't have. From advertising to attitude, we face a discontented culture. How much money does it take to be content? Usually just a little bit more. Money cannot buy contentment or happiness. It is hard for us to be satisfied with what we do have, but we need to strive for contentment and contend for happiness.

Finally, the book touches on the very practical issues of life and the very fundamental financial decisions that must be made. When you have debt, change is necessary. You must make a decision to change your attitude, lifestyle and spending habits and invest in a new you. When your debts are high and your monthly income is not enough to cover the payments, there are ways to solve your debt problem. However, the road to financial recovery takes a total commitment.

When you make a decision to change, it must be firmly rooted in the knowledge of what got you there in the first place. You must know why you feel like you work your entire week just to serve a lender. It's really nothing new, as the Bible clearly summed up this same situation many years ago. Proverbs 22:7 says, "The rich rule over the poor, and the borrower is servant to the lender."

If you are going to rescue your life and liberate your future by breaking free from your bondage of debt, not only will you be repaying current debt, but you must also not add any new debt. You ought to decide once and for all that you will not take on new debt and not become a slave to your old habits. Decide that you will not borrow new money for any reason or purchase additional merchandise on credit. When it comes to personal finances, the Bible clearly teaches that debt is a big fat negative and it is to be avoided if at all possible.

It will be impossible for you to get out of debt and stay out of debt without a written budget. A written budget helps you plan for your expenses in advance, before your income arrives. By planning in advance and following your predetermined budget, you will not spend money on things not already in your budget. The most important part of making a budget work is not how the budget is set up. The most important part of the budget process is you! You are the only one who can make it work.

Becoming debt free is only the beginning. The simple truth is that getting out of debt is only the first step. That is how you get to the starting point. Staying out of debt and moving forward to financial independence—that's the bigger challenge. And that's where the big rewards await.

People can become disciplined, pay off their existing debt and make it to the starting line. Are they progressing or did they mistake the starting line for the finish line? How many of them grabbed the prize and went back to their old ways of living and thinking?

Many people have repaid a boatload of debt, only to fall back into the temptation and into the old ways of piling up debt. How can we encourage people not to stop…but to move on to the next level and beyond? Is it possible to win over debt for a lifetime?

You have to get to the starting line, establish your long-term goal of reaching financial freedom, define that goal in terms of steps and then change gears from debt-recovery to debt-prevention. You have to think specifically, not generally, about how you're going to get there and then rejoice because each step from now on will be one of progress, not repair.

There is a planning process that you should be aware of. What is involved in the planning process? Planning is outlining a course of action in order to achieve a goal, thus fulfilling a desired objective. It is predetermining today a course of action for tomorrow. It is throwing a net over tomorrow and making something happen. It is being tomorrow-minded rather than yesterday-minded.

The only way to reach a financial goal is to work at it. The most important step in reaching that goal is to develop a plan to achieve it. That's why it is so important to plan ahead for your retirement and your financial future. While the idea of planning ahead and building a solid financial strategy for success can sometimes be intimidating and overwhelming, once you get started, it will become easier. With a little planning and a better understanding of what your investment options are, you too can successfully manage your money and pursue your financial goals.

So there you have it. Only *you* can make a difference in your financial life. You can be led to the well, but only you can quench your thirst. If you desire real change in your life and are tired of the crushing load of debt from poor decisions you have made and bad habits in your past, then read on. There is hope for you and light at the end of your financial tunnel. You are about to rescue your life and liberate your future!

Rich Brott

Section One

The
Key

Stop Spending on Yourself

*L*et me be very forthright and direct with you. You already have enough. Stop buying more things! You don't need everything. You don't need the latest, the greatest, the biggest or the best.

Quit watching television commercials. Stop listening to those who are trying their best to convince you that you just have to buy their product. After all, it will help you live a better, more fulfilled, more satisfied life, will keep you in better health and make everyone else want to be your friend. They don't care a flip about your well being; they just want your money, or your credit card.

Now I want to get right in your face and say this: Living below your means *is* possible. It is just a matter of making different choices; right decisions.

How much is enough? How many things are sufficient? Specifically, just how much money do you need to spend on yourself and just how many things do you need to live in this world? How many possessions must you accumulate to feed your appetite for having it all?

Are you happy only when you indulge your every whim to spend more money on yourself, or can you actually be happy curbing your craving for more and more? Is it possible to place self-imposed limits on your current lifestyle and restrict your personal spending? Are you spending your cash for need or greed?

If you find that your spending is out of control and you cannot resist buying more things for yourself, building up your resistance to impulse buying is a discipline you need immediately. The traits of godly people are characterized by the spiritual disciplines to which they submit. Whether it be prayer, purity, integrity, humility, diligence, faithfulness and obedience or selflessness, leadership, servanthood and financial stewardship. These are all important. Economic disciplines include time management, wise spending, hard work, financial stewardship and debt restraint.

What is the key to achieving success in all these areas? The key to success is that of personal discipline. Just as the daily disciplines of exercise, training and hard work successful athletes must practice, so you must approach your desire to stop spending money on yourself. Often it simply comes down to this: Say "no" and have the steadfastness to keep yourself out of temptation's path.

Rescue your life and liberate your future!
Stop spending on yourself!

Start Giving to Others

*G*iving to others brings indescribable pleasure. An inward joy comes to you when you have reached out and helped others. Whether it be in monetary gifts or simply rolling up your sleeves and helping out the old-fashioned way, the act of giving brings its own reward. When you give first, your own personal needs will be automatically taken care of. After all, giving is the Lord's work. It is Christianity in action. Jesus Christ had something to say about giving to others.

Matthew 25:35-40

"'For I was hungry and you gave me something to eat, I was thirsty and you gave me something to drink, I was a stranger and you invited me in, I needed clothes and you clothed me, I was sick and you looked after me, I was in prison and you came to visit me.' Then the righteous will answer him, 'Lord, when did we see you hungry and feed you, or thirsty and give you something to drink? When did we see you a stranger and invite you in, or needing clothes and clothe you? When did we see you sick or in prison and go to visit you?' The King will reply, 'I tell you the truth, whatever you did for one of the least of these brothers of mine, you did for me.'"

In the verses, Jesus was not just speaking about seasonal giving. Of course, during the holiday season of Thanksgiving and Christmas many of us tend to think more often about giving to others. Some people think of giving only around these holidays. It is pleasant to give gifts to children and family, but how much more desirable is it to give gifts to someone who cannot return the favor, to someone who is not expecting anything from you? What about your giving the other 11 months of the year? How can you be a giver during that time?

Many Scriptures in the Bible talk about giving. They instruct us how to give, when to give, where to give, why we give and what to give. All these verses are not meant to bring us down, point a finger in our face or discourage us. They are there to bring us happiness, merriment and a sense of well being! It is wonderful to be a giver in every sense of the word! The unhappy people in life are those who keep everything for themselves. They are the discontented ones who are selfish, living life only to please themselves and chase after their own personal wants.

Giving is fun! Giving is exciting! Just try to give something away without feeling wonderful. The non-giver is a very miserable individual. When you are feeling blue and discouraged, try giving of yourself to others. Give away something and discover what you receive in return. You will receive happiness, hope, a sense of peace and well being, and instant encouragement will come your way. Give even to your enemies. Drive them absolutely crazy with your selflessness and love.

BE A GOOD STEWARD

Stewardship is a biblical requirement for all Christians. It is all about blessing others, giving to others and practicing the art of putting good intentions to action.

Matthew 25:21

"His master replied, 'Well done, good and faithful servant! You have been faithful with a few things; I will put you in charge of many things. Come and share your master's happiness!'"

The Bible is clear that our position in regard to property is as stewards, not owners. A steward is a guardian of the interests of another. The steward owns nothing, but carefully guards, protects and increases the property of the One he serves. The essential quality of a steward is faithfulness. When we are faithful, God gives us more because we have proven we are diligent to use what He gives us wisely and generously.

1 Chronicles 29:11-14

"'Yours, O LORD, is the greatness and the power and the glory and the majesty and the splendor, for everything in heaven and earth is yours. Yours, O LORD, is the kingdom; you are exalted as head over all. Wealth and honor come from you; you are the ruler of all things. In your hands are strength and power to exalt and give strength to all. Now, our God, we give you thanks, and praise your glorious name. But who am I, and who are my people, that we should be able to give as generously as this? Everything comes from you, and we have given you only what comes from your hand.'"

 The non-giver is a very miserable individual.

This prayer of David reflects the heart of a humble steward. He acknowledges that everything in heaven and earth belongs to God. He recognizes God as the head and ruler of everything, the giver of wealth and honor. God gives us things we may use, but ultimately everything belongs to God. The steward understands total dependence on God and gives generously to the Lord, simply from understanding that everything comes from Him.

GIVE YOUR TIME

Your personal time is very valuable. We know that. In our busy world of work, children, family, school, church and the like, our time might be the hardest thing to give. Yet it is probably the most precious commodity we have. After all, our time on earth is short lived, and we have only so much allotted to us. What we don't use wisely is gone forever. When you give your time to others, they value it strongly. One of God's greatest gifts is time. Time is our tool. It is a wonderful gift. You can give this gift to others. Here are some examples of how you can give your time to others:

- Clean up litter in a neighborhood park.
- Take your family to a church maintenance day.
- Serve your church as greeter, usher, teacher, filing clerk, in visitor follow-up, etc.
- Gather and collect household items for the poor and needy.
- Clean an area of the church, either inside or outside.
- Bake a pie and deliver to your local firemen.
- Mow the grass of an elderly person.
- Visit the sick and incarcerated.
- Volunteer at a soup kitchen.
- Change the oil in the vehicle of a person who has been ill.
- Bake cookies or bread and take them to a shut-in or elderly person.
- Fix broken toys for children.
- Provide childcare for a single mother.
- Gather coats in the fall and distribute to needy families.
- Befriend a lonely person.
- Rake a neighbor's leaves in the fall.
- Prune rosebushes, plant flowers and help older people.
- Write a thank you note and send to your neighborhood police or fire station.

The list of what you can do with your time in service to others is endless. When you give to others, you make a difference in their lives. Often you give them hope and encouragement they cannot find anywhere else. One should always have an attitude of service. This means being aware and anticipating the needs of someone else. This means offering to help instead of waiting to be asked. You serve God by helping others. God is always giving to us continually. We can express His love to others by showing them genuine generosity.

GIVE YOUR MONEY
Exodus 35:5

"From what you have, take an offering for the LORD. Everyone who is willing is to bring to the LORD an offering of gold, silver and bronze…"

This verse advises us that a willing heart is a must for giving offerings. God gave us a free will so we would love Him voluntarily. The same applies to our offerings. He doesn't demand we give more than the tithe, but when we give of our free will, we are telling Him we love Him and our desire is to worship Him with our offerings.

It is required you give to God the tenth of your increase that already belongs to Him, and it is always in our best interest to give above and beyond in offerings and designated gifts, so how else can we be involved in giving? I offer the following suggestions to consider in your giving perspective.

- Give to an overseas missions project.
- Give toward feeding the poor in your city.
- Give to help an unemployed family with their house payment.
- Give to a worthy charity.

Endless special projects and numerous charities could use your money and financial support. So how does one determine to whom to donate hard-earned money? We cannot help all the world, but we can help those with whom we are closest and those whom we have become aware of. Of course we can love the world or help some overseas mission project, but can we love and help our neighbor? What kind of special needs do you have in your own neighborhood?

GIVE YOUR RESOURCES

A Mayan woman in Belize, Central America desired to give a gift to the missionary who had brought her the gospel. She knew the missionary's greatest need was money, though she had none to give for they did not use money in her village. She did not have livestock to give that could be eaten or even an extra portion of vegetables for the missionary to enjoy. All she had was the skill of her hands. She made a living by weaving intricate tapestry, and it took her 40 hours a week for an entire month to produce one. She decided she would work twice as much to produce an extra carpet to give. This offering blessed the missionary's heart more than any sum of money could have because it represented the woman's time, her skill and her heart.

Perhaps you do not have money to give. You can honor the Lord by offering your time and your skill. What are your skills? Are you good at typing? What about volunteering at the church office? Are you good at reading aloud to children? What about volunteering for story time in your church's children's ministry? Your church will probably be very blessed by the offering of your time and skill. There is always a way to give an offering—no matter how tight things are financially—so give with your heart.

Everyone has resources for giving. No, I am not talking about money, nor am I necessarily referring to time, though it could involve our time. I am speaking of those things that can be given for a specific purpose or at a specific time.

What if you are a professional nurse and you know of an elderly person who could use a medical visit from time to time? You can give the gift of your vocation to those you know. Perhaps you are a carpenter and a single mom's porch is badly in need of repairs. Maybe you are a landscaper and you could lend a hand to a disabled household. Maybe you own a truck and a poor family needs a helping hand in moving to a new home. You may be a whiz at science or math and a young neighbor needs some extra tutoring. Get creative in giving your personal resources.

GIVE YOURSELF

We, as the Body of Christ are responsible for the health and welfare of all the parts of the Body. We are also responsible for reflecting the heart of Christ to those in need in our society. One of the most important ways we can give an offering to God, as revealed by the following passage, is by meeting a need. Check your local church to find out if you might be able to meet any needs.

Hebrews 13:16

"And do not forget to do good and to share with others, for with such sacrifices God is pleased."

GIVE BECAUSE GOD IS GOOD
Matthew 12:35

"The good man brings good things out of the good stored up in him, and the evil man brings evil things out of the evil stored up in him."

When our hearts are filled with the goodness of God, we will give from that goodness. Let's allow our hearts to be filled with the following truths about God's goodness.

- God wants to bless your work. (Deuteronomy 28:12)
- God wants to make your work increase and prosper. (Deuteronomy 30:9)
- God will keep His promises to you. (Joshua 21:45)
- The Lord's mercy endures forever. (Ezra 3:11)
- The Lord wants to put His good hand upon you. (Nehemiah 2:8)
- God is good and upright. (Psalm 25:8; 34:8; 100:5)
- God does that which is good. (Psalm 119:68)
- God wants to show you His loving kindness. (Psalm 69:16)
- God is good to the pure in heart. (Psalm 73:1)
- God wants to give every good thing to you. (Psalm 84:11)
- God wants to give you good things and increase your business. (Psalm 85:12)
- God will be abundant in mercy toward you. (Psalm 86:5)
- God wants to give good gifts to you. (Matthew 7:11)
- God is gracious and compassionate. (Exodus 33:19; 34:6)
- God wants to bless you. (Psalm 21:3)
- God wants to allow His goodness to be with you always. (Psalm 23:6)
- God prepares good things for those who fear Him. (Psalm 31:19)
- God gives the power to get wealth. (Deuteronomy 8:18)
- God gives strength and power to His people. (Psalm 68:35)
- God gives life to the world. (John 6:33)
- God gives us richly all things to enjoy. (1 Timothy 6:17)

- God has the power to do anything. (Isaiah 40:21-22)
- God has the power to create something from nothing. (Psalm 33:6-9)
- God is sovereign and there is nothing too hard for Him. (Jeremiah 32:17-19)

Rescue your life
and liberate your future!
Start giving to others!

Discipline Your Cash Attitude

*L*et's get serious about disciplining your cash attitude. The bottom line is this: When you pay with cash, you will buy less. You will pay less. You will want less. The professionals are quick to point out that consumers purchase one-third less when paying with cash. The flip side is that when you use credit for purchases, you may buy more than you could possibly need or use, pay more for the item and pay more interest. When you overspend, you not only pay much more, but you also severely retard your ability to save and invest.

All the places that are trying to sell you everything from cars to furniture to plasma TVs, also entice you to sign on the dotted line by offering so-called "free financing," 90 days same as cash, interest-free credit, no payments until...etc. Often if you will open an account, they promise a gift. Of course, we've all heard the saying "There is no such thing as a free lunch." And so true it is. Nothing in life is free. It all costs you something. You will pay for everything, and sometimes very dearly.

When you are about to be enticed by these sales clerks, TV marketing or newspaper advertisements, pause and think it through. Ask yourself what is the real cost of the item if you purchased it via a credit account. Is it really something you need, or are you just buying on impulse? Exactly why do you want this item? Just how much and how long will you really use it? If you think that you need it, stop and think, *If you had not gone shopping today, would you even be considering it right now?*

If you truly do need it, is this the best price? If this store is able to offer "interest free" credit, will the next store discount it if you pay cash? Can you afford this purchase? Does it make good money sense? What will happen if you cannot repay the loan? Will making this purchase bring you closer to your financial goals? Is this really such a good deal? If it all seems too good to be true, then perhaps it is.

What are the advantages of paying cash?

Consider the following list:

- You will be less inclined to think you really need the item.
- You will delay your purchase as long as possible to preserve your cash.
- You won't be the impulse buyer you would be when using credit.
- You will always attempt to purchase at a discount to use less of your cash.
- You won't have to worry about destroying your planned budget.

- You won't have to worry about making payments.
- You will choose your purchases more carefully.
- You will not purchase your wants before your needs.
- You will be at peace and the purchase will seem more satisfying when you pay with cash.
- You will take better care of your purchase when you pay with cash.

 ## When you pay with cash, you will buy less.

Some of you may try to excuse yourself and think cash could be dangerous to use for it could be stolen. Yes, perhaps that is true, but using a debit card, which is drawn against your bank account that has the cash, is safe indeed. A debit card has the same purchase safeguards as any credit card. When using a debit card, the amount of the purchase is automatically deducted from your checking account as if you had written a check.

Think about it. If you paid cash for an automobile, would you buy a brand new one with all of the extra bells and whistles, or would you be more inclined to purchase a great used model? It's a good feeling to use cash to make major purchases. I don't remember when I last purchased a vehicle on credit. It has been too many years ago. Yes, it does keep me from trading vehicles every year, but

who needs to drive the biggest and the best all the time? Only those whose egos need to be maintained. I purchased all four of my vehicles with cash. Because of that, I don't have a lot of cash, but they were all purchased new without credit. In our family we have a boat, a pickup, an SUV and a family van. Because we all work in different areas of the city, it makes having three separate vehicles a necessity. If the city bus came near our neighborhood, we wouldn't need all three.

It is a great feeling to pay with cash. I was born in the 1950s. Back then, 33% of all vehicles were purchased with cash. My first five cars were purchased with cash. All five were purchased during my high school and college days. I was raised with the attitude that you did not buy something unless you could afford it. You certainly could not afford it unless you could pay in full before taking the purchase home. If you didn't have the money, you saved for it first. It is much better to fund your dreams instead of servicing your debt.

How do you stop adding to your debt load? You simply begin to pay cash for all purchases. If you do not have the cash, you walk away. Using common sense is the best way to stay out of debt. Have the common sense to stop buying on credit and start paying with cash. If you want to freeze the level of your debt, you simply freeze spending.

I took a cyberspace trip to Bankrate.com, used the online calculators and developed the

	MAKING MINIMUM PAYMENTS OF 2%	MAKING MONTHLY INVESTMENTS
	$34.24	$34.24
Total Purchase Cost:	$18,931	$0
Total Investment:	$0	$18,931
Money at Age 65:	$0	$933,682

following calculations. If you have credit card debt of just $5,000 at an interest rate of 18% and make a minimum payment of 2% of the unpaid balance, it will take you more than 46 years to pay it off. During that time, the $5,000 purchase will cost you an additional $13,931.13 in interest. If you took on this debt at age 19, you will have it paid just in time for retirement at age 65. This makes your purchase cost a total of $18,931.13. I hope it was worth it!

As if that doesn't hurt enough, another cost is involved here. It is the opportunity cost of what those minimum payments invested at a mere 12% would have brought to you. Divide the total cost of your purchase ($18,931) by the 553 months it took to pay it in full, and you have an average monthly cost of $34.24. Investing that monthly for the same time period in a tax-free account would earn you at least $933,682. So it's quite simple. The choice is yours. Do you want to purchase something at age 19 for $5,000, make the minimum payment and have it paid for at retirement? Or would you rather skip that important credit card purchase and have a cool million at retirement with the very same monthly investment?

These simple statistics will be a wake-up call for many. Time can be a curse or a blessing.

Which will it be for you?

**Rescue your life and
liberate your future!
Discipline your cash attitude!**

Begin to Live Below Your Means

*A*n oft-quoted axiom is "Live within your means." That is good beginning advice for those who dive into heavy debt from living beyond their means, but such advice will hardly provide financially over the long haul.

To live a life that is debt free, bondage free, and to head happily toward a comfortable retirement requires a different pattern of living. Financially, you must live *below* your means.

If you have been living above your means, you are already in serious debt and have no hope of becoming debt free unless you quickly change your financial habits. If you have been living within your means, you may be debt free, but you have little or no savings or investments to carry you through your retirement. What you must begin to do is live below your means.

Why is this important? Unless you believe you will be in excellent health to work in your 90s to provide food for yourself, shelter and the other necessities of life, you need to save and invest for your retirement years. Doing this is not possible if you are living above your means or simply living within your means.

If you spend more than you earn, you have a very serious problem on your hands—the problem is you! Most people do not have an income problem; they have a spending problem. It' s not what you make; it's what you spend. If you have managed to tame the spending tiger within you and are living within your means, you still have further cutbacks to make in your family cash flow. You need to spend below your available income stream. You need to be planning for your retirement. Your government social programs won't provide adequate income for your retirement days—that will be left up to you. It is your responsibility, not your friends', family or government.

Okay, now you understand the necessity of living below your means. What does that really mean? In a nutshell, it simply means you have to spend less money than you earn. It means you do not allow yourself to spend money on things you don't absolutely need or things that just make you happy for a moment or two. It means you save money instead of spend it. It means investing the money that is left over.

The picture of retiring early, gaining wealth and having plenty of money to give to worthy causes is a picture of a happy life. You are the lender, not the debtor. You are the master, not the servant, because you have learned to master yourself. You have learned to discipline your sudden impulses and you have learned the difference between wants and needs. It's not complicated; it's very straightforward. It's living a simpler lifestyle.

A couple of weeks ago, my wife asked me if I had heard of the financial talk-show host Dave Ramsey. I had not. On her way home from work each day, she regularly tunes into the show. My twelve-year-old son also listens to and likes the show. My son, Nathaniel, has always been a money-conscious young man who has been aware of price comparisons, spending habits and financial matters. Since about the age of two, he has always been interested in and commented about things having to do with money. At the early age of about four, he chastised me for purchasing a box of ice cream bars when I could have purchased another box with more bars in it for less money. Of course, at that age, he didn't understand the difference between bars containing ice milk or real ice cream. To this day, he continues to ask questions almost daily about what we spend, how much we owe, will we be able to retire, etc. He seems to have been born with some kind of financial interest gene. At any rate, I now tune my radio to the Dave Ramsey Show on Sundays during our drive home from church. Nathaniel delights in anticipating the answers to the call-in questions before the host responds to the caller.

I like what Dave Ramsey says about living simply. He often notes, "If you will live like no one else, later you can LIVE like no one else." It's a great maxim and one that is true!

The authors of *The Millionaire Next Door*, Thomas Stanley and William Danko, have spent considerable time researching the lives of the affluent and the wealthy. Their research led them to the following conclusions about how the rich in America arrived there and how they continued to stay that way. From their conclusions, they believe the first point is the most important.

- They live below their means.
- They allocate their money, free time and energy to wealth accumulation.
- They prefer achieving financial independence over displaying/flaunting their social status.
- Their parents did not give them free and frequent handouts of money.
- Their children usually become self-sufficient.
- They are skilled in targeting business opportunities.
- They carefully select occupations that complement their skills and talents and that lead to building wealth.

Their studies show that typical millionaires own their own homes but do not live in multi-million-dollar homes or drive expensive cars. More often than not, they buy used cars, bargain for other purchases and live simple lives. They do not live extravagant lifestyles. They usually live frugally.

Seldom do inheritances or advanced degrees build fortunes. The wealthy in America are usually living far below their means and working very hard. Typical millionaires are willing to give up status to instead invest for financial security. The greatest percentage of millionaires are self-made. They are some of the most efficient and resourceful people around. In many cases their children are unaware of their family's wealth. Instead of living in plush New York garden apartments, Beverly Hills or on the Florida waterfront, much of the time, they just live next door in comfortable neighborhoods. Many millionaires are ordinary people who work dull jobs. They have learned important truths: Nothing is more valuable than working hard, saving large sums of money and living well below your means. They have learned the important lesson of living on a budget, accounting for their expenditures and paying close attention to their investments.

The only way for you to provide for your later years is to live below your means. If you want to have any hope of achieving financial independence, you must live far, far below your means. This is not a difficult concept to understand. Although it is very simple, few people do it. Because it is so simple, people tend to discount its effectiveness. The bottom line is this. There is no free lunch, no schemes by which you can get rich quick, no ship coming your way, no lottery with your name on it, and no alternative to plain, old-fashioned hard work.

 Studies show that typical millionaires live frugally.

In our culture, impulse buying is predominant. In years predating the present easy credit, you would walk into a department store, see an item you would like to purchase, and put a small cash down payment toward it and then pay it off monthly until the item was paid for. Once paid for, you took it home and began to enjoy it. Many today fear that without the newest cars, latest toys and exotic vacations, they are missing the train. They find out later that, by buying these things, they risk being run over by the train; the fast charging, mounting-debt train that's about to steamroll over their lives.

In our culture, credit purchases are the norm. Often, before an item has been paid for, it has been discarded. If you think you must have it all now or you cannot be happy, a paradigm shift

must be made in your thinking. In our culture, going in hock up to our eyeballs is the normal thing to do. Our culture and society is all about promoting credit, spending, debt and an "I can have it now" way of life. Buy now; think it through later. Buy now; worry about payment later. Live for today; let tomorrow's worries come later. Beginning a debt-reduction program almost seems countercultural.

Living above your means creates high stress levels. High stress levels affect your health, your spiritual life, your emotional health, your marriage and your financial life. Living within your means lessens this stress. Living below your means decreases the normal stress of life much more. Living far below your means gives you peace of body, soul and spirit.

You can build a huge nest egg for your later years simply by living below your means. Does it mean driving a car that should be abandoned in a junkyard? Not really. Does it mean eating oatmeal seven days a week and drinking only water? Not really, but perhaps that would help you with your weight-loss goals. It does mean monitoring your spending, watching your cash and accounting for every penny spent. It means making conscious financial decisions based upon need and stopping your impulse spending. It means waiting 30/60 days before purchasing, giving you time to come to your senses.

Rescue your life
and liberate your future!
Begin to live below your means!

Start Saving for Your Future

You may be reading this book at a very young age, but you'll get old very quickly, trust me. Someday all of us want to relax and not have to focus on earning money every hour of every day. The best way to prepare for that time in our lives is to begin saving at an early age. Saving while young is simpler, requires less, is habit-forming and is much, much easier. This is not rocket science; it's just simply having time on your side.

What kinds of thoughts come to your mind when I mention the word *saving* to you? Are you immediately having thoughts of dislike, pain, going without, not having any fun, or living cheap? Does it seem you just aren't ready to cope with great sacrifice? Or does the word *saving* have a different feel? Maybe for you it means being prepared for emergencies or planning for retirement. Maybe to you it feels like financial freedom and easy living in your later years. It might even give you dreams of wealth and prestige. Regardless of whatever thoughts come to your mind when you think of beginning a savings plan, the fact remains that there is a definite relationship between saving now and future wealth. You may give up a little of your spending power now, but doing so will yield a whole lot more later. Continually and consistently saving and investing money now will lead to big rewards later.

The secret to becoming wealthy is steady plodding, putting away a few dollars at a time, consistently, week after week for the rest of your life. Adjusting your lifestyle to do this is not only important, but also absolutely necessary. To start saving for the future, you also have to find some money to save. This, of course, mandates that you live below your means; i.e., spend less than you earn.

"How can I begin to save?" you ask. "Where will I get the money?" Basically, you can begin your savings or increase your savings in three ways. First, you can find savings money by reducing your regular expenses. Do without some things you normally buy. Perhaps it's that daily latte or the fast-food snacks. Second, you can find savings money by increasing your income. This may mean a part-time job, or some weekend service you can provide. It might even be a raise or bonus from your regular job. Third, you can find money to save by converting unused/unneeded possessions (assets) into cash. This may be as simple as selling something to a friend or family member (one man's trash is another man's treasure), it may mean having a garage sale, or it can mean getting rid of that adult recreational toy you rarely use. Either way, these three basic options can put savings money into any person's pocket.

Savings and investments are necessary for you to take full responsibility for your future. You provide for your future by accumulating enough wealth to take care of your needs independent of any other person or entity. You accumulate wealth by investing. You invest by first saving dollars for that purpose. You save dollars by finding money to set aside in a savings vehicle. You find money to set aside by living below your means. You live below your means by spending less than you earn. It is very important to begin setting aside money NOW. It does not matter whether you are old or young—now is the time to begin. Tomorrow never seems to come. Of course, by starting at an early age, time is on your side. The following chart shows the annual return on an investment in five-year increments. Of course, one could start at age 50 and have $132,683 by the time he reaches the age of 75. Later, I will chart for you the benefits of starting very young and what the effects of a life of investing will do for you. If you were to begin saving now, an amount of $100 per month, the chart below details your possible investment return showing a variety of percentages and years.

After looking forward to it for many years and planning for it with anticipation, your years of retirement should be a time of enjoyment and a wonderful season in your life. But when the time comes, will you have all of the resources accumulated to allow you to live the life you imagined?

Most people will have to replace 70-80% of their current income at retirement age. Many will want to replace 100% of their pre-retirement income. Because we are living longer and healthier lives, we can expect to live 20-plus years after retirement and to be more active at an older age than previous generations. Then there is the inflation factor. Your accumulated nest egg will be worth much less in purchasing power because of it. Suppose we have an average annual rate of inflation of 4%. If you have $20,000 in current savings, that $20,000 would have to grow to $43,800 to have the same purchasing power 20 years from now.

> The secret to becoming wealthy is steady plodding, putting away a few dollars at a time, consistently, week after week for the rest of your life.

There are a number of ways that derail the best of intentions. Many find themselves on track with their savings and investments and well on their way to financial independence...then something happens. It might be something as simple as your "wants" getting in front of your "needs." One of your "needs" is to provide for your future. It may be a major health problem that sucks up your savings and investments. It is important to do preventive maintenance in this area. Be sure to have adequate health insurance at all times. Don't ever be without it. You also need disability insurance coverage.

Annual Return	5 Years	10 Years	15 Years	20 Years	25 Years
1.5% Bank Account	$6,226	$12,938	$20,171	$27,968	$36,372
5.0% Money Market Fund	$6,800	$15,528	$26,728	$41,103	$59,550
10.0% Stock Mutual Fund	$7,743	$20,484	$41,447	$75,936	$132,683

Other possibilities that might drain your savings are short-term emergencies. Financial emergencies happen in life. You will never be able to predict just when it will happen, how it will happen or where it will happen. But it is a fact of life that it will happen. Without an emergency fund set aside, you are unprepared, and it can be costly and worrisome.

These needs might be new tires for your vehicle, a shortfall in seasonal income, an unexpected house repair—the list could go on forever. Many people face these inconvenient expenses by raiding their savings or retirement funds.

Though cash flow challenges are sure to surface, the answer is not to dip into savings or investments. The answer is to have a separate savings account that is pre-designated for such emergencies. Even before saving for your retirement or preparing for investments, it is of utmost importance to set aside an emergency fund. Though ultimately you will want to have three to six months income set aside in this fund, beginning with at least $500–$1000 will get you started. Depending on your education, experience, job skills, time on the job, etc., you will eventually need up to six months of income saved. Of course, if you are paid on commission or are self-employed, six months might be a minimum to set aside in an emergency fund.

Investing while you are still young has many pluses. If, for instance, you invest at age 22, even if your total contribution is limited, observe what you can still end up with after just putting aside $2,000 per year for only six years. In this example I am using an average return of 12%.

Now let's assume you don't begin to invest early. Note the following chart to see what would happen if you spent all your money from age 22 to age 27 and then decided that you should be investing $2,000 per year.

When you begin saving/investing at an early age, you have a lot of time on your side.

Contribution Amount	Total Accumulation	Age/Number of Years
$2,000	$2,240	22/1
$2,000	$4,509	23/2
$2,000	$7,050	24/3
$2,000	$9,896	25/4
$2,000	$13,083	26/5
$2,000	$16,653	27/6
$0	$18,652	28/7
$0	$20,890	29/8
$0	$23,397	30/9
$0	$41,233	35/14
$0	$72,667	40/19
$0	$128,064	45/24
$0	$225,692	50/29
$0	$397,746	55/34
$0	$700,965	60/39
$0	$1,235,339	65/44
Total Cash Contribution	$12,000	Contributing 6 Years

Compound interest and/or investment growth can put a lot of money into your retirement pocket.

I have a 12-year-old son. Let's say I make a one-time investment into a S&P 500 mutual fund of $1,000 at his current age. (An S&P 500 index fund is a group of stocks considered to be generally representative of the stock market. This index is composed of 400 industrial, 20 transportation, 40 utility and 40 financial companies.) Assuming that neither he nor I ever placed another dime into his account, by the age of 65, at an annual growth rate of 12%, he would have an investment portfolio worth $406,027. Actually, this is exactly what I did for him this year.

Let's look at another scenario. What if I started with that initial investment of $1,000 in a mutual fund that averages a 12% return, compounded monthly. Now say that I set aside $150 each month to add to the fund. My son, should he continue adding to it in the same amount after I am gone, at the young age of 65, assuming he has no other investments whatsoever, his net worth would be $8,949,244.81. This also is what he and I are doing together. He contributes from his earnings and I pitch in with the rest. At age 75, he would have $29,570,476.09.

Rescue your life
and liberate your future!
Start saving for your future!

CONTRIBUTION AMOUNT	TOTAL ACCUMULATION	AGE/NUMBER OF YEARS
$0	$0	22/1
$0	$0	23/2
$0	$0	24/3
$0	$0	25/4
$0	$0	26/5
$0	$0	27/6
$2,000	$2,240	28/7
$2,000	$4,509	29/8
$2,000	$7,050	30/9
$2,000	$25,130	35/14
$2,000	$56,993	40/19
$2,000	$113,147	45/24
$2,000	$212,598	50/29
$2,000	$386,516	55/34
$2,000	$693,879	60/39
$2,000	$1,235,557	65/44
Total Cash Contribution	$74,000	Contributing 37 Years

Section Two

The Attitude

I Can Be Debt Free

*C*an you be debt free? One person says, "I can;" another person says, "I cannot." Which person is correct? Both are correct. If you think you can, most likely you will. It's not so much the power of positive confession or positive thinking as it is the sheer determination of the human spirit to accomplish what he or she sets out to do.

Being in bondage through debt is sort of the modern-day equivalent to ancient times when a peasant served his lord. Debt is probably one of Satan's best natural weapons. Debt binds so many individuals and families that it is hard to think of a stronger bondage. Debt is the source of strife, heavy burdens and marriage problems. Debt keeps us from being free to fulfill the purposes of God in our lives. Debt also keeps us from giving generously, which can heap enormous blessings upon our lives.

Benjamin Franklin said, "When you run in debt, you give to another power over your liberty." Living within your means is simply not going into debt for any purchase. It means you purchase only things you need, not what you want, and you pay cash for things you need instead of trapping yourself in debt by using credit.

The good news is that everyone can become debt free! By not doing so, you are robbing yourself and robbing your future. Instead of going into debt, would it not be better if the money you pay in interest went into a savings account to help you reach your personal financial goals? By purchasing things now on credit, you are limiting your choices and continuing the unfortunate situation of paying for yesterday's unwise decisions with today's income. You are borrowing from tomorrow to satisfy the whims of today.

It is scriptural to become debt free. Romans 13:7-8 tells us, "Give everyone what you owe him: If you owe taxes, pay taxes; if revenue, then revenue; if respect, then respect; if honor, then honor. Let no debt remain outstanding, except the continuing debt to love one another, for he who loves his fellow-man has fulfilled the law."

You can be debt free if you want it badly enough. However long it may take you, it is worth it to begin the journey now. Commit today to become debt free. Don't fill the pockets of the lenders. Instead, fill your own pockets and fund your own dreams.

What is debt? What is a deficit? Do the two words mean the same? We often hear the two used wrongly and completely out of context. In simple terms, we can explain the differences in this way. A deficit is the amount by which a sum of money falls short of the required or expected amount—a shortage. For example, if you have a monthly spending budget that equals your monthly cash inflow, then you are within budget and have no deficit. However, if your spending exceeds your cash income, then you end with a deficit equal to the amount of the excess spending. The government annual budget deficit is the difference between the amount of money the government spends and the amount it collects.

In the previous example, if you continue deficit spending, the accumulated deficit becomes your debt. This debt, of course, is in addition to all other debt you may have. Debt is an obligation or liability to pay or render something to someone else. It is something owed, such as money, goods, or services. Does debt really matter? Does it affect our lifestyles and us? Why should we be interested in becoming debt free?

Why do people go into debt? Usually it is from ignorance of the eventual financial consequences. True enough, sometimes, unforeseen disasters occur that are completely out of a person's control. This may include the loss of a job or gigantic health and medical bills that come out of nowhere. Usually these are rare exceptions. For most people, debt comes by personal choice: having a personal choice, but making the wrong financial decision.

Some people go into debt because they are not aware of the biblical principles that concern the bondage of debt. Others are fully aware of what the Bible says, but, by their actions, imply they believe these are not commands or requirements, rather suggestions to take or leave. First of all, if Scripture records only suggestions, then is the entire Bible a take-it-or-leave-it opportunity? Second, if it were merely a suggested pattern for living, would you not trust it to be the very best advice you could possibly get?

A lot of denial takes place when it comes to the subject of finances, debt, responsibility and financial accountability. You may deny that debt is bad. You may deny that you really have debt. After all, isn't debt just being past due on your payments? Isn't a loan just a contract? Or you may be thinking, *Sure, I owe some money, but it is manageable and my spending really is not out of control.* Or you may say you are young and have plenty of good years to pay off the debt; you can always start reducing your spending tomorrow, or next week, next month or even next year. The problem is that the discipline of tomorrow never comes. I am suggesting that you change your spending behavior right now, today—and make sure that when tomorrow does come, you are well on your way to becoming debt free.

Why do people go into debt? Usually it is from ignorance of the eventual financial consequences.

Why should you become debt free? After all, we needed that new car. Our house must have furniture in it. A closet would be useless without a good stock of new shoes and clothes. Of course, we don't have the money now, but we do have credit cards. I am willing to work hard and put in some occasional overtime so that I can put a little extra toward my debt from time to time. The problem with that kind of thinking is that, every time you attempt to get ahead, you will probably be hit with some other unexpected expense. This is the unintended consequence of debt. Perhaps it is car trouble or an unexpected health-related bill, and because you had neither planned nor budgeted for any unexpected expenses, you seek more credit. This might be another credit card, an extended personal loan or a higher line of credit. At some point though, the deficit spending must stop, the debt must be paid and the savings begun.

Can you become debt free? Yes! Yes, you absolutely can! Why should you desire to become debt free? What should motivate you to stay within a planned budget, pay off debt and keep it paid off? Of course, we could list literally hundreds of reasons, but here are a few to get you started:

1. **To stay physically healthy.** Debt can cause stress, sickness, depression, illness and poor health. Serious illness can occur when you are stressed out and worn out and your will to fight is diminished. Will you be able to have the money to eat properly or will you and your children be malnourished? How about affording to purchase vitamins, minerals and other health supplements? Can you pay for the proper medicines your physician prescribes for you and your family?

2. **To stay emotionally healthy.** Long after the pleasure of the purchase is gone, the emotional baggage of repayment goes on and on. If you decide to go ahead and sell the item you were so excited about owning, it is worth a fraction of what you originally paid for it. That is, of course, assuming that someone actually wants to buy it from you and that it has any value at all. Many of your purchases do not. Much debt is brought on by purchases one cannot even recall.

3. **To stay mentally healthy.** Clear thinking and peace of mind cannot be taken for granted. It is hard to have clarity of thought and difficult to make good, logical and well-reasoned financial decisions when you are stressed under a burden of heavy debt.

4. **To maintain a healthy marriage.** Finances are said to be the number one cause of divorce today. This isn't having money or not having money. It has to do with how we handle our money, our discipline, our integrity, our responsibility for it and our accountability in handling it. Match that with the stress from the weight of debt, along with other communication challenges, and it's a recipe for potential marriage disaster.

5. **To have money for repairs.** If you own or even rent a home, you will need money for repairs and general upkeep. Some examples of possible repairs are a leaky roof, a squeaky furnace, household appliances such as the washer, dryer and refrigerator, and other necessary repairs on vehicles, computers, etc. If you are maxed out on credit card debt and other payments, you won't have the money to pay for unexpected repairs.

6. **To pay for college without adding more debt.** Many kids and adults never have the opportunity to go to college because of heavy debt loads, even though it is a necessity in today's world. The average American household pays $100 a month in just credit card interest alone. Just think what could happen if that same amount were invested in a stock mutual fund for several years until a child goes off to college. Not only would the child's college tuition be paid for, but there would also be enough money left over to help with other education-related expenses like room and board or textbooks.

7. **To enjoy life.** Debt has a way of diminishing our quality of life. It often takes the enjoyment out of the simple things in life. After

piling up debt after debt, we spend half our lives just paying the cost of interest, in addition to repaying the debt.

8. To fulfill dreams. Debt has a way of dashing our hopes, dimming our vision and destroying our dreams. The more debt we incur, the less chance we have of implementing our goals, executing our ambitions and realizing our dreams.

9. To enjoy retirement. When will you retire? Will it be 15 to 20 years after your friends retire?

Understanding that a lot of choices do come your way and that you have within you the power to improve your financial condition, you will soon understand that you too can be completely debt free. So what is the answer? Let's start by making sure you know you have too much debt now and need to get out from under the debt burden. In my opinion, any debt is too much debt. To begin your journey out of debt, you must not borrow anymore from this point on. This means saying no to anything but survival needs; i.e., food, water, shelter. Sacrifice all other purchases even though you feel you need them. Things such as tools, clothes, manicures, hairstylists, movies, eating out, lawn furniture, gifts, going out of town on weekend trips, etc, are definitely out. No more purchases of these kinds. Even some grocery spending should be examined. Specialty foods/drinks and other extras can be trimmed, and a great deal of savings can immediately be realized from your food budget.

Of course, you think you have worked hard and deserve some extras, and perhaps you do—but don't! Now is the time to say no and now is the time to give up the extra things you purchase that make you feel good. Will some of this involve saying no to some of your friends? Probably, in the sense that you may not be with them to go shopping, to the beach, to the mountains, to Starbucks, etc. Just let them know you will be "out of commission" for a while until you get your financial house in order. It is up to you and you alone to decide whether or not your debt is spinning out of control and how you are going to manage it. Cut up the credit cards and get rid of them. Out of sight, out of action and out of mind. This will keep the temptation to spend at a distance.

Though that will stop the bleeding, it does nothing to correct past mistakes. You still have to handle past purchases, past loans and other debt you have incurred. Now that you have stopped the bleeding by saying no to new debt, take all extra cash you have and apply it to old debt. Take any extra money and wipe out all your small debt first. It can be discouraging to limit your wants and not enjoy a few extras as you have in the past, but by doing so, you will soon make some real progress. As you wipe out smaller debts one by one, you will soon be encouraged and energized to pick up some speed and move ahead to the next debt casualty. Will it be hard work to make these difficult but necessary no-spending choices? Certainly! But keep the bigger picture in mind. Someday you will be debt free and on your way to a better, stress-free life.

Break free from financial bondage.
Get the right attitude!
Discover that you can be debt free!

I Can Break Bad Spending Habits

*B*eing in control of your finances means a whole lot more than just earning a greater income, having a better job and controlling your money. It means getting a handle on your bad habits. These might be habits of bad thought, wrong decisions, wrong choices and bad spending habits.

What is it that is motivating you to take on more debt? What is driving your desire to spend until you are out of control? Second Peter 2:19 mentions this, "For a man is a slave to whatever controls him" (*TLB*).

How we manage our money affects not only our present, but also our future. It affects how we feel about ourselves and how we react to others. Many of us find ourselves with dismal spending habits that need to be broken. The good news is this: Regardless of your past, your future is a clean slate. Recognizing a problem doesn't always bring a solution, but until we recognize that problem, there can be no solution. Many times the difference between your accomplishment and your failure is your attitude. If you have the attitude that you can take control of your finances and you can break bad habits, then I am confident you will.

You already have all the income you must have to meet your basic needs of food, shelter, and so on. It is amazing how much money we spend on everyday things. Forget all the unnecessary purchases you make. You can save significant dollars just on housing, food, clothing and transportation costs.

Much of a bad spending habit involves seemingly little and simple insignificant purchases. You burn a lot of unaccounted-for cash. Is it a need or is it a want? If it is possible to live life without it, then it's definitely a want. If it is possible to delay the purchase, it's also probably just a want. You must know the difference between a need and a want. Knowledge is good, but your choices must reflect that knowledge. If the potential purchase is a want, then don't buy it. Knowing the difference puts you in control. In the chart (next page), take the test and see if you know the difference.

Maybe you purchase things just to impress your family, friends and neighbors. Don't worry about keeping up with the Joneses. The only reason you should ever buy something is because you need it, not to impress someone else.

Old bad habits are always hard to break. New good habits are hard to form. The good news is that you CAN break bad spending habits and you CAN get rid of your debt. With the right information, coaching and self-discipline, you CAN move to a much better life of financial stewardship. If you have good

Need	Choice	Want
	Winter Coat	
	Larger House	
	Milk, Bread, & Water	
	Cable TV	
	Transportation	
	Lottery Tickets	
	Shoes	
	Designer Jeans	
	Furnace	
	New Patio Set	
	Call Waiting, Voice Mail	
	Kid's School Supplies	
	Large Screen TV	

financial stewardship in your life, you will be blessed. You see, the result of good stewardship is ongoing and continuous biblical prosperity.

Becoming debt free and honoring God by becoming a person of financial integrity is pleasing to Him. Thus, we may need to begin with a heart transformation and a change in our approach and attitude about managing what He has entrusted to us.

Remember that we own nothing and that we are nothing more than managers of what God has placed in our hands. If we mess up on the little money we have to manage, I cannot imagine God will want to heap more upon us only to see it disappear through bad spending habits, poor purchasing choices and bad financial stewardship. It is clear that breaking bad spending habits will take some personal discipline. In Proverbs 13:18, we are admonished in this way, "He who ignores discipline comes to poverty and shame, but whoever heeds correction is honored."

Freedom from bad spending takes personal discipline to be sure, not only the discipline of self-restraint, but also the discipline of a good work ethic, careful time management, wise choices and good decisions. Breaking free from poor spending habits takes the personal discipline of knowing where you can go and where you should not go, where you spend your time and the wisdom of how to live below your means. This means utilizing resources already available to you before jumping into your car, heading for a shopping area and pulling out the credit card to purchase what you perceive you need. This is an example of a bad spending habit you need to break.

Often we form bad financial habits because we are discontent with what we have. Scripture speaks clearly about our bad spending habits when it tell us in Hebrews 13:5, "Keep your lives free from the love of money and be content with what you have."

The end result of continual spending and bad financial habits can eventually lead to bankruptcy. This is something you NEVER want to do. It is dishonest not to repay your debts, and it will also cause financial havoc and personal pain for many years to come. According to Reuters (11/14/2003), bankruptcies are at a record high. Nonbusiness bankruptcies rose 7.8% in fiscal 2003 to 1.63 million. Since 1994, when filings totaled 837,797, bankruptcies in federal court have climbed to an astonishing 98%.

Bad spending habits flourish when we fail to turn down the radio during advertisements, turn off the television during commercials, spend our day off visiting shopping malls, new car dealer lots, etc. Use your free time in productive areas far away from people and places that exist to separate you from your money. Bad spending habits make you spend hundreds or thousands of dollars without really giving much thought to what you are buying. To stop the process, begin to write down everything you buy for two or three months. Record every nickel, every dime, every cup of coffee and every burger. This simple inconvenient exercise alone will help you to retard your out-of-control spending.

You can break bad spending habits if you will understand all that God has already given to you. If you take the time to appreciate His goodness, you won't always be on the lookout to get something more. First Timothy 6:6-10 says this: "But godliness with contentment is great gain. For we brought nothing into the world, and we can take nothing out of it. But if we have food and clothing, we will be content with that. People who want to get rich fall into temptation and a trap and into many foolish and harmful desires that plunge men into ruin and destruction. For the love of money is a root of all kinds of evil. Some people, eager for money, have wandered from the faith and pierced themselves with many griefs."

This verse pretty well puts it all into the proper perspective. We have been given so much already—after all, we came into this world with nothing. If we have food, clothing, shelter, family and friends, we have all we need. Second Corinthians 9:8 lets us know God will always be looking out for us: "And God is able to make all grace abound to you, so that in all things at all times, having all that you need, you will abound in every good work."

Break free from financial bondage.
Get the right attitude!
Discover how you can break free
from bad spending habits!

I Can Choose to Pay Cash

*P*aying cash for a purchase is not generally promoted in our society. In many cases, it is outright discouraged. Why pay cash when you can lease the item? Why pay cash when you can enjoy low-interest financing? Why pay cash when you could be building your personal credit rating? Why pay cash?—you may need it for something else.

Of course, all these statements about not paying cash are just silly. If you buy into this notion that paying cash is bad, you are buying into a lifetime of debt. You are becoming the debtor while someone else is becoming the creditor or lender. The timeless biblical proverb still remains credible and truthful. According to Proverbs 22:7, "The borrower is servant to the lender." The principle is black and white: There is no room for an alternate interpretation or explanation. You are either a borrower or a lender.

Let's contrast a real-life scenario of the borrower versus the lender that happens tens of thousands of times every day. A person walks into an auto show room and falls in love with that new car or truck that has everything he ever desired. The design is superb, the model fits his personality, the safety features are comforting, the interior is sleek and the instrument panel comes with satellite navigational features. Not to mention the surround sound, satellite radio and leather interior. Just sitting behind the wheel makes you feel rich and successful and gives you a sense of well being.

Of course, in reality, if you do not have the cash to pay for it, and you are not already completely debt free, you are headed for financial disaster. At the very least, you are falling for a lifestyle of debt that has been disastrous to many people today. Current marketing culture paints a glorious picture of the rich and famous as opposed to the down and out. Yet millions have bought into the payment-poor, debt-bondage lifestyle.

Look at the difference between the borrower and the lender in purchasing just one moderately priced vehicle. Given a very common loan repayment schedule of six years, a huge gap occurs between the two situations. Here are the two choices: 1) making vehicle loan payments or 2) taking that very same payment and investing it in the equity market yielding average equity returns over the past 40 years.

The real difference is this: The borrower makes the same payment the lender (investor) does for the exact same time period. When the time period is up, the borrower stops making all payments; so does

It's Your Choice	Your Total Cost	Value in 6 Years	Value in 10 Years	Value in 20 Years	Value in 30 Years	Value in 40 Years
Auto Loan	$37,872	$5,000	$1.00	$0	$0	$0
Invest Instead	$37,872	$55,741	$90,082	$299,081	$992,985	$3,296,826

the investor. At the end of the six years, the borrower has a used vehicle of questionable value. At the end of six years, the person who chooses not to borrow for a new car or truck, but instead invests the exact same payment, has a total sum of $55,741. This is just for the onetime purchase of just one vehicle.

Wait, that's not all. Both persons have made the very same monthly payment. However, the investor (the one who does not borrow) makes no more payments, but continues to let the accumulation of his or her six-year payments grow in the marketplace, gaining return upon compound return at the very same rate.

In just four additional years, the lump sum of payments has now turned into $90,082. Add on another 10 years and it becomes $299,081; yet another 10 years and the total is now $992,985. Finally, after another 10 years it has grown to $3,296,826.

Amazing! All the accumulation has come from just six years of monthly payments. The borrower described in Proverbs 22:7 has a used vehicle of questionable value after six years. But with absolutely no additional contributions, look what the wise person of Proverbs 22:7 has accumulated! This is a clear reminder that the Bible really does make a lot of sense.

Here are the details for your review:

VEHICLE LOAN

Cost of Vehicle:	$30,000
Interest Rate:	8%
Number of Monthly Payments:	72
Monthly Payment:	$526.00
Total of Payments:	$37,872
Year 6 Vehicle Value:	$5,000
Total Loss on Payments:	($32,872)
Year 10 Vehicle Value:	$1.00
Total Loss of Payments:	($37,871)

INVEST INSTEAD

Interest Rate:	12%
Number of Monthly Payments:	72
Monthly Payment:	$526.00
Total of Payments:	$37,872
Year 6 Investment Value:	$55,741
Total Gain on Payments:	$17,869
Year 10 Investment Value:	$90,082
Total Gain on Payments:	$52,210
Year 20 Investment Value:	$299,081
Total Gain on Payments:	$261,209
Year 30 Investment Value:	$992,985
Total Gain on Payments:	$955,113
Year 40 Investment Value:	$3,296,826
Total Gain on Payments:	$3,258,954

Why are you encouraged to use credit instead of paying with cash? Two reasons are clear to me:

1. If you pay cash, you are likely to be more careful in your purchase.

   a. You may not make the purchase at all.

   b. You may delay the purchase until you have enough cash.

   c. You may decide there are other priorities for you cash.

   d. You may press the vendor for a better deal.

   e. If you do not get a substantial discount on the potential purchase you may just walk away.

2. If you pay cash, the dealer, the vendor, the store, etc., will not get more benefit from your purchase by gaining from a financing deal.

   a. Carrying your financing increases the value of your purchase.

   b. Carrying your financing provides ongoing interest income.

   c. Offering you credit helps push you toward a purchase.

   d. Offering you credit helps you make a quick decision.

   e. Offering "easy credit terms" gets more types of people in the door to make a purchase.

   f. Offering to finance the deal gets you into the store or showroom much quicker.

   g. Offering to loan you the money makes you think about a purchase you would not have previously considered.

You need to know that vendors who are offering you easy financing for your purchase don't do so for YOUR benefit. It is not offered to you because you are so well liked that the store or dealer just wants to make your life a bit easier. Offering to finance your purchase is purely in the self-interest of the vendor.

Many people, even so-called consultants, will tell you that there is "good debt" and "bad debt." Wrong! Please don't buy into the "good debt"/"bad debt" discourse. ALL debt is bad! Yes, at times we are swayed into a purchase because we don't have the cash, but that does not make the debt good! The only debt that even comes close to making some short-term sense is a home mortgage. If you cannot make the payments on a 15-year mortgage however, you are probably buying too much house. My recommendation is to limit your home mortgage to 15 years and then do everything in your power to shorten that debt period by making extra payments toward your principle balance.

Some go into debt for so-called investment purposes. They are buying second homes, seaside properties, even speculating in commercial development or in the house rental market. This is a volatile place to put your personal finances. Unless you have substantial cash available to cover an enormous potential loss in income, run away from such so-called investing.

Coming from the corporate world, I can tell you of faulty thinking firsthand. During the boom and subsequent bust of the nineties, a common practice was to make large purchases via leasing contracts. Virtually everything was leased. Fleets of trucks, manufacturing equipment, buildings, and so on were all leased instead of purchased outright.

This produced a couple of scenarios. First, it encouraged buying even when no cash was available. Second, it kept the "corporate debt" off the Statement of Financial Condition, commonly called the balance sheet. Third, many assets owned outright by the company were sold for cash and then leased back from the new owner. This supposedly freed up corporate cash for other things. I saw great companies with substantial real estate and other corporate assets proceed to sell off the assets, receive the cash, and then watch the cash simply disappear over a short time period. The company was left with long-term leasing debt and a huge burden to bear for many years to come.

The bottom line of the leasing scandals I witnessed was that the greedy corporate executives boosted the value of their corporate parachutes and boosted the value of their personal stock options. They received unprecedented amounts of company bonuses because of their wonderful achievement of improving the corporate financial condition. After many great personal bonuses and benefits, the executives would move on to other companies and new opportunities to do the same all over again.

The real sadness of going into corporate debt was that the investors never knew what was happening to the companies in which they had invested their life savings. The leasing debt was never a part of the corporate balance sheet and because of loopholes in the law, the company auditors never disclosed the debt in the financial reports.

If corporate debt is good, then why is one of the most successful companies ever to grace planet earth completely debt free? If debt is so good and provides so much so-called tax relief, why is the company that produced the richest man in the world debt free? Of course, I am talking about Microsoft, which has no debt and more than 50 billion in cash! That's a cool fifty-

thousand-million dollars. Not only this company, but also many others are debt free.

 ## Paying cash for a purchase is not generally promoted in our society.

Thousands of others like it have chosen to have absolutely no corporate debt. These companies include Walgreen, Cisco Systems and William Wrigley. Cisco Systems has never borrowed money and does not plan to. Cisco Systems, the networking company, funds its own expansion instead of borrowing money.

Not having debt helped companies survive during the dot-com bust. As I write this, Cisco earned $772 million during its most recent quarter, while Lucent (a company in great debt) lost $7.9 billion. Lucent pays interest each quarter on $3.2 billion. Walgreen expands its drugstores by the monthly cash it generates. Its corporate philosophy, according to a company representative, is "We're a pay-as-you-go type." A competitor of Walgreen is Rite Aid, which struggles with paying interest on a heavy debt load of $3.7 billion.

Wrigley, the chewing-gum maker, has never had any long-term debt since it was founded some 110 years ago. Ross Stores don't borrow any money to expand. Each new store costs $1.3 million to open, but generates an average of $6 million in revenue the first year of business. In the northwest US, where I live, 34 major companies alone have no debt.

Use the information I have just provided to think about paying cash. If you don't have the cash, don't make the purchase! Use the "cash paying" model of these companies to improve your own personal family financial balance sheet. Perhaps you have made some mistakes in the past. Yes, you must now dig yourself out of debt. Your past is important, but not nearly as important to your present as the way you see your future.

So is there really good debt? Not in my opinion. Perhaps, at best, some debt is tolerable for a short time period if we you need a roof over your heads or a yard for the kids to enjoy. Make a commitment to your future and the future opportunity of your family. Choose now to pay cash.

**Break free from
financial bondage.
Get the right attitude!
Discover how you can
choose to pay cash!**

I Can Renew My Thinking

*D*o you suffer the consequences of bad financial decisions because you have faulty thinking? Do you need to renew your thinking? Life seems busy as we hurry through our hours, days, weeks, months and years. At various seasons of our lives we need to stop and reassess what we have been doing, where we are now and the direction we are headed.

Proverbs 14:12

"There is a way that seems right to a man, but in the end it leads to death."

Proverbs 3:5

"Trust in the LORD with all your heart and lean not on your own understanding."

Proverbs 3:7

"Do not be wise in your own eyes; fear the LORD and shun evil."

What past financial decisions have you made that affect the way you are now living? Many of those in financial difficulty really don't know just how they got into trouble. They know that all of a sudden they found themselves in financial jeopardy. It is easy to let our decision making be based upon our current surroundings and the circumstances in which we find ourselves. Is your financial future being influenced by your season in life, your current friends and your need to be accepted? If so, this influence can be positive and productive if you have the right influences, or it can be negative and devastating if you are keeping the wrong company.

Our culture often pushes greed, materialism and a mind-set of "you've got to have it all right now." Our judgment and decision making are easily influenced by the commercials we see and hear, by the friendships we keep and by our inability to distinguish our needs from our wants.

Proverbs 23:4 says, "Do not wear yourself out to get rich; have the wisdom to show restraint." We need to be on guard against personal greed that will lead us to want everything we see and cause us to spend all our energies in a futile attempt to have it all. We must restrain ourselves from seeking things even when we have enough money to purchase them. Additionally, we should also restrain ourselves from purchases for which we have no money and have to go into debt to obtain.

Going into debt for wants certainly suggests that a person needs a renewal of the mind and a change in the thinking process. Debt is potentially enslaving and we should avoid it at all costs. Proverbs 22:7 makes this very clear to us when it says, "The rich rule over the poor, and the borrower is servant to the lender."

Whether we want to admit it or not, we are influenced by the common thinking prevalent in our "get it now" society. Every once in a while, even normally rational people have to step back and review how we are affected by our surroundings.

Do you have a faulty system of input and thinking? Are you influenced by others to make bad financial decisions? We may find that we need to "renew our thinking." In Romans 12:2, the apostle Paul says we are not to conform or go along with the thinking that is prevalent in our world, but we should think differently, or be transformed. He tells us that this is accomplished by renewing our mind; i.e., our patterns of evaluation, our outlook, our wisdom on any matter, our thoughts, our assessment, our thinking, etc.

Our culture often pushes greed, materialism and a mind-set of "you've got to have it all right now."

Romans 12:2 says, "Do not conform any longer to the pattern of this world, but be transformed by the renewing of your mind." The word *transformation* is translated from the same Greek word that also gives us the word *metamorphosis*. This word means to change. If we are not to have the same materialistic mind-set that is prevalent in our culture and society today, then we must change our thinking. The changing of our attitudes about matters of personal finance will not come without a renewal of our thinking.

Break free from
financial bondage.
Get the right attitude!
Discover how you can
renew your thinking!

I Can Change
My Flawed Value System

*H*ave the priorities in your financial life been influenced by a faulty system of values? Is your spending out of control because principles of integrity are out of alignment in your life?

A key indicator of strength of character is a person's system of values. Values help each of us determine what is important in our lives. Values set our parameters and provide us with directional guideposts. Our core values and set principles help us make decisions and determine our responses to what life hands us. Our actions come from our value system.

A value is a mission, a belief and a set of principles upon which to live our lives. Whether or not values are clearly defined or written upon some paper or e-file, we all live our lives based on some set of personal rules and values. Very few notable people have achieved great accomplishments, enjoyed enormous success or distinguished careers without implementing personal values and underpinning their daily lives with certain principles.

What do you value in life? Is having things more important to you than becoming debt free? Is your work more important to you than your family? Are business contacts more important to you than your friends? Is climbing the corporate ladder of success more important to you than enjoying life itself?

Of course we are not talking about a lack of motivation, laziness or failing to work diligently for our employers, but we are referring to the values we hold close and getting our priorities right. Having a good value system does not come without a monetary cost.

Is accumulating vast resources of money so you can live on Easy Street for the rest of your life part of your value system? Is driving the latest car so you can impress your neighbors and friends part of your value system? Does a sense of pride drive you to continuously outdo others? Are you driven to do more, have more, buy more and show more?

In Luke 12:15 Jesus says, "Watch out! Be on your guard against all kinds of greed; a man's life does not consist in the abundance of his possessions."

A sense of self-worth and all the things that are important in life is directly connected to the core values a person possesses. If you are to be at peace with yourself, your family and your God, you need to rest upon an established base of good personal values, and those values need to drive your every thought, action and reaction. Anything less than that will lead to a violation of the real you. This will lead to confusion, discouragement, frustration and depression.

What are some good core values? What do you value in life? Some important values to consider are as follows:

financial responsibility
loyalty
self-respect
concern for others less fortunate
adventure
effectiveness
decisiveness
respect for others
friendships
security
affection
close relationships
love
family
humor
creativity
freedom
justice
independence
honesty
good health
purity
spirituality
reputation
responsibility
stability
hard work
self-reliance
selflessness
accuracy

excellence
personal growth
diligence
fairness
accountability
orderliness
accomplishment
achievement
truth
wisdom
nature
helping others
positive attitude
teamwork
doing God's work
trust for others
inner peace
emotional well-being
knowledge
meaning in life
faith
service to others
resourcefulness
tradition
gratitude
simplicity
and so on . . .

An important personal value that has nothing to do with money, possessions or things is personal integrity. When you lose your personal integrity, you have lost one of the great personal values available to every person alike. This value comes at no economic cost. Compromising integrity for social, economic or financial gain is the fast track to an unhappy life.

Another important personal value that has no economic cost to you is to leave your world (globally and locally) a better place for someone else. Whether you leave a room organized and clean for the next person, a project completed competently, a system working efficiently or a life lived righteously as a model for your children and grandchildren, leave something for someone else. George Bernard Shaw said, "Life is no 'brief candle' to me. It is a sort of splendid torch which I have got a hold of for the moment, and I want to make it burn as brightly as possible before handing it on to future generations."

Compromising integrity for social, economic or financial gain is the fast track to an unhappy life.

Sometimes we find ourselves in conflict with our chosen core values. If you say you value charity, but rarely give of yourself, your time or your money, you are in conflict with your core values and not living your life to its fullest. If you say you value family life, but never spend any time at home, a conflict is occurring in your life. If you say that you value good health, but you have poor eating habits and you never exercise, another conflict is in progress.

I began with the following two questions. Have the priorities in your financial life been influenced by a faulty system of values? Is your spending out of control because principles of integrity are out of alignment in your life? If you have found that your desires and ambitions have centered on accumulating more and more possessions and keeping ahead of your neighbors, then you have been making financial decisions based upon a defective system of values. Cracks have formed in your foundation. The good news is that those cracks can be repaired.

Financially responsible people who discover that improvements in their value system are needed make changes and seek changes in the following ways:

- Saying, "I'll do it."
- Finding an answer for every problem.
- By accepting, "I can change."
- Looking for a way to make it happen.
- Acknowledging, "Why not?"
- Saying, "It may be difficult, but it's possible."
- By determining, "I can do all things through Christ who strengthens me" (Philippians 4:13).

You can change your faulty financial value system. Instead of valuing things, you can value life. Instead of desiring the latest, the greatest, the best and the rest, you can change yourself and change your life. You can do it with just a bit of encouragement and support.

You really CAN
rescue your life and
liberate your future!

I Can Rise Above
My Burden of Debt

*D*ebt is a burden, a weight, a concern, a worry, and comes with a certain amount of uneasiness. The burden of coping with a large amount of debt is strenuous. Coping with debt-related problems is no picnic. The stress of carrying debt crosses over from your business life, to your personal life, to your marriage and family life, to your spiritual life, as well as to your personal health. All the various challenges in each of these areas become greater and more intense when you add in the debt factor.

If you are self-employed or own your own business, carrying a personal debt burden becomes a major distraction from other areas that need your undivided attention. Even if you are employed by someone else, if you are constantly worrying about debt, you are not performing your job to your fullest potential. Without looking closely into your financial history, I can say confidently that to rise above your burden of debt, you will have to reduce and eliminate the plaguing debt. When it comes to debt, you slide into it and slowly climb back out. Benjamin Franklin is quoted as saying, "Rather to go to bed supperless than to rise in debt." Debt puts your personal living in jeopardy, and makes your spiritual discipline defenseless.

A recent survey on Monster.com asked the question, "How much does your personal debt affect the amount you earn?" Out of a total of 1,522 responses, the answers were broken down as follows:

1. 8%   It doesn't: I can save as much of my paycheck as I want.
2. 10%   Enough: But it doesn't hinder my savings.
3. 40%   A lot: The amount I earn makes it hard to save.
4. 41%   Far too much: I can barely meet my bills—never mind trying to save anything.

Recent numbers released by the Federal Reserve indicate that personal debt (credit cards, auto loans, consumer debt, etc.) exceeded $1.6 trillion. Businesses continue to write down and write off unpaid consumer debt. Bankruptcies are on the rise. More alarming is the fact that more and more of a person's paycheck is being used to pay off debt. Wage earners are devoting an all-time high of over 15% of their take-home pay toward paying down debt. Unfortunately, the good times rarely last. We live in a cyclical economy where ups and downs are commonplace. When the economy cools and husbands and/or wives lose their jobs, unemployment rises and debtors find themselves head over heels in debt.

What is causing the steep increase in percentages? Many professionals believe that the good times and the great economy of the past led consumers to feel they were untouchable. Nothing bad could happen to them. Because their investments seemed to be unstoppable and their jobs secure during the good times of market bullishness and optimism, more consumers took on debt, assuming that to pay it off would never be a problem. It is easy for most people to get caught up in the euphoria of good times and to overextend themselves with credit card and revolving credit-line debt.

What happens when personal debt is high and a recession overtakes the economy? Major firms lay off workers, blue collar and white collar alike. Manufacturing companies close assembly plants and unprofitable firms go out of business. Workers remaining employed face cuts in wages and dwindling benefits. Less money in consumer pockets means fewer goods and services are purchased. This leads to more job cuts and higher unemployment. The result becomes an even deeper recession, a continuing bad economy and an ongoing crisis.

Often this scenario presses individuals and families to purchase more things on credit, things they could not afford even before the faltering economy. They spend today's wages AND tomorrow's wages on things they think they need today. Of course, this does not work in the long term because at some point a person simply cannot take on any more debt and has no additional cash flow to service the debt. The burden of personal debt turns difficulty into hardship and hardship into personal crisis.

To cope, individuals often pay only the monthly minimum required on revolving consumer debt. This barely covers more than the interest due, and usually takes 40 or 50 years to pay off. No, that was not a misprint you just read. It really does take that long to pay off by making minimum payments, no matter how large or small the debt may be. Personal debt in working-class families has crippling power over their lives. It becomes a great source of anxiety and stress.

> The burden of personal debt turns difficulty into hardship and hardship into personal crisis.

I will attempt to relate a story about crabs to carrying a heavy burden of debt. It goes like this. If you put one crab into a pot, it will climb right out. However, if you put several crabs in a pot at the same time, they will all stay there—not one will climb out. That's because as soon as one crab starts to climb out of the pot, the others grab it and drag it back down. In a sense, debt is like a pot of crabs. When you face a personal obstacle in the area of business and try to climb out, debt pulls you down again. When you try to get out of some personal struggles and wrong habits, the burden of debt pulls at you until you start to slide backward. When trying to improve your marriage and family relationships, it seems that the stress of debt reaches out and pulls you down from your upward climb.

Debt is a heavy weight and must be eliminated. It must be expelled, driven out of your life and banished forever. It creates all kinds of debilitating pressure. It can become unbearable and weaken even the strongest person, strongest marriage, strongest business, strongest relationships and strongest financial planning. When plagued with debt that has become out of control, it is often difficult to see the whole picture of any situation, whether it be spiritual, relational or financial. Often the person carrying this kind of stress is unable to make good decisions, has clouded judgment, reacts instead of acting proactively and seeks only short-term solutions.

Of course, all these descriptions of debt may be familiar to you. After all, that is why you purchased this book. Debt has become close to you. Although you can't exactly call it your friend, you do have an intimate relationship with it. It is on your mind every day and keeps you from enjoying the life you should be living. It has taken over your thought life and taken control of your daily living. You have been forced to spend a great deal of time thinking about it. You devote a great deal of your paycheck to it and it keeps you from being the loving, giving person you should be.

Because of your personal debt, your life is owned by someone else or something else. Your life is not your own. You must work at that job because you need the income. You are not able to spend time in furthering your education or pursuing a career or vocation you would enjoy because you are too busy working at a job you don't like or appreciate because you need the money to pay your debt. Should you lose your present job, it would become a financial emergency in your life.

When you become debt free, for the first time perhaps, you will truly own your life. You can make money-related decisions based upon what you want and not on what others want from you. You don't have to think of the creditors first and your family second. The new situation becomes family first, all else after that. When you become debt free, losing a job will be difficult, but not insurmountable. Yes, maybe there will be a shortterm dip in your cash flow, but it won't become a financial crisis in your life. You will still be able to exist. You will still have food on the table, a roof over your head and utilities to make your living tolerable.

The good news is that you CAN rise above your burden of debt! Yes, you can! Let me tell you how. It starts with recognizing *The 5 Keys, The 10 Attitudes, The 15 Personal Responsibilities, The 30 Biblical Principles* and the *35 Practical Applications.*

We have already talked about the "5 Keys": *Stop Spending on Yourself, Start Giving to Others, Discipline Your Cash Attitude, Begin to Live Below Your Means* and *Start Saving for Your Future.* Change your perspective by identifying with the 10 "I CAN" attitudes. Genesis 18:14 reminds you of help from above when it says, "Is anything too hard for the Lord?"

Dedicate your resolve to being personally responsible in 15 different areas, line up your life with 30 principles from the Word and then follow the 35 area of practical, hands-on, real-world advice. By doing all these things, you CAN rise above your burden of debt! Yes, you can!

Break free from financial bondage.
Get the right attitude!
Discover how you can rise
above your burden of debt!

I Can Be Financially Accountable

You can be a responsible person and you can become financially accountable for every decision you make. What is the best way to dig yourself out of a financial hole? The answer is simple—one small painful step at a time. It is easy to get into debt and difficult to climb back out of debt. People who are in debt are usually enslaved to the advertising and marketing of our day. They have bought into the cultural attitude of "I want it, and I want it now!" Some view a pocket full of credit cards and credit lines as having financial freedom, when it really is financial bondage. Real freedom comes from being debt free.

What does accountability mean anyway? *Webster's Dictionary* defines accountability as "the state of being accountable, subject to the obligation to report, explain, or justify something; responsible, answerable." The *Merriam-Webster's Collegiate Dictionary* defines accountability as "The quality or state of being accountable; especially: an obligation or willingness to accept responsibility or to account for one's actions."

Financial accountability comes down to discipline, discipline and even more discipline. When you say "no" to credit cards and needless spending, you can then say "yes" to your financial future. Debt robs you of your dreams. Debt robs you of a vision and purpose you have for your life. Debt can drain your strength, rob your marriage and take away the good things that were designed for your life. Debt will crush the life out of you. This is why you must be careful to stop it before it has a death grip on your life.

One person reports that he had purchased enough merchandise to overextend his credit cards to more than $40,000. He said that by cutting every possible expense, he has reduced it by 15%. He reports that the weight of debt increases his stress and the heavy burden of interest is almost unbearable. Another person notes that she has reduced her credit card debt by $15,000. Life for her now is much less stressful and she comments that she uses ONLY cash these days. She also noted that by staying focused, a rainbow is now visible just beyond the clouds.

What is the lesson to be learned here? First of all, if you don't have money, don't spend. You cannot spend money you don't have. Don't go into debt! Debt is not your friend. It is your enemy. Credit is NOT your friend. It is your enemy. Debt sucks the life out of many marriages. Become financially responsible today, for tomorrow comes much too quickly. You don't want to be old and in debt and have little or nothing to show for it.

Debt is not fun, nor is it exciting. Being financially responsible is not some game to play. Being financially responsible is a very serious commission and should not be taken lightly. Being responsible makes you accountable. Being accountable raises questions. Anytime you are tempted to make a purchase or sign a contract, before doing so ask yourself this question: "What would happen to me if I decided to postpone this purchase for 90 days?" If the honest answer is "nothing in particular," then don't proceed with the purchase. Because we are impulse buyers, we tend to disengage our brains before we commit to spending more money we don't have on things we do not need to impress people we really don't like. So go without all the luxuries and extras you think you may need. Most of the time you will never miss them and probably won't give them another thought.

What should you do when you are overwhelmed with debt and there seems to be no easy way out? First of all, you certainly do not want to ignore debt. Ignoring your debt problem will not make it go away. Ignoring your personal spending problem will not curb your appetite for more and more. If you need help in specific areas, seek it. Many people with problems of all kinds are ashamed and embarrassed and resist finding help. This is exactly what you should not do. Do you want to be cured? If so, swallow your pride, confess your faults and seek professional help. Don't let anything prevent you from making the needed changes in your life. With a little help, you too can become financially accountable. Become accountable for every money decision you make each day, accountable for every purchase, every dollar and every penny. Believe me,

it's worth setting aside any personal obstacle to get your life turned around.

Okay, so you have made some mistakes and have not always been financially accountable. That is unfortunate, but just remember you CAN change your behavior. It is never too late. I usually recommend paying off all debt first, assuming you have a couple of month's living expenses set aside should something happen to your job or health.

If, however, you have not yet accumulated three to six months for an emergency fund, here is another way for you to proceed. Once you have paid off one debt, take half the usual payment and add it to the payment on another debt. Take the other half of the payment and put it into a savings account. Let this accumulate each month until you have enough set aside should you experience a financial emergency. The best way to speed up this process is to get a second job and earn a second income.

What does financial accountability and responsibility feel like? How does it feel to have worked so hard and to have been successful? Try closing your eyes and getting a mind picture of a life without debt. How does it feel to be financially free? Can you feel the stress leaving your body? All of a sudden your emotions are soaring to new highs as you see all debt disappear; no credit card debt, no car payments, no personal loans, and even no mortgage payments because your house has just been paid in full. Wow, what a great picture that is purely the result of impulse restraint. This is the result of a financially accountable person.

Get the right attitude!
Discover how you can
be financially accountable!

I Can Enjoy Life
Without Spending Money

Most of the real treasures of life can be had without spending a single penny. We all have rich resources available to us without cost.

What is the value of a great friendship or loving relationship? Everyone can extend friendship to some acquaintance. If not, endless opportunities to offer friendship can be found. How many senior citizens are living in care facilities that would love to feel the warmth of a compassionate relationship?

In the past, people lived from birth to the grave enjoying the blessings of life, yet never had to spend real money to enjoy them. Currently, we think that to enjoy life we must have money to spend.

At what monetary cost is our freedom? Our freedom of mobility, worship, independent thinking, etc., may have come at a cost to past generations, but for us we enjoy them without personal financial cost.

At what monetary cost is a walk through the forest, a rest by a rippling stream, a gaze toward a beautiful sunset, staring upward at showers of stars, a warm gentle breeze, a good read from a book of interest, a trip to the park, etc.? Equally free are enjoying the autumn colors, the white winters, the colorful spring and warm summer nights. What about the endless puffy clouds of white that fill our sky, a glorious sunrise, and the squirrels that run from tree to tree? These are all priceless treasures of life that bring endless hours of enjoyment to us, all without costing us a dime.

Many people think that it takes money to enjoy life and all it has to offer. I am not of that crowd. Life is all about what you have inside, not what you see and accumulate on the outside. You don't need 25 years of education to take advantage of the opportunities available to you. Watch any immigrant culture and see how industrious and prosperous they can become with some hard work and simple ingenuity.

A story is told about a former prisoner of the Vietnam war. His name is Charlie. Charlie used to give speeches and presentations across the country. When he first came on the stage, he took a couple of chairs and placed them about two feet apart. As he began to talk he paced back and forth between the two chairs again and again. Of course, the listeners were a bit puzzled, yet fascinated at the words he was speaking. They watched and listened intently. Back and forth, silently he paced. At a particular moment in his speech, Charlie then told his audience that for a period of six long years, he paced, just as he was doing now, back and forth, back and forth in his three-foot-wide North Vietnam prison cell.

Then he continued his story. It seems he was shot down by the enemy and was captured wearing only his tattered flight suit. It was all he had with him at the time of the capture. He was placed into a very tiny prison cell with only the clothes on his back. He didn't have much. Or did he?

At this point in his presentation, Charlie engaged the audience, attempting to broaden their thinking and help them appreciate all they had at their disposal. He asked the listeners what else he had with him besides his flight suit. With their input, he then listed other great assets at his disposal more important than his flight suit. Some of the items on his list were as follows:

- his knowledge
- his acquired skills
- his training and experience
- his ability to think
- his courage
- his creativity
- his imagination
- his ability to reason
- his ability to remember

On and on the list grew until the audience suddenly began to understand that some of the best things in life are free. Some of his best assets were not the clothes on his back or the things in his possession, but rather the intangible strengths that were his.

Life is all about what you have inside, not what you see and accumulate on the outside.

If each of us were to do a similar exercise, we could count thousands of ways we could enjoy life without spending money.

Get the right attitude!
Discover how you can enjoy life
without spending money!

I Can Find Financial Solutions

You cannot tailor-make the situations in life, but you can tailor-make the attitudes to fit those situations. For many people, the income never seems to cover the outflow. This leads to arguments and high family stress. The stress often comes from deciding how much money to spend, what things to spend it on and when to spend it.

Some of us spend more time reacting to the fact that we have a problem than we do solving the problem—problems are inevitable. Some problems can be anticipated. Some are surprises. The idea that problems occur regularly need never be a surprise.

The good news is that for every problem, there's a solution. Sometimes the solution is immediate. Sometimes, it takes awhile to discover. Sometimes, the solution involves letting go. When you leave your financial problems unsolved, you in essence are leaving them to chance. You need a plan, a budget and action steps, or your financial problems will never go away.

Sometimes problems are a warning sign that you are on the wrong track. You can learn to identify which problems are trying to lead you in a new direction and which ones simply ask to be solved.

All of us have definite ideas about how we are doing financially and just what we want our money to do for us. All of us must take those ideas and commit them to a plan, a financial road map, if you will. This financial plan becomes the written answer, the on paper solution to our financial challenges. You can learn to focus on the solution rather than on the problem and maintain a positive attitude toward life. Things work out best for those who make the best of the way things work out.

What kind of financial solutions do you need to find in your life? Do you have excessive debt? Are you facing college bills for yourself or your children? Are you single, but need to save for marriage? Are you planning to purchase a house or are you simply facing the financial challenge of preparing for your long-term future? The way to connect all these dots is through the design of a good financial plan. This plan, like a good road map, shows you exactly your current financial picture, where you are now, where you wish to be in the future, and what steps to take to get you there. It answers the standard questions of how, what, why, when and where.

What is your solution? What is your plan? Let me suggest an uncomplicated beginning plan that sounds so simplistic that it just might work for you. You can condense it all down to just five words. That is: spend less and save more.

Spending less is a simple answer, but it's not so easy to accomplish. Perhaps you have formed bad money management habits that have haunted you for years. Don't you think now would be a good time break the bands of bondage? You can spend less by eliminating wasteful spending. Do you really need those expensive toys you only use a few times a year? Sometimes the maintenance and insurance alone for SUVs, motorcycles, boats, RVs, guns, wave runners, snowmobiles and other cash-draining hobbies can run into the hundreds if not thousands of dollars (this amount, of course, is after the initial purchase cost).

Saving more is the financial solution. Of course you cannot save until you eliminate the debt and payments to service your debt. That frees up cash to save more. If you are a consumer with bad spending habits, you are probably adding to your debt load every month. If so, now is the time to rein in your spending and change those bad habits. Change those bad-spending habits into good-savings habits.

> **Things work out best for those who make the best of the way things work out.**

When you find solutions to your financial problems, your personal stress level goes way down. When you waste less money, you have more cash to pay down debt. Paying down debt frees your cash to be saved and invested. Your hard-earned dollars won't be spent on frivolous purchases. This means your long hours and work-filled weeks will be used to make your retirement years more comfortable instead of your current days and weeks more stressful.

Break free from financial bondage. Get the right attitude! Discover how you can find financial solutions!

I Can Change My Attitude—
I Can Change My Life

ATTITUDE isn't simply a state of mind; it is also a reflection of what we value. Attitude is more than just saying we can; it is believing we can.

Attitude requires believing before seeing, because seeing is based on circumstances and believing is based on faith. Attitude is contagious, especially when we ready ourselves for our tomorrows.

We have total ownership of our attitudes. No one else has the power to alter our attitudes without our permission. Our attitude allows us to become more empowered than money, to rise above our failures and accept others for who they are, and what they say.

Attitude is more important than giftedness, and is the forerunner of all skills needed for happiness and success. Our attitudes can be used to build us up or put us down—the choice is ours.

Attitude also gives us the wisdom to know that we can't change events of the past. I am convinced that life is 10% what happens to me and 90% how I respond to it—and with this state of mind, I remain in charge of my attitude.

Attitude is a choice! We have the power to choose our responses to any situation. Two kinds of choice-point filters have a profound impact on our responses: those within and those outside of our control.

Some choice influences, such as gender and age, are outside our control. Others, such as values and education, are within our control. Through our attitude, we can empower the elements within our control while minimizing the effect of those outside our control.

OUTSIDE OUR CONTROL	WITHIN OUR CONTROL
Race	Feelings
Sex	Thoughts
Age	Attitudes
Country of Origin	Values
Birth Family	Desires
Physical Attributes	Education
Other's Choices	My Choices

Whether within or outside our control, our attitude can greatly influence our response to the circumstances of life. Do financial setbacks come our way? Of course. Do they have to keep us down? Certainly not!

> **Attitude is more than just saying "I can;" it's believing you can.**

Your attitude is one of the few things in life you can control. Although you can't foresee the ups and downs you'll experience, you can control how you'll react to them.

THE BUCKETS

I read a story about two little buckets who were on their way to the well. These were talking buckets!

"You look mighty sad," said one bucket to the other.

"I was just thinking about the uselessness of what we do," said the sad bucket. "Time after time we go down to the well and get full, but we always come back to the well empty."

"You've got the wrong slant," said the other bucket. "I enjoy what we're doing. The way I look at it, no matter how many times we come to the well empty, we <u>always</u> <u>leave</u> <u>full</u>."

Attitudes are highly contagious. They can have a profound effect on the people with whom we live and work. Choose to be a positive person!

OPTIMISTS AND PESSIMISTS

Have you heard this story? What does the optimist say about the glass and the water? *(It's half full!)* And what does the pessimist say? *(It's half empty!)* Finally what does the process reengineer say about it? ("It looks like you've got twice as much glass as you need there.")

All of us have the freedom to make choices in life. No one tells us which choices to make; we have complete freedom to make our choices. Attitude is a choice. Don't choose negativity. Choose to be an optimist—to believe in yourself and others. Associate with positive leaders. Seek advice from those who are firmly in control of their finances. Get advice from those who have become debt free. If they have become successful in this area of their personal lives, then you can too!

Watch your financial attitude! Are you seeking a solution or just looking for more problems? Do you tend to see the dark side of things or the bright side of things? Are you trying to be an optimist or a pessimist?

THE FARMERS

Here is a very old but humorous story: There were two farmers. One was a pessimist, the other an optimist. The optimist would say, "What a beautiful day, lots of sunshine." The pessimist would respond, "Yes, but I'm afraid too much sunshine will scorch the crops." The optimist would say, "We had such a nice rainfall." The pessimist would respond, "Yes, but I'm afraid too much rain will flood the crops."

One day the optimist said to the pessimist, "Have you seen my new bird dog? He is the finest dog money can buy!" The pessimist answered and said, "You mean that mutt I saw penned up behind your house? He didn't look like much to me!"

The optimist said to the pessimist, "How about going hunting with me tomorrow?" The pessimist agreed to go. The two farmers went on a hunting trip. They shot some ducks. The optimist ordered his dog to get the ducks.

The dog obediently responded. But instead of swimming in the water after the ducks, the dog walked on top of the water, retrieved the ducks, and then walked back to his owner still walking on top of the water.

The optimist turned to the pessimist and said, "Now, just what do you think of my dog?" After pondering the question, the pessimist replied, "Hmmm, your dog can't swim, can he?"

Aren't we all like that at times? We can't see the good in our financial world because we focus on faults or problems. Someone once said, "In the middle of every difficulty lies opportunity."

The Bible speaks about focusing on the right things.

Philippians 4:8

"Finally, brothers, whatever is true, whatever is noble, whatever is right, whatever is pure, whatever is lovely, whatever is admirable—if anything is excellent or praiseworthy—think about such things."

Attitude is more than just saying "I can"; it's believing you can. It requires believing before seeing, because seeing is based on circumstances, and believing is based on faith.

Break free from financial bondage.
Get the right attitude!
Discover how you can
change your attitude and
you can change your life!

Section Three

The Responsibility

The Responsibility
of Acknowledgment

*A*re we the owners of our money and possessions, or is God? The correct answer is that God owns it all. As creator of the world and owner of all that it possesses, He is in complete control of everything. God owns the world. God owns me. God owns my money. God owns my possessions. He owns me because He created me. He owns me because He bought me again when He purchased me with His life. I need to acknowledge His ownership!

It is also true that if God owns it all, He has the right to control it all. If He has the right to control it all, does He not also have the right to delegate some responsibility to us? The Bible calls us stewards. Our role today is that of manager. A steward or manager is someone that has been put in charge of possessions he or she does not own.

If everything truly comes from God (and it does), then He owns it all. If He owns it all, then we have been placed in charge of possessions that belong to someone else. We, as stewards or managers, are accountable to the owner (God) for the quality of managing. What kind of results are we producing? How good of a money/possession manager are you? Is there room for improvement?

GOD OWNS IT ALL

What then belongs to God? Of course, the real personal struggle usually accompanies the money He allows to flow through our hands and the material possessions we often try to accumulate. It all comes from God.

THE EARTH

1 Chronicles 29:13, 14

"Our God, we thank thee, . . . For all things come of thee, and of thine own have we given thee" (*KJV*).

Exodus 9:29

"The earth is the Lord's."

Isaiah 66:1, 2

"Thus saith the Lord, 'The heaven is my throne, and the earth is my footstool: For all those things hath mine hand made'" (*KJV*).

Acts 7:49, 50

"Heaven is my throne, and earth is my foot-stool: Hath not my hand made all these things?" (*KJV*).

2 Kings 19:15

"Thou art the God . . . thou hast made heaven and earth" (*KJV*).

Nehemiah 9:6

"Thou, even thou, art Lord alone; thou hast made heaven, the heaven of heavens, with all their host, the earth, and all things that are therein, the seas, and all that is therein, and thou preservest them all" (*KJV*).

Jeremiah 27:5

"I have made the earth, the man and the beast that are upon the ground, by my great power and by my out-stretched arm, and have given it unto whom it seemed meet unto me" (*KJV*).

Hebrews 1:10

"And, thou, Lord, in the beginning hast laid the foundation of the earth; and the heavens are the works of thine hands" (*KJV*).

Acts 17:24

"God that made the world and all things therein, seeing that he is Lord of heaven and earth, dwelleth not in temples made with hands" (*KJV*).

Job 12:9, 10

"Who knoweth not in all these that the hand of the Lord hath wrought this? In whose hand is the soul [life] of every living thing, and the breath of all mankind" (*KJV*).

Psalm 89:11

"The heavens are thine, the earth also is thine: as for the world and the fulness thereof, thou hast founded them" (*KJV*).

Psalm 95:3, 5

"For the Lord z a great God. . . . The sea is his, for he made it, and his hands formed the dry land."

Daniel 4:17

"The most High ruleth in the kingdom of men, and giveth it to whomsoever he wills, and setteth up over it the basest of men" (*KJV*).

John 19:11

"Jesus answered, 'Thou couldest have no power at all against me, except it were given thee from above'" (*KJV*).

Revelation 4:11

"Thou art worthy, O Lord, to receive glory and honour and power: for thou hast created all things, and for thy pleasure they are and were created" (*KJV*).

OUR POSSESSIONS (MATERIAL AND MONEY)

1 Timothy 6:17-19

"Command those who are rich in this present world not to be arrogant nor to put their hope in wealth, which is so uncertain, but to put their hope in God, who richly provides us with everything for our enjoyment. Command them to do good, to be rich in good deeds, and to be generous and willing to share. In this way they will lay up treasure for themselves as a firm foundation for the coming age, so that they may take hold of the life that is truly life."

Note here that God "richly provides" us with everything for our enjoyment, but it does come with some conditions; to do good, be rich in good deeds, be generous and be willing to share.

OUR ABILITIES

God gives us talents and abilities so we can use them for His kingdom. We are accountable for His giftings.

Romans 12:6-8

We have different gifts, according to the grace given us. If a man's gift is prophesying, let him use it in proportion to his faith. If it is serving, let him serve; if it is teaching, let him teach; if it is encouraging, let him encourage; if it is contributing to the needs of others, let him give generously; if it is leadership, let him govern diligently; if it is showing mercy, let him do it cheerfully."

OUR TIME

Ephesians 5:15, 16

"Be very careful, then, how you live—not as unwise but as wise, making the most of every opportunity, because the days are evil."

OUR BODIES

1 Corinthians 6:19, 20

"Do you not know that your body is a temple of the Holy Spirit, who is in you, whom you have received from God? You are not your own; you were bought at a price. Therefore honor God with your body. "

Romans 12:1, 2

"Therefore, I urge you, brothers, in view of God's mercy, to offer your bodies as living sacrifices, holy and pleasing to God—this is your spiritual act of worship. Do not conform any longer to the pattern of this world, but be transformed by the renewing of your mind. Then you will be able to test and approve what God's will is—his good, pleasing and perfect will."

Having the knowledge that God owns it all is the first step to becoming an honorable steward. It is crucial that you take a moment to reflect and confess to yourself and to God that He is in control and that you want to be a reputable steward of His possessions.

Although head knowledge and confession are good, it is more important that you live a lifestyle of fulfilling this principle. These words should be embedded in your heart and their fruit exemplified in your daily decisions: What I do with my possessions reveals what is truly in my heart.

Learn the right way to live.
Understand the responsibility
of acknowledgment!

The Responsibility
of Understanding Creation

*B*ecoming debt free takes a lot of hands-on hard work and persistent labor. It is never an easy task. It is rewarding, but challenging. Only God has the power to speak the word and cause something to happen instantly, but with man, work is necessary to accomplish an end result. In the book of Genesis, Adam was the sole steward appointed over all natural resources, as well as plant and animal life—a substantial entrustment from God. So when Adam disobeyed and lost that leadership, it affected a lot more than his descendants; it affected the sea, the air, the earth and life as well.

When the steward (Adam) went astray, that which had been entrusted to him was severely injured. According to Romans 8:22, the whole earth groans in travail. When Adam and Eve sinned, God judged them. Humans were required to leave the plush Garden of Eden. God commanded in Genesis 3:19, "In the sweat of thy face shalt thou eat bread, till thou return unto the ground" (*KJV*).

Robert Ingersoll once said, "Every man is dishonest who lives upon the labor of others, no matter if he occupies a throne." The famous poet Robert Frost once gave an insightful quotation regarding work and people. He said, "The world is filled with willing people. Some willing to work, and the rest willing to let them."

In the United States, unlike Third World countries, we do not have a lower class. Though many think otherwise, all healthy people who want to work can do so, provide for themselves and have plenty to eat and shelter for sleep. There are, of course, economic cycles of employment, job availability, discomfort and times when growth opportunity is limited. When compared to the poor of this world, however, those who lack the most in this country are far better off than almost anyone anywhere else in the world.

In the Western world, a great deal of emphasis is placed upon having fun, spending time in leisurely activity and taking care of the whims of "me." Many are content to put as little into their work as they think they can get away with. Far too many employees are receiving a full paycheck for less than a full day's work. Scriptures note in 2 Thessalonians 3:10, "If any would not work, neither should he eat" (*KJV*).

One sure sign of progress in your journey to becoming debt free is simple recognition and understanding that there is no easy solution to a difficult challenge. While others are looking for their "ship to come in" or an easy path out of their mounting debt, you are quietly affirming to put your hand to the plow, get serious about debt relief and carve out a good financial future for yourself. Only God can speak a word that can create something new. For all of us, getting out of debt and remaining debt free takes a lot of effort and determination.

Learn the right way to live.
Understand the responsibility
of understanding creation!

The Responsibility of Reflection

2 Timothy 2:7

"Reflect on what I am saying, for the Lord will give you insight into all this."

How often do you take the time to reflect upon your financial responsibilities and stewardship obligations? Your stewardship defines your relationship with the Lord. How you manage what God has entrusted to you is an accurate reflection of your heart. Does your heart reflect a good understanding that everything you are and everything you have are nothing more than stewardship gifts from heaven? We are nothing more than managers of God's good gifts.

What is your relationship to God? Do you have a good personal relationship with Him? Do you spend time developing this relationship? A good relationship is built upon trust. A good relationship is built upon faith, confidence and expectation. God expects you to do a good job taking care of your gifts—gifts of talent, time, health, possessions and wealth. Many things come and go in our life, but gifts given by God are with us virtually every minute of every day. Having said that, our daily decisions and daily walk should reflect the trust relationship we have developed with God, and this relationship should be growing closer and maturing continually.

Our life's stewardship should reflect God's interest in all He has entrusted to us. Genesis 1:26 records that God made us to rule over all the earth and all life on earth, both plant and animal. In Genesis 2:15, man was made steward over the Garden, in which there was gold, precious stones and rivers. In other words, we were created for more than going to heaven after a lifetime of waiting. We were created to be faithful stewards over the work of God's hands, His creation.

God places in us a lot of trust; it is more than just money and finances. Our entire being and how we handle faithfulness, responsibility, accountability, honesty and integrity are involved. Stewardship is bringing everything we have to offer under the Lordship of Christ. What kind of a person makes a good steward? A person who has great respect for God and His creation. Are you a good steward?

Is your relationship with God reflected in every financial decision you make? When you receive income from the job God has blessed you with, do you pause to reflect on His goodness before you do anything else, or do you quickly spend it on nonessentials without regard to making the wise money-management decisions you know you should be making? Do you mirror the image of God? Do you reflect the wisdom of God in your financial life? Are you replicating His will in your financial world? Are you seeking insight and understanding before you initiate what seems right in your own eyes?

2 Corinthians 3:18

"But we Christians have no veil over our faces; we can be mirrors that brightly reflect the glory of the Lord. And as the Spirit of the Lord works within us, we become more and more like him" (*TLB*).

Learn the right way to live.
Understand the responsibility
of reflection!

The Responsibility
of Gifting Stewardship

Each of us has been given access to gifts from God. Are you developing those gifts? Are you using and exercising the gifting of God? If God has blessed you with houses and lands, businesses and possessions, are you trusting only in them and pursuing more of the same or are you developing good stewardship over them? If these things mean a lot to you and you give all your time and all your money to seeking more, than be careful, because you won't have them forever. However, if you are pursuing God and the things of His kingdom, God will probably trust you with more.

If we are idle and lazy, we will be judged accordingly (Ecclesiastes 10:18). At judgment day we will give account for every idle word we speak (Matthew 12:36). If we must account for an idle word, what about idle time? The apostle Paul encouraged the Ephesians to redeem the time (Ephesians 5:16). The Greek word is *exagorazo* and means "to buy up" or "rescue from loss" (*Strong's Concordance*).

A great lesson can be learned from the Matthew 25:14-25 parable of the talents. When God invests something in our lives and allows us to have stewardship over it, we must use it for His glory and His kingdom. If we do nothing with it, God will take it away and give it to another. If we do not know how to invest it into the kingdom or how to take care of it, we had better seek some wisdom. God is very interested in our caretaking ability and what we do with our time, money, possessions and ministry giftings. What we do, where we go and the actions we take are very important to God. Remember, we are not the owners of all God has given us; we are only stewards—we are managers and therefore responsible for the gifts and accountable for their use.

In addition to the stewardship of our giftings, consider the gifting of our stewardship. The biblical story of the poor widow models how our gifting stewardship should be.

Luke 21:1-3

"As he looked up, Jesus saw the rich putting their gifts into the temple treasury. He also saw a poor widow put in two very small copper coins. 'I tell you the truth,' he said, 'this poor widow has put in more than all the others. All these people gave their gifts out of their wealth; but she out of her poverty put in all she had to live on.'"

The widow was poor, perhaps destitute. She had a couple of coins to pay for her next meal or two, but that's it. Her desire to give to God was so powerful that she pulled both coins from her pocket and gave all she had.

She gave cheerfully to the work of the kingdom. No one saw her do it. No one knew what she gave. No one understood that she gave it all. No one even noticed—no one, except Jesus. Jesus knows the depth of her sacrifice. Jesus knows what it cost her. All of the other givers on that day gave out of their abundance, out of their wealth. She gave out of her poverty.

This woman is a model for us to have the right motivation in giving. When Jesus spoke about giving in His Sermon on the Mount, He taught that the motivation for giving should not be to receive the praise of men or to impress people with our wealth or generosity. Instead, we should be so focused on pleasing God (more than men) that we do not even allow others to see that we are giving.

When God invests something in our lives and allows us to have stewardship over it, we must use it for His glory and His kingdom.

Matthew 6:1-4

"'Take heed that you do not do your charitable deeds before men, to be seen by them. Otherwise you have no reward from your Father in heaven. Therefore, when you do a charitable deed, do not sound a trumpet before you as the hypocrites do in the synagogues and in the streets, that they may have glory from men.

Assuredly, I say to you, they have their reward. But when you do a charitable deed, do not let your left hand know what your right hand is doing, that your charitable deed may be in secret; and your Father who sees in secret will himself reward you openly'" (*NKJV*).

Learn the right way to live. Understand the responsibility of gifting stewardship!

The Responsibility
of Productivity

ood stewardship is not merely an occupation or a profession, rather it involves being productive. In Jesus' parable of the talents in Matthew 25, the stewards reported their earnings. One servant, however, merely hid his entrustment, and earned no increase—he lost his portion. The faithful ones not only had increases but also received more because of their faithfulness. From the very beginning, God commanded creation to be fruitful. God is energetic, creative and imaginative and is the life giver. Stewards are also to be concerned with productivity and so cultivate God's creation to be productive.

It is wonderful to live in a productive society. Productive societies are composed of many productive individuals. When my days are full of productive tasks, I enjoy life. My normal going-to-sleep activity is to close my eyes and mentally survey all the productive things I accomplished during the day. If I have had an efficient and industrious day, I fall right to sleep.

A warning about being productive is seen in Jesus' story about the unfruitful branch of His kingdom, which He says will be cut off by the husbandman (John 15:1-5). God wants to have a productive kingdom and stewards who will be faithful.

As good stewards, we are required to work hard. If you work for someone else, you need to do it with everything you have. Give more than is required; go the second mile and the third and fourth. Proverbs 6:6-11 says, "Go to the ant, you sluggard; consider its ways and be wise! It has no commander, no overseer or ruler, yet it stores its provisions in summer and gathers its food at harvest. How long will you lie there, you sluggard? When will you get up from your sleep? A little sleep, a little slumber, a little folding of the hands to rest and poverty will come on you like a bandit and scarcity like an armed man."

Check out the ant. The ant has no one to tell it what to do—not supervisor, nor overseer, and yet it is a self-starter, a self-motivator. The ant works all summer long gathering food for the harvest season. The Scripture extends a wake-up call to the sluggard hoping for some kind of response. It says to the sluggard, "Have you not slept enough?" "How long can you possibly sleep?" "Do you want to go hungry? Do you want to go through life looking for handouts because you have not the wherewithal to earn your own keep?"

SCRIPTURES ON PRODUCTIVITY

1 Thessalonians 4:11

"Make it your ambition to lead a quiet life, to mind your own business and to work with your hands, just as we told you, so that your daily life may win the respect of outsiders and so that you will not be dependent on anybody."

Proverbs 22:29

"Do you see a man skilled in his work? He will serve before kings; he will not serve before obscure men."

Ecclesiastes 9:10

"Whatever your hand finds to do, do it with all your might."

Proverbs 20:4

"A sluggard does not plow in season; so at harvest time he looks but finds nothing."

God is energetic, creative and imaginative and is the life giver.

According to the above Scriptures, we should approach life and work like the ant. Although the ant has no boss, it still works extremely hard to provide for its needs. A lot of people today could learn a valuable lesson from the ant. Some today have the attitude that if I can get someone else to do the work for me, then why should I exert myself? Why not let someone else do the work; why not let the government provide for me? Many today have little or no initiative, are not able to put themselves to work and must always have someone else instruct them and supervise them in order to keep them working. The biblical way is for each person to accept the personal responsibility to be a contributor to society and a person of productivity.

Learn the right way to live. Understand the responsibility of productivity!

The Responsibility
of Time Management

*B*ecoming debt free requires efficient and productive use of our time. We are required to redeem the minutes and capture the hours. We should be filling efficient days and occupying industrious weeks. Our effective and productive months should result in progressive years. We have a responsibility not to waste the precious little time we have been given.

Several years ago, I traveled to a small town with a couple of friends. Our mission was to paint the house of a dying man. The house was in need of a fresh coat of paint and we had wanted to pay him a visit. Instead of just standing around watching his pain, we intended to help brighten his day by painting the house.

As we were saying our good-byes at the end of the day, he made a profound statement I still remember as if it were yesterday. He said, "It pays to give it all you've got while you're on stage, because you never know when your act is up." Soon afterward, he died of cancer.

Time is our tool. It is a wonderful gift. We should not be a slave to it; we should put it to proper use as an investment for the future.

God is the giver of life and the giver of time. He has the right to expect us to use it wisely. We have a responsibility to make the most of it. Good stewards of time and finance are not only faithful and responsible, but also have an honesty and financial integrity about them.

God is the God of the past, present and future. He has no time constraints. He is not bound by the limitations of time. Time means nothing to Him. See what the Word says about it.

2 Peter 3:8

"But do not forget this one thing, dear friends: With the Lord a day is like a thousand years, and a thousand years are like a day."

On earth, we (you and I) are constrained by time. Our lives are but a few years, at best. Our time is limited. Time means a lot to us. God has allotted us just a limited amount of years and, therefore, is very concerned how wisely we spend those years.

Job 14:1, 2

"Man born of woman is of few days and full of trouble. He springs up like a flower and withers away; like a fleeting shadow, he does not endure."

Psalm 90:10

"The length of our days is seventy years—or eighty, if we have the strength; yet their span is but trouble and sorrow, for they quickly pass, and we fly away. "

Ephesians 5:15, 16

"Be very careful, then, how you live—not as unwise but as wise, making the most of every opportunity, because the days are evil."

John 9:4, 5

"As long as it is day, we must do the work of him who sent me. Night is coming, when no one can work. While I am in the world, I am the light of the world."

Time is valuable and utterly irretrievable; it is a priceless commodity. Suppose your bank credited your account each morning with $86,400.00, carried no balance from day to day, and allowed you to keep no cash in your account. Then suppose every evening the bank canceled whatever you failed to use during the day.

We all have this kind of bank; its name is time. Every morning it credits us with 86,400 seconds. Every night it considers lost whatever time we have failed to invest for good during the day. It carries over no balance. It allows no overdrafts. Each day it opens up a new account. Each night it burns the records of the day. If you failed to use the day's deposits, the loss is yours.

We are all given 1,440 minutes each day, 168 hours each week. This makes 52 weeks each year for which we must account. In spite of its value and unique characteristics, we probably waste time more thoughtlessly than anything else.

Adlai Stevenson once said, "It's not the days in your life, but the life in your days." In other words, it's not how much you do that counts, it's how much you get done that has purpose and lasting benefit.

This seems to be the great paradox in life. We generally feel as though we don't have enough time, yet we have all the time there is. Time is NOT the problem; the problem is how we use our allotted time.

Learn the right way to live.
Understand the responsibility
of time management!

The Responsibility of Planning Ahead

*D*ebt reduction will never take place without the assistance of a written plan. Planning ahead for an eventual result provides a road map to follow with predesignated milestones. If you don't have a plan, how will you know when you are successful? Without a predetermined road map, how do you know where you are going? Without a target in your crosshair, how will you know if you are pointed in the right direction? It is your responsibility to have a written plan that continually measures your debt-reduction progress.

Planning for the future is biblical. Joseph told the people of Egypt to prepare for the coming famine. During the years of surplus, Joseph was wise enough to gather the excess and store it for later use. He was a great model of advance preparation in process. The preparation done by the Egyptians cared for their needs during the years of lack.

Genesis 41:48, 49

"Joseph collected all the food produced in those seven years of abundance in Egypt and stored it in the cities. In each city he put the food grown in the fields surrounding it. Joseph stored up huge quantities of grain, like the sand of the sea; it was so much that he stopped keeping records because it was beyond measure."

While we are in good health, we too have the opportunity to be employed and should be living below our means. We should be setting aside money to help should there be a time of financial drought in our lives. We should be living the principle of advance preparation and planning.

Here is a biblical story about a man about to lose his job, planning ahead for his future well being, even though he does so in an unscrupulous way:

Luke 16:1-8

"Jesus told his disciples: 'There was a rich man whose manager was accused of wasting his possessions. So he called him in and asked him, "What is this I hear about you? Give an account of your management, because you cannot be manager any longer." The manager said to himself, *What shall I do now?*

My master is taking away my job. I'm not strong enough to dig, and I'm ashamed to beg—I know what I'll do so that, when I lose my job here, people will welcome me into their houses. So he called in each one of his master's debtors. He asked the first, "How much do you owe my master?" "Eight hundred gallons of olive oil," he replied. The manager told him, "Take your bill, sit down quickly, and make it four hundred." Then he asked the second, "And how much do you owe?" "A thousand bushels of wheat," he replied. He told him, "Take your bill and make it eight hundred." The master commended the dishonest manager because he had acted shrewdly. For the people of this world are more shrewd in dealing with their own kind than are the people of the light.'"

Sensible people look ahead and plan for the future. They manage money to provide benefit for the present, as well as the future. Christ is suggesting that in doing good works we should consider our future with just as much ingenuity as the dishonest steward considered his future. As stewards of Jesus Christ, we are mandated with the responsibility to use every means at our disposal to spread the Good News to all. In doing so, our gains will have great effect in eternal matters.

The shrewdness with which the unjust servant negated his responsibility to his lord was commended. He promoted his cause with the utmost care and effort. With an unprincipled passion he sought to use his master's money in securing advantage after his inevitable dismissal. Christ was simply asking those to whom he spoke to be just as inventive, but for a better cause. This can happen only when we look down the line a bit and seek to plan ahead. The message is clear. In our stewardship responsibility to God, we should be at least as wholehearted and energetic as the misguided steward was in prosecuting his own interests.

Learn the right way to live.
Understand the responsibility
of planning ahead!

The Responsibility
of Disciplined Living

*I*f we are to lead prosperous and successful lives (prosperity is not to be thought of as just having money), we have to apply biblical instruction to work hard and lead a disciplined life. Clearly, we are to do the very best we possibly can with the talents and strengths God has given us. A lot of people think that the world (that just means you and me) owes them a living. This kind of attitude destroys the work ethic in our society. Our country's welfare system does little to build character and establish the needy into better life-changing environments. To give money year after year to those who are idle and not expect any change in lifestyle does little to improve society for future generations.

Although in Matthew 26:11, Jesus said "Ye have the poor always with you" (*KJV*), the Western world has been blessed beyond measure. Those we consider poor by our country's standards could be considered rich by the measurements of the entire world. How many families in our society are without a television set or two or three? How many in this country do not have access to transportation? How many do not have shelter when they want it? How many do not enjoy the basics of life? Yes, we are a very blessed people.

Living a responsible and disciplined life requires financial discipline. Larry Burkett, a Christian economist who went to meet his heavenly reward in 2003, once noted that in 1929, the majority of all home purchases were made in cash. Roughly 95% of purchase transactions were paid in cash. Today, only 5% of homes are purchased with cash and 95% are mortgaged.

In the years prior to 1945, almost no cars were financed. It was almost unthinkable to purchase a vehicle with loaned money. If you didn't have the cash, you didn't purchase a car. Yet, by contrast today, the average person has seven credit cards, at least one financed vehicle and a mortgaged home loan. Credit card debt is at an all time high; nearly 72% of people never pay off their credit card balances each month. Where is the financial discipline of people today? It seems it doesn't exist.

It is sad when Christ has called us to be free people, yet many become enslaved to debt.

Galatians 5:1

"It is for freedom that Christ has set us free. Stand firm, then, and do not let yourselves be burdened again by a yoke of slavery."

Accepting the responsibility of a disciplined life is accepting the responsibility of financial discipline. Accepting this financial responsibility will ultimately result in reducing major stress in our lives. It will give us unequaled freedom, the flexibility to come and go and live anywhere and enormous personal fulfillment. I believe God wants us to have the freedom to respond to His call. This means we can be flexible and mobile in a relatively short time period. That is simply not possible when you live undisciplined financial lives. When we live from paycheck to paycheck and payment to payment, we simply do not have mobility.

God has given us dominion over the earth. But we have taken our God-given freedoms and submitted ourselves to the bondage of burdensome debt. Instead of serving God, we live to serve our lenders. Instead of being debt free and having a great testimony that God is taking care of our needs, we show our friends, family and neighbors that we have a lack of trust and confidence in God's ability to care for us—so much so that we go into debt to get things He has not supplied.

Learn the right way to live.
Understand the responsibility
of disciplined living!

The Responsibility of Diligence

Proverbs 21:25, 26

"The sluggard's craving will be the death of him, because his hands refuse to work. All day long he craves for more, but the righteous give without sparing."

Romans 12:11

"Not slothful in business; fervent in spirit; serving the Lord" (*KJV*).

Proverbs 24:30-34

"I went past the field of the sluggard, past the vineyard of the man who lacks judgment; thorns had come up everywhere, the ground was covered with weeds, and the stone wall was in ruins. I applied my heart to what I observed and learned a lesson from what I saw: A little sleep, a little slumber, a little folding of the hands to rest—and poverty will come on you like a bandit and scarcity like an armed man."

It is everyone's responsibility to be hard working, persistent, and diligent. The person who has no diligence is lazy—a sluggard, if you will. The sluggard. What can be said about this kind of person? Is he self-centered or lazy? Does he rest; does he do what he wants to do without regard to others? Certainly all these things probably describe a sluggard, but much more could be said.

At the very least, a sluggard has a major problem with procrastination. His motto would be to "Never do today what you can put off until tomorrow"; always with good intentions; always just about ready to start a job, but not quite. The sluggard probably gets started on a few jobs, and with some of those tasks he may even get some things done, but never quite gets them finished or brought to completion.

What is his excuse? Maybe he didn't have all the tools to finish the job. Maybe he wasn't feeling well. Maybe the rain was on its way or it could be just that the sun was not shining brightly enough. Perhaps his excuse is that the job became bigger than he was expecting or it became more time consuming than he was willing to commit to. Whatever the excuse, the sluggard always finds a reason for not finishing the job.

The sluggard as portrayed in Proverbs is an example of what not to be like and presents a valuable lesson for us to learn. Proverbs 20:4 tells us that the sluggard is too lazy to pull a plow in the springtime, and therefore has no harvest in the fall. In Proverbs 22:13, he lets his mind wander, but refuses to move his body. He has a great reason why he can't get it into gear.

He says there could be a lion outside, and if he goes out to work, he could be murdered in the streets! Whatever the situation, when the sluggard makes up his mind that he doesn't feel like working today, he will find an excuse to justify his inaction. He will find some kind of plausible explanation for his decision. He will leap to shirk his responsibilities, for he has a quick mind and a lazy body.

The ancient Chinese philosopher Confucius once said, "The expectations of life depend upon diligence; the mechanic that would perfect his work must first sharpen his tools."

Samuel Johnson noted, "If your determination is fixed, I do not counsel you to despair. Few things are impossible to diligence and skill. Great works are performed not by strength, but perseverance."

William Penn equated faith and diligence when he said, "Patience and diligence, like faith, remove mountains."

Proverbs 12:27 says, "The lazy man does not roast his game, but the diligent man prizes his possessions." Here is the picture of a sluggard who is not only lazy, but also wasteful. Not only does he do what he wants to, when he wants to, but he is also is a great waster of resources and provision. He goes out, he hunts his game, he kills his game. But after the fun of the hunt, the work never begins. He could prepare the provision for his family or the poor, the needy and the hungry, but he instead chooses to walk away from it, lets it die and lie and does not make the food available for the hungry.

Diligent people don't waste God's provision. They thank God for the provision and prepare the meat for future use. They share it with others. They continue diligently using the resources available to them.

Sluggards are not like that. They are not interested in saving resources and helping others. To them it is all about the fun of the sport. They are wasteful about everything. Sluggards proclaim that when their ships come in, they will begin to give. Herein lies the problem: If you never sent your ship out to begin with, you cannot expect it to come in. For what kind of ship are you waiting? Money does not fall from heaven. God does not give money miracles to a lazy, slothful person.

If you are not going to live the life of a sluggard, you need to get your act together. You need to start working, using godly wisdom and insight. You need to understand your calling and purpose in life and set out objectives that will allow you to live that fulfilled life. Then, and only then, will you reap with joy what you have sowed with tears.

THE SLUGGARD

'Tis the voice of the Sluggard: I heard him complain,
"You have waked me too soon! I must slumber again!"
As the door on its hinges, so he on his bed
Turns his sides, and his shoulders, and his heavy head.

"A little more sleep, and a little more slumber!"
Thus he wastes half his days and his hours
without number;
And when he gets up he sits folding his hands,
Or walks about sauntering, or trifling he stands.

I made him a visit, still hoping to find
He had taken better care for improving his mind:
He told me his dreams, talk'd of eating and drinking
But he scarce reads his Bible, and never loves thinking.

—*Issac Watts (1674–1748)*

Learn the right way to live.
Understand the responsibility
of personal diligence!

The Responsibility
of No Waste

*M*any people, deep in debt, complain that their employers don't pay them enough, their taxes are much too high, their business costs have skyrocketed, or render some other excuse why they cannot plan for their financial future. Of course, some of these excuses may have a certain amount of legitimacy to them, but they don't excuse a person from the responsibility of "no waste." The problem is not a lack of money; it is a problem of lack of money management.

In Luke 16, the story is told of a dishonest steward who wasted his lord's goods, for which he was liable, and was judged by his master.

In times past, I thought this steward was expelled from his job because of fraud. But the verses do not say this. If it were fraud, the master never would have let him stay around long enough to make alternate arrangements with the master's debtors. The verses simply infer that he was a bad money manager. If the steward had not been so fiscally challenged, the master could have had a better return on his investments and not wasted the investment return he never received.

Today, we also are responsible to our Master for His creation and blessing. The scope of the parable suggests to us that it is important to manage our possessions and life on earth in such a way that will benefit us in eternal life. It's not that eternal life is our sole reason for managing our possessions judiciously. We should do this from our obedience, appreciation and love for God.

We are wrong to make bad decisions when we waste the finances God has allowed to flow through our lives. All of us are stewards of what has been entrusted to us. We have a fiduciary responsibility to employ our wealth in acts of charity and good works, seeking an eternal return much the same way the dishonest steward employed his abilities to achieve the greatest temporal profit.

A lot of wasteful spending is incurred on perfectly good purchases, but more often than not, many purchases are for things we neither need nor use. How many attics, basements and garages are full of great buys that were never used? If they were used, maybe they were rarely used. I could tell you about some exercise equipment I purchased that falls into this category. When all is said and done, the amount spent on these items, although seemingly legit, was very wasteful.

In Luke 16, the steward's lord commended him because he finally showed some ingenuity and ambition, even though it was for his own personal gain and benefit. The steward is not commended because he showed good credible sensitivity, rather because he had done wisely for himself. The steward who was about to be dismissed made every attempt to better his cause through any means available—even though that cause was self-serving.

Most people today live far above and beyond their means. Their spending exceeds their earnings. Many people earn large incomes, but because of wasteful spending habits, little goes to personal investment, debt reduction or charitable contribution.

By not spending wisely, or watching every dime spent and knowing for what it was spent, you will be led to poor financial decisions. Bad money management leads to a lot of debt and a lot of debt usually causes a tremendous amount of strain and anxiety on an otherwise good marriage. This kind of pressure can lead to anger, fighting and possibly even divorce.

Learn the right way to live.
Understand the responsibility
of no waste!

The Responsibility of Handling Our Possessions

W hat a person does with personal possessions is important to God."

"Alas, how many, even among those who are called believers, have plenty of all the necessities of life, and yet complain of poverty!"—John Wesley

The manner in which we obtain, hold and disburse our possessions and finances is of utmost importance to God. Jesus said in Luke 16:11, "If therefore ye have not been faithful in the unrighteous mammon, who will commit to your trust the true riches?"(*KJV*). Mammon means "gain or wealth."

What is so much better than money that God calls them "true riches"? True riches could be a lot of things, but certainly they include the gift of salvation, the gift of grace, the gift of mercy and the gift of the Holy Spirit. The Scriptures present a wonderful reality. Second Peter 1:3 notes, "According as his divine power hath given unto us all things that pertain unto life and godliness" (*KJV*).

Accepting the responsibility of handling our possessions means we must be willing to place all we have at God's disposal. Not everyone is successful in this matter, even in biblical days, as is recorded in the following story:

Matthew 19:16-22

"Now a man came up to Jesus and asked, 'Teacher, what good thing must I do to get eternal life?' 'Why do you ask me about what is good?' Jesus replied. 'There is only One who is good. If you want to enter life, obey the commandments.' 'Which ones?' the man inquired. Jesus replied, 'Do not murder, do not commit adultery, do not steal, do not give false testimony, honor your father and mother, and love your neighbor as yourself.' 'All these I have kept,' the young man said. 'What do I still lack?' Jesus answered, 'If you want to be perfect, go, sell your possessions and give to the poor, and you will have treasure in heaven. Then come, follow me.' When the young man heard this, he went away sad, because he had great wealth."

Wealth can keep us from inheriting the kingdom of heaven if it steals our hearts from their rightful place in God's hands. In the story of the rich young ruler, Jesus could see clearly what was lord in his life. He was willing to obey Jesus until it came to money, obviously the true ruler of his heart. God does not ask each of us to sell our possessions and give to the poor, as He did this man, but the principle is still true today. It is about a willing heart. When we are truly surrendered to God's will in our lives, we have a heart that is willing to give everything to God. When our hands are too busy grasping what God has given us, we are unable to receive more. Instead, we should live in such a way that we hold what God has given to us with open hands facing towards heaven. Such a posture says, "Whatever you've given me is Yours, Lord. I freely offer it." Notice though that when we offer, we are also in a position to receive.

To handle possessions well, we must have something for which to be responsible. To have something, we must have been receivers of something. Everything we have we received from someone else. Everything we have came from somewhere. Our automobiles, our home, our furniture, our money, our jobs: they all came from outside of us. Paul makes this point in 1 Corinthians 4:7, "For who makes you different from anyone else? What do you have that you did not receive? And if you did receive it, why do you boast as though you did not?"

Our responsibility to handle our possessions properly means understanding that as we have received with open hands we also give with open hands. Once in receipt of possessions, we don't respond by clenching our fists and holding tight all we have been given. This would indicate an abnormal love for things, making us self-centered, proud and selfish. When we have been blessed with possessions, it becomes our responsibility to care for them and share them as the need arises.

If God can trust us with the least possessions, then He can trust us with great possessions. Once we have received, we cannot get anymore until we have proven responsibility to handle what we have, whether that is money or other possessions. Once we are found faithful with little we can create the capacity to handle more. When we have an open hand, God will fill it. If we close it to others, we close it to God. When we give away, we fill up again. This creates the cycle of stewardship. This is the way God intended for us to live.

Luke 16:10

"Whoever can be trusted with very little can also be trusted with much, and whoever is dishonest with very little will also be dishonest with much."

God gives us things to extend His kingdom. They are kingdom property and we have become mere caretakers. The possessions entrusted to our management are but for a temporary time period. God has given them to us for use in our ERA. No, that's not an Individual Retirement Account, but something much more significant. It is an Eternal Return Account. How we use these possessions is an indicator of how good we are as managers.

Have you reached your limit of responsibility, or can God trust you with more?

Learn the right way to live. Understand the responsibility of handling our possessions!

The Responsibility of Individual Accountability

*C*hristians have access to unlimited and unimaginable resources. Along with this access comes accountability. One of the greatest motivators, and probably the biggest single need regarding stewardship, is accountability.

Accountability begins with the person, not the gifts. Accountability in the human sense is recognized favorably by any society and rewarded accordingly. If you don't take care of that old clunker of a vehicle you now own, how can you take care of a new car? If you goof off during the day at your current job, why would God want to bless you with a better one? If God cannot trust you with $100, how can He trust you with $1,000 or $100,000? If you cannot take good care of your apartment or rental house, how can you be trusted with your own property? A principle is at work here! We must prove that we can be good stewards!

A profound illustration of this principle taken from biblical times is found in the life of Joseph. It seems that in every job he had, he started at the bottom and eventually landed at the top (see Genesis 39-41).

Joseph was tested severely on many occasion; he was lied about, cheated on and forgotten for two years by a man for whom he had done a great favor. What was his secret of success? Joseph was a hard worker, and no matter what job he was assigned, he went after it with efficiency, enthusiasm and energy! And to his credit, Joseph never allowed temporary adversity to make him bitter. He always had a great positive attitude and he maintained a devout trust in God. God honors effort and He will always bless those who are giving their best.

Accountability is the responsibility of people in all economic situations. It doesn't matter how rich, how poor, how educated or how illiterate. The Old Testament includes a story of a very poor woman's accountability. This woman had very little by way of possessions, yet obedience and accountability were required of her.

1 Kings 17:8-16

"Then the word of the LORD came to him: 'Go at once to Zarephath of Sidon and stay there. I have commanded a widow in that place to supply you with food.' So he went to Zarephath. When he came to the town gate, a widow was there gathering sticks. He called to her and asked, 'Would you bring me a little water in a jar so I may have a drink?' As she was going to get it, he called, 'And bring me, please, a piece of bread.'"

"'As surely as the LORD your God lives,' she replied, 'I don't have any bread—only a handful of flour in a jar and a little oil in a jug. I am gathering a few sticks to take home and make a meal for myself and my son, that we may eat it—and die.'"

"Elijah said to her, 'Don't be afraid. Go home and do as you have said. But first make a small cake of bread for me from what you have and bring it to me, and then make something for yourself and your son. For this is what the LORD, the God of Israel, says: 'The jar of flour will not be used up and the jug of oil will not run dry until the day the LORD gives rain on the land.'"

"She went away and did as Elijah had told her. So there was food every day for Elijah and for the woman and her family. For the jar of flour was not used up and the jug of oil did not run dry, in keeping with the word of the LORD spoken by Elijah."

This story is about a woman who was accountable to God in faith and obedience to meet the need of another with what she had in her household. Elijah was dependent on God's provision through this poor widow, one who had almost nothing and was ready to die. This woman was in a famine, a time to be very careful and self-protecting, but the famine was not in her spirit. She had a generous and giving spirit. The famine could not break her; her generosity could not be bound. She gave from her need and poverty from what she had in her household.

This story shows that even if you think you are lacking, God can use the things you do have

to meet a need. You may think you just don't have the money to give right now or you may think that because you have very little, God will excuse you from your responsibility to be fully accountable with what you do have. Not so. God expects accountability from people of all socioeconomic classes.

If you cannot afford to give largely, you must not despise the day of small beginnings. God never asks us to give what we do not have. He only asks that we be willing to give all we do have. Second Corinthians 8:12 shows us that it is the heart that matters: "For if the willingness is there, the gift is acceptable according to what one has, not according to what he does not have." We can look to the needs and then look to our own household, listening to and obeying the voice of the Holy Spirit when He says, "Give."

Like this widow, we too will experience seasons of testing. Enduring such seasons will teach us faith and trust in God. We must not allow a spirit of poverty to bind us, choke us or keep us from giving. If you are experiencing a season like this right now, I encourage you to take the words of Elijah to heart. In 1 Kings 17:3, he tells the widow, "Do not be afraid." When in doubt, we must believe the words of hope that fill the Scriptures, not fearing what our minds or circumstances may say to us. As we put fear aside, we move into the realm of faith, trusting God to provide for us, just as He did for the widow of Zarephath.

Learn the right way to live.
Understand the responsibility
of individual accountability!

The Responsibility of Giving Generously

*G*iving generously is expected of all Christians. After all, we have freely received much—forgiveness of sins, salvation, relationship with God, and the list goes on. Scripture offers the following suggestions:

1 Corinthians 16:2, 3

"On the first day of every week, each one of you should set aside a sum of money in keeping with his income, saving it up, so that when I come no collections will have to be made."

A godly perspective of giving is found in this setting. In it, Paul gives a direction and a formula for consistent, regular giving. Note Paul's appeal for consistency. He asks for regular giving on the first day of the week. He asks specifically that a sum of money be set aside. Finally, he asks for a proportionate amount that is in keeping with one's income.

Giving, like savings, needs to be regular and be designated for your place of worship. Your local church has financial challenges that must be met regularly.

In the book of beginnings, Jacob made his commitment to giving known.

Genesis 28:20-22

"Then Jacob made a vow, saying, 'If God will be with me and will watch over me on this journey I am taking and will give me food to eat and clothes to wear so that I return safely to my father's house, then the LORD will be my God and this stone that I have set up as a pillar will be God's house, and of all that you give me I will give you a tenth.'"

Early in biblical history we see a picture of Jacob, a man who promised God he would return a tenth of all his increase. Jacob was beginning a journey, apparently leaving his family for a period of time, making his bed under the stars. God came to him in a dream, promising him great blessings in the future, which He, of course, did. Jacob promised a tenth, as he understood the principle of giving.

Luke 6:38

"Give, and it shall be given unto you; good measure, pressed down, and shaken together, and running over, shall men give into your bosom. For the measure you give will be the measure you get back" (*KJV*).

Giving is God's trigger for financial miracles. We gain by giving. When you give to the kingdom of God, it will be given back to you. But where will it come from? Who will give to you? Will God cause money to float down from the heavenlies so your needs will be met? No, the *second* part of verse 38 says, "shall men give into your…[life]" (*KJV*). This is how the cycle of blessing works. *When you give to God, God in turn causes others to give to you.* They could be in the form of new customers to your business, new products to sell, and so on. When God owns your business, He will make sure it prospers!

Nothing happens in the economy of God until you give something away. It is a universal law of God. Paul very appropriately reminds us:

"Remember this: Whoever sows sparingly will also reap sparingly, and whoever sows generously will also reap generously. Each man should give what he has decided in his heart to give, not reluctantly or under compulsion, for God loves a cheerful giver. And God is able to make all grace abound to you, so that in all things at all times, having all that you need, you will abound in every good work" (2 Corinthians 9:6-9).

How much money should a Christian give to the Lord? God is not so much interested in how much we give, whether it be the minimum of 10%, 15%, 20% or even 50% of our income, but He is interested in how and why we give. Giving begins with tithing. Tithing is all about obedience.

Tithing has everything to do with trusting God and His promises. Tithing is done in faith. We tithe because He says to. We tithe because we trust Him. Our act of faith brings results.

Disobedience is a serious matter. God had a great future planned for King Saul. He wanted to bless his life and fill it with great authority, power and riches. But then Saul chose to disobey.

1 Samuel 15:19

"Why did you not obey the LORD? Why did you pounce on the plunder and do evil in the eyes of the LORD?"

1 Samuel 15:23

"For rebellion is like the sin of divination, and arrogance like the evil of idolatry. Because you have rejected the word of the LORD, He has rejected you as king."

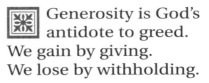 Generosity is God's antidote to greed. We gain by giving. We lose by withholding.

1 Samuel 15:25, 26

"Now I beg you, forgive my sin and come back with me, so that I may worship the LORD." But Samuel said to him, "I will not go back with you. You have rejected the word of the LORD, and the LORD has rejected you as king over Israel!"

Saul was rejected as king of Israel because of his disobedience. Everything God had planned for Saul now was given to David. Everything meant for Saul became David's. Be careful that you do not keep what belongs to God.

Second Corinthians 9:7 tells us how we should

give: "Each man should give what he has decided in his heart to give, not reluctantly or under compulsion, for God loves a cheerful giver." We must be completely honest with ourselves. Do we honestly get a lot more enjoyment from giving than receiving? Too many people put more emphasis on receiving than they do on giving.

Generosity is God's antidote to greed. We gain by giving. We lose by withholding. The person who wants blessing upon life is one who understands giving generously.

God expects us to be generous and to also give with balance. David wrote in Psalm 112:5, 9, "Good will come to him who is generous. . . . He has scattered abroad his gifts to the poor, his righteousness endures forever; his horn will be lifted high in honor." The true spirit and attitude of giving is at the heart of Jesus' instruction in the Sermon on the Mount. It talks about helping the needy. In Luke 6:35 we are told not to expect anything in return for our kindness: "without expecting to get anything back. Then your reward will be great."

So should we then give just to get? Absolutely not! A giving person gives from a spirit of genuine generosity. When the person receives, it is treated as a totally unexpected blessing and he turns around and gives some more! Seeking to get is disastrous to the spirit of giving! Remember, Jesus Christ, Son of Man, Son of God, said, "It is more blessed to give than to receive" (Acts 20:35, *KJV*).

Why is it more blessed to give than to receive? When we give freely and generously, we put God first and ahead of our own selfish interests. By doing this, we are obeying His Word and this obedience will cause Him to bless us. When we give freely and generously, this shows that we trust God. The degree of our giving is a clear indication of our freedom from fear. Freedom from fear is always a blessing.

Freely giving protects us from the pitfalls of greed and materialism. Generous giving comes from a humble, loving heart. Greed and selfishness are derived from a prideful "me first" attitude and this serves to put barriers between us and the blessings of God. First Peter 5:5 says, "God resisteth the proud, and giveth grace to the humble" (*KJV*).

Our giving must be bountiful and with the knowledge that our kindness and generosity will ultimately be of much help to those in need. It is not the amount of our gift, but it is our motive behind the gift. We are not to give grudgingly, or out of necessity or sorrow. Don't give large gifts if you feel obliged to do so. Don't give sorrowfully, because you are giving out of regard for public opinion. Give out of a sense of need and a pure motive. This is the kind of giving in which God delights—giving cheerfully, with laughter, delight, exuberance and joyfulness. When we manage to grasp these principles, giving really does become a blessing. "Each one must do just as he has purposed in his heart, not grudgingly or under compulsion, for God loves a cheerful giver" (2 Cor. 9:7; *NASB*).

Learn the right way to live.
Understand the responsibility
of giving generously!

The Responsibility of Seeking Wisdom in Matters of Finance

*S*cripture is very clear about matters of stewardship. It is also clear that when we struggle in areas of finance, we are to seek help from those who have knowledge and experience. Not understanding how to handle your finances correctly does not excuse you from the responsibility of good stewardship. Proverbs 17:16 says, "Of what use is money in the hand of a fool, since he has no desire to get wisdom?"

Proverbs 24:3-6

"Any enterprise is built by wise planning, becomes strong through common sense, and profits wonderfully by keeping abreast of the facts" (*TLB*).

Proverbs 15:22

"Plans fail for lack of counsel, but with many advisers they succeed."

Later on in this book, one of the practical applications I write about is getting professional help. Seeking wisdom and getting help is a personal responsibility, a biblical principle and a practical solution to your debt problem. It is your responsibility to get spiritual advice and wisdom about your financial decisions.

Proverbs 4:5-7

"Get wisdom, get understanding; do not forget my words or swerve from them. Do not forsake wisdom, and she will protect you; love her, and she will watch over you. Wisdom is supreme; therefore get wisdom. Though it cost all you have, get understanding."

One of the most practical persons I know of who dispenses advice to millions of people daily via a national radio talk show is Dave Ramsey, author of many books, seminars and financial programs, etc. As I mentioned before, my wife, in commuting to and from her office, made me aware of Dave's ministry. Since then, whenever I can, I try to find his show on the radio and glean some practical and spiritual insights. His advice is spiritual, biblical, practical and full of wisdom. For a listing of his books, radio show, etc., go to daveramsey.com.

Dave Ramsey often quotes his grandmother as saying, "Those convinced against their will, are of the same opinion still."

You can have the best intentions regarding a bright financial future, but without input from others, your intentions will fail.

What people do you know in your own life (a church friend, coworker, pastor, CPA) that obviously have their finances in order? Approach them and ask for their advice. People love to share their ideas and strategies with others.

Matthew 7:7, 8

"Ask and it will be given to you; seek and you will find; knock and the door will be opened to you. For everyone who asks receives; he who seeks finds; and to him who knocks, the door will be opened."

Humble yourself and learn from those around you.

Learn the right way to live. Understand the responsibility of seeking wisdom in matters of finance now!

The Responsibility
of Learning to Save

*H*ave you ever noticed that after you pay your monthly bills, buy groceries and cover your other expenses, you have little left over from your paycheck? Consider contributing to your savings plan first, not last, each month.

SAVE EARLY

You can save through personal discipline. It isn't easy to save! One must make a commitment to start saving and stick to it. There will always be something waiting to take your money. But no one else will save for you, so you have to do it for yourself. Saving small amounts now is relatively painless. Waiting until later and having to save large amounts regularly can be painful. The following chart shows the advantages of saving early. Let's make some assumptions.

Let's say a young person at the age of 20 invests a mere $2,000 a year for 10 years. At age 30, he or she stops contributing, but the percent money remains invested for the next 35 years until retirement. At an average return of 12% over the long haul what will the result be?

By contrast, let's say the same person invests for the same period of 10 years, with the same annual contribution of $2,000. The average annual return remains at 12%. But because this person at a young age was more interested in cars, motorcycles, eating out, daily lattes and other personal indulgences, he decides to live it up and not worry about saving or investing until later. The truth is, if you begin at age 20, saving will probably be easier than if you wait until later on in your life when you are married, have children, have all the expenses of a house, vacations and many other unanticipated expenses.

So the beginning point of that 10-year savings contribution period is not started at the age of 20, but at the age of 40—just 20 years later. What would the result be? Take a look at this.

AGE AT BEGINNING OF INVESTMENT	INVESTMENT VALUE AT AGE 20	INVESTMENT VALUE AT AGE 40	INVESTMENT VALUE AT AGE 65	ANNUAL CONTRIBUTION
20	$0	$177,277	$3,898,254	$2,000
40	$0	$0	$ 337,559	$2,000

INVESTMENT DETAIL

- Interest Rate Compounded Continuously
- Annual Payment Made at Beginning of the Period
- 10 Years/$2000 Per Year
- Interest Rate of 12%

How much money should you be saving? Professionals suggest that at least 10% of take-home pay should go into savings. I take it a step further and suggest you save 15% of your take-home pay. Savings mean setting aside money for investment. This includes such investments as stocks, mutual funds and bank accounts. But this is only a guideline.

STRATEGY FOR SAVING MONEY

Saving money is hard work. The hardest part is simply getting started. The earlier you start, the greater the potential. If you're beginning from scratch, consider this three-part strategy:

First, put your money into a rainy-day fund: four to six month's worth of living expenses. In case you lose a job or are injured and have no income, this rainy-day fund will become necessary. If you have worked in a successful company for several years and both your position and the company's position in the marketplace appear to be secure, then a rainy-day fund, or emergency fund as many call it, might be the equivalent of only four months income. However, if you are self-employed or paid on commission, six months is an absolute necessity. Take no chances with this money. Keep it readily available, in a bank account or a money-market mutual fund.

Second, save for long-range expenses: a new home or college for the kids. Be more flexible with this money. Keep it in long-term certificates of deposit or in Series EE Savings Bonds. You'll earn more interest than in a conventional bank account and you can time your investment so the money is available when you need it.

Third, save for retirement. That can mean an Individual Retirement Account, a company retirement plan or other solid financial investments. A conservative mutual fund that invests only in top-quality stocks is one possibility. Or you might risk a little more for a greater reward by investing in a mutual fund that buys growths stocks.

The following strategies can help you make this practice automatic. Set up an automatic payroll deduction. Thanks to payroll deduction programs, such as Credit Unions or 401(k) plans, part of your paycheck can go directly into your investment account.

Saving is easy. What you don't see, you won't spend. Set up an automatic bank transfer. Many investment companies will transfer money automatically from your bank account to your investment account according to a schedule you specify. Such a program can make saving for retirement as natural as paying the mortgage.

Invest all salary increases. Direct half of your next raise into an investment account before it reaches your wallet and you get used to spending the extra income.

Invest lump sum payments. Invest a portion of bonuses and tax refunds; you'll turn the extra money into added savings—not increased spending. You can begin saving now!

SAVING GOALS

Set savings goals. Start with 10-15% of every paycheck. It's easiest if your employer deducts it from your check because you don't miss money you don't see. You could also ask your bank to move it from checking to savings every month or make automatic investments into a no-load (no sales charge) mutual fund.

Saving is more certain when someone else arranges it for you. The goal may be college for the kids. It may be retirement in a few years. It could be a new car, a boat or a summer place. A real key here is that it forces you to think ahead—beyond the next paycheck. Any successful business is one that plans for the future; many times 5 and 10 years ahead. Japanese companies project plans even longer.

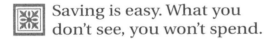

Saving is easy. What you don't see, you won't spend.

Pay yourself first. After taking care of your tithing obligations, the next person in line to be paid is you. Although this seems hard to do with our other obligations, just get started by forming a regular habit. It will get easier as you progress.

Throw stumbling blocks in the path of spending. Most of us save too little because we spend too much on impulse items. Control that urge to splurge. Keep a list of all the things you really need—coats for the kids, a new refrigerator, tires for the car, etc. Wait to buy until those items go on sale. If you're drawn to something not on the list, give yourself a week to think about it.

Save all extra money. Once you have paid off a loan, start paying yourself by putting an equivalent amount of money directly into savings. If

you have a car loan you're about to pay off, and you've been paying $250 a month, keep the car for a couple more years, and save that $250 each month. Some people plan so they receive a tax refund each year, but most financial planners suggest handling your taxes so you don't overpay. After all, Uncle Sam doesn't pay any interest on the overpayment.

Thrift used to be a basic part of the American ethic. Before we were a nation, Ben Franklin said this; "A penny saved is two pence clear." All of us would benefit by returning to that thinking.

Make your savings grow faster! Put cash you don't need right away in three- or five-year CDs (Certificates of Deposit). If you need the money and have to break into the CD before it matures, you might pay a six-month interest penalty. But that's nothing compared to the penalty you're imposing on yourself by settling for today's low short-term rates "just in case."

1. Money market funds are possible cash storage vehicles. Keep the cash you use for big bills in a money market mutual fund instead of a bank account. You may get free checks, and your money continues to earn interest until the check clears. As a rule, money funds pay from 0.5 to 2% more than the highest rate you can receive from most banks.

2. Stock mutual funds are also possible ways to store extra cash. Buy a mutual fund that invests entirely in U.S. Treasury securities. These are even safer. If you live in a high-tax state, they're a better deal. Although Treasury Funds often yield a little less than other money market funds, you owe no state or local income taxes on your earnings, so your return is much higher.

3. **Consider purchasing U.S. Treasuries.** Buy Treasury securities instead of CDs if you live in a high-tax state. You can buy Treasuries free through the nearest Federal Reserve bank or branch. Check your telephone book under U.S. Government or ask your own bank for the address. The minimum investment in Treasuries maturing in one year or less is $10,000; in two or three years, $5,000; in four years or more, $1,000.

Check your tax bracket carefully before buying tax-exempt mutual funds. You'll generally net more after taxes by investing in higher-yielding taxable funds if you're in the 15% federal tax bracket. Sometimes taxables pay for people in the 25 and 28% brackets, too, but in the highest brackets, tax-exempts are usually best.

You have a responsibility to learn how to save. Of course there are many demands on your paycheck and it is not always easy to save. But it is imperative to find the cash to do so. When saving for big items like college, a house or retirement, the most important rule is to begin saving now—the sooner the better. The younger you are, the easier it will be. Why? Because you can develop great savings habits at an early age and time will be your greatest ally. The longer you invest, the greater the opportunity and potential for gaining substantial wealth.

Learn the right way to live.
Understand the responsibility
of learning to save!

Notes

Section Four

The
Biblical
Principle

The Biblical Principle of Knowing That God Owns It All

Psalm 50:10

"For every animal of the forest is mine, and the cattle on a thousand hills."

1 Chronicles 29:10-12

"'Praise be to you, O LORD, God of our father Israel, from everlasting to everlasting. Yours, O LORD, is the greatness and the power and the glory and the majesty and the splendor, for everything in heaven and earth is yours. Yours, O LORD, is the kingdom; you are exalted as head over all. Wealth and honor come from you; you are the ruler of all things. In your hands are strength and power.'"

Don't make the mistake of thinking your job or your business is what provides your income. God is the source of your abundant supply. Jobs disappear; customers in your business come and go. It is God who sees to it that your needs are being met. Everyone and everything else is just His instrument for getting it accomplished. God uses many vehicles to get the job done, but in the end, it is not us, but God's blessing upon our lives.

Haggai 2:8

"The silver is mine and the gold is mine, declares the LORD Almighty."

Billy Graham said, "If a person gets his attitude towards money straight, it will help straighten out almost every other area of his life. Tell me what you think about money, and I can tell you what you think about God, for these two are closely related. A man's heart is closer to his wallet than almost anything else."

Jesus taught that we must be responsible in our finances. God is the source of all wealth. He is the original owner of all things, for He made all things. As Scripture says, He owns the cattle on a thousand hills. In addition to the ways God provides for us supernaturally, God also gives us the ability to earn a living (see Deuteronomy 8:18).

When you partner with God in business, He not only will bless it, but He also will let you enjoy prosperity. But there is a caution not to keep everything to yourself. Instead of trying to figure out how little you can give to God, try giving it all to Him and ask Him how much you should keep. When you partner with God, He will prosper you! When God becomes your source, then your well will never run dry. When we become Christians, we become children of God, and the Bible says God wants to give gifts to His children.

A successful business person by the name of R. G. LeTourneau was in the business of manufacturing earth-moving equipment. As his business grew and prospered, he decided to increase his tithe over and above the tenth. In time, he eventually increased his giving to 90% of his income and lived on the rest. *Instead of giving the tenth, he lived the tenth.* God blessed this man bountifully and used his inventive God-given genius and creativity to reach the world with the gospel. The Bible provides many great giving Scriptures, but none seem more specific than that of the directive that every person should give what is in his heart, not reluctantly or under compulsion. Mr. LeTourneau certainly recognized the value of 2 Corinthians 9:7 and acknowledged that it was God who gave him the power to gain wealth.

Someone once said that the real measure of your wealth is how much you'd be worth if you lost all your money.

In the sixteenth century, Izaak Walton said, "Look to your health; and if you have it, praise God and value it next to conscience; for health is the second blessing that we mortals are capable of, a blessing money can't buy."

What does God already own that you are trying to keep absolute control over by refusing to acknowledge God's ownership? What about your business or your house? What about your transportation vehicles, your recreational vehicles, your clothes, toys and other worldly goods?

What about your body? According to Romans 12:1, your body belongs to the Lord. Does your time belong to you or to God? What about your income, your savings, your investments and your other possessions? Do these things belong to your or to God? Have you been allowed oversight of them for the purpose of showing good stewardship or have you taken them over, assuming they are yours only? Everything you say, every decision you make, every action you take must be accountable to the principles of God.

What about your entire life? Your dreams, your goals, your visions—are they born of God or have you allowed your carnal nature to take complete control? Are you a thief or a steward? If a steward, then what kind of steward are you? Are you one that God can trust with complete care or are you careless in your stewardship?

Not only are the silver and the gold the Lord's, so is everything else. Everything belongs to God. So why not give it all to Him? In 1 Corinthians 4:2, Paul says it is required that those who have been given a trust must prove faithful. In other words, we are all stewards and must be the kind of stewards that are faithful. A steward is simply a manager of someone else's money and possessions. We must acknowledge God's ownership and manage it or use it as He would have us use it. We gain by giving; we lose by withholding.

Begin now to live
a principled life. Determine at
this moment to live the principle
of knowing that God owns it all!

The Biblical Principle
of Seeking First

*T*he biblical principle of seeking first is all about proper perspective and proper motives. If your sole purpose in life is to make money and accumulate stuff for yourself, then you are already headed down the wrong path. Jesus said the kingdom of God is to be sought first. This does not mean to seek first for a while and then to switch to a second goal of accumulating vast amounts of material possessions second. It just means that our focus must always be on kingdom matters and kingdom priorities. As we keep our priorities in line, the things we need will be provided.

Jesus knew that men and women would have trouble keeping their hearts focused on their real purpose for being here. That's why, on the Sermon on the Mount, He said:

Matthew 6:19-21

"'Do not store up for yourselves treasures on earth, where moth and rust destroy, and where thieves break in and steal. But store up for yourselves treasures in heaven, where moth and rust do not destroy, and where thieves do not break in and steal. For where your treasure is, there your heart will be also.'"

Matthew 6:33

"But seek first his kingdom and his righteousness, and all these things will be given to you as well."

Putting God first in our lives alleviates us from the task of having to worry about everything else. Seeking His kingdom and righteousness first is simply making God the priority in our lives. Verse 33 outlines for us a priority, a principle and a promise. Our priority is to seek God's will and way first. The principle is to focus on kingdom activity. The promise is that when we seek Him first and focus on the business of the kingdom, God will take care of all our other needs.

There is always the temptation to put our money first. Do you remember the rich young ruler who came to Jesus and said he wanted to follow Christ? How Jesus responded to Him didn't make him very happy. Jesus told him to give his money away and follow Him. You see, it wasn't the money that was wrong; it was that this young man placed his money ahead of and above all else.

"When wealth is lost, nothing is lost; when health is lost, something is lost; when character is lost, all is lost."—*Billy Graham*

If we have too much money, there is always the danger that we can depend upon it ultimately. Does your life reveal your desire to put God first? The Lord admonishes us to seek first His kingdom, His way of doing things, and not to worry about possessions. Acquisition of possessions never satisfies. We only want more and more. That is why our focus must be on needs, not wants.

What do we need? Generally that would include food and water, sunshine and air, rain and shelter. Beyond these basic survival needs could come the need for friends, family, relationships, self-esteem, etc. What we don't need is more *things*. Materialism is a focus on things of matter rather than on the things of God. Before we put all our time, energy, interests and life into what we deem valuable, Jesus is telling us to stop and get your focus on things of eternal value.

Moses considered the reproach of Christ as greater riches than all the treasures in Egypt.

If we have too much money, there is always the danger that we can depend upon it ultimately.

Hebrews 11:26

"He regarded disgrace for the sake of Christ as of greater value than the treasures of Egypt, because he was looking ahead to his reward."

The biblical mandate is to seek first the things of the kingdom. The lives of believers are spoiled if they are completely wrapped up in possessions and absorbed in the pursuit of material accumulation. We must ask God to help us develop an attitude of serving Him faithfully and a life that is free of debt so we can pursue the extension of kingdom priorities instead of human wants. After all, our whole purpose in life is to give to others, share with others and bless others just as we have been blessed.

Begin now to live a principled life. Determine at this moment to live the principle of seeking first!

The Biblical Principle of Giving, Not Getting

2 Corinthians 8:7

"But just as you excel in everything—in faith, in speech, in knowledge, in complete earnestness and in your love for us—see that you also excel in this grace of giving."

WEALTH

Is having a lot of money the key to everything? Does money bring happiness? Does money bring solutions to life's problems? If you had a limitless amount of money and could buy anything you wanted, what would you buy? When would you stop buying, gathering, grasping and grabbing? Our wealth does not come from what we accumulate in life, but from what we give in life.

Some of the wealthiest men in the world gathered in 1923 at the Edgewater Beach Hotel in Chicago. This group of seven was worth more than the entire U.S. Treasury in their time. These were great financial men with records of success who had achieved great prosperity.

But this was not the end of their story. Within 25 years the president of the largest steel company had died penniless. A millionaire wheat speculator had also become poor. Another, who was the president of the New York Stock Exchange, had already spent many years in prison. Yet another of the wealthy seven who was a member of the president's cabinet had spent time in prison, but was pardoned so he could die at home instead of prison. The fifth of the seven committed suicide; the sixth man, who headed one of the world's largest companies, also took his own life. The seventh, and last of the world's richest men, also took his own life.

Acts 20:35

"Remembering the words the Lord Jesus himself said: 'It is more blessed to give than to receive.'"

Luke 6:38

"Give, and it will be given to you. A good measure, pressed down, shaken together and running over, will be poured into your lap. For with the measure you use, it will be measured to you."

"When it comes to giving until it hurts, most people have a very low threshold of pain."
—*Anonymous*

Mother Teresa was a woman of God who never stopped giving of herself. She said, "Never worry about numbers. Help one person at a time, and always start with the person nearest you."

GRACE

True givers are not motivated by competition; they are motivated by grace. What is this grace? In 2 Corinthians 8–9, it is referred to as a divine favor that is displayed in generosity. It is the divine enablement to participate greatly in giving. An act of grace as used in this passage means an act of giving. Grace causes pleasure and is delightful; it means to be regarded favorably; it is a mercy that causes joy. Grace is that which makes one ready, quick, willing and prompt to give freely. Grace dignifies and lifts people up in its gift of favor; it honors and blesses and supplies all that is needed. Grace is the initiator of giving. Neither biblical law, a set of rules, nor guilt or competition should make you give. It is grace that creates the desire to give, grace that gives us the ability to give and grace that causes us to move into the realm of faith. Second Corinthians 8:6, 7 says that giving is something we need to excel and abound in, but it must be motivated by grace.

"Never measure generosity by what you give, but by what you have left." —*Fulton Sheen*

CHEERFUL GIVING
1 Chronicles 29:9

"Then the people rejoiced, for they had offered willingly, because with a loyal heart they had offered willingly to the LORD; and King David also rejoiced greatly" (*NKJV*).

Giving should never be burdensome. It should never be stressful. Our gifts should not be presented in doubt, clothed in reluctance or reservation. In fact, giving, as seen in this passage, should be an occasion for great joy! Our gifts should be presented in faith, presenting them to God with confidence in His Word. If we give with a grudging spirit and attitude, does it hinder God from giving us full blessing? I don't know. But what I do know is that God just simply loves one who gives cheerfully and wholeheartedly.

2 Corinthians 9:7

"Each man should give what he has decided in his heart to give, not reluctantly or under compulsion, for God loves a cheerful giver."

In this verse it is clear that giving (we are not talking about returning God's tenth to Him) should not be coerced. No one should be intimidated into giving. No one should be pressured into giving. Giving must not be compulsory or motivated by guilt; it is to be exercised out of one's free will and love.

Giving is a personal decision to bless others as God has blessed us. We do this through supporting the various ministries of our local church. Yes, there are other giving opportunities, but be careful to first sustain the place where you are fed week in and week out. Take care to give willingly and cheerfully.

 Our gifts should not be presented in doubt, clothed in reluctance or reservation.

HOW SHOULD I GIVE
TO THE WORK OF GOD?

Many churches offer opportunities to give to the Lord in a variety of ways. Check with your church for an avenue to give:

- To the poor.
- To the needs of children.
- Toward retiring any debt the church has.
- Toward new churches being planted.
- Toward strategic, creative evangelism.
- Toward constructing new buildings to be used for the purposes of God.
- Toward Christian education (schools and colleges).
- Toward the needs of the community (pregnancy centers, counseling, child abuse centers).
- Toward the purchase of necessary equipment for your church.
- Toward capital improvements for the church.
- In the inheritance you will leave behind.

John Wesley donated to mission causes by sacrificing personal comforts. Living simply, he was able to give more than $500,000 to missions in his lifetime. When asked about this personal sacrifice, his answer was, "Gladly would I again make the floor my bed, a box my chair, a box my table, rather than that men should perish for want of the knowledge of the Savior."

During the World War II, Winston Churchill, then prime minister of Great Britain, set out to "win with words" over Hitler by raising the morale of the nation. Not only did he visit the troops and factories, but he also went to the out-of-the-way coal-mining towns. On one visit to the hard-working coal miners, the prime minister urged them to see their significance in the total effort for victory. He told them:

"We will be victorious! We will preserve our freedom. And years from now when our freedom is secure and peace reigns, your children and children's children will come and they will say to you, 'What did you do to win our freedom in that great war?' And one will say, 'I marched with the Eighth Army!' Someone else will proudly say, 'I manned a submarine.' And another will say, 'I guided the ships that moved the troops and supplies.' And still another will say, 'I doctored the wounds!'"

Then the great statesman paused. The dirty-faced miners sat in silence and awe, waiting for him to proceed.

"They will come to you," he shouted, "and you will say, with equal right and equal pride, 'I cut the coal! I cut the coal that fueled the ships that moved the supplies! That's what I did. I cut the coal!'"

We can all do our part. Maybe we are not on the frontlines, just like the coal miners in this story. However we can supply the fuel for these efforts. Our part is just as necessary as that person overseas; so let us partner together to fund God's kingdom.

Begin now to live
a principled life. Determine
at this moment to live the
principle of giving, not getting!

The Biblical Principle of Supernatural Provision

1 Kings 17:15, 16

"So she went away and did according to the word of Elijah; and she and he and her household ate for many days. The bin of flour was not used up, nor did the jar of oil run dry, according to the word of the LORD which He spoke by Elijah" (*NKJV*).

Supernatural provision happens when the natural is not enough. If we can make it happen on our own, there is no need for faith. No need for trusting God. And it follows that if we do not have faith and have no need for God, He will not step into areas we have reserved for our own self-control. The principle of supernatural provision is that He is strong when flesh cannot be.

Philippians 4:19

"And my God will meet all your needs according to his glorious riches in Christ Jesus."

Notice that the Scripture does not say, the company that employs you will provide for your needs. Neither does it say the local banker or loan officer will supply your needs. Nor does it say that the welfare department of your government will supply your needs. It says that God, and no one else, will supply your needs. God is your only Source! It's not your job that provides your income. It is God who provides your needs.

This story has been told for many generations. It is about a Christian family that was going through some tough times. They were so destitute that they didn't even have food for their next meal. The father and mother got down on their knees and cried out to God for food so their children would not go hungry. A man who was not a Christian was walking by their house and heard their prayer. Instead of feeling bad for them, he decided to play a trick on them.

He went down to the grocery store and bought a huge box of groceries, put it on their front porch and rang the doorbell. When the Christian parents saw the groceries on the porch, they immediately began to thank God for it. Just then the unbeliever walked up and said, "Why are you thanking God? I'm the one who placed the groceries there." The Christian father replied, "Oh no, it was God who answered our prayer and provided the groceries. But I do want to thank you for being His delivery boy and bringing them to us!"

God is your sole source, your only provider. Through Him and Him alone are all your needs met. Your professional employment is just that, it's not an end-all. When the economy tanks, so do jobs. When the industry sector that employs you goes bust, your job disappears with it. Don't trust your education, don't trust your experience, don't trust your job; trust God.

Begin now to live a principled life. Determine at this moment to live the principle of supernatural provision!

The Biblical Principle
of Open Heavens

Deuteronomy 28:12

"The LORD will open the heavens, the storehouse of his bounty, to send rain on your land in season and to bless all the work of your hands. You will lend to many nations but will borrow from none."

One way God opens the windows of heaven is by keeping us from untold financial disasters.

Malachi 3:10-11 says, "Bring ye all the tithes into the storehouse, that there may be meat in mine house, and prove me now herewith, saith the LORD of hosts, if I will not open you the windows of heaven, and pour you out a blessing, that there shall not be room enough to receive it. And I will rebuke the devourer for your sakes, and he shall not destroy the fruits of your ground; neither shall your vine cast her fruit before the time in the field, saith the LORD of hosts" (*KJV*).

What does it mean to "rebuke the devourer"? Many things create havoc in our financial lives. It may be the loss of a job, auto repair expenses, house maintenance, appliance breakdown, or healthcare related expenses. From time to time we all can acknowledge some difficulty in these areas. And when "out of nowhere" expenses come alongside us, they can be burdensome and costly.

However, what we don't know is all that God keeps away from us. When we are faithful in our giving, the Word simply states that our crops will be large and that He will keep the insects and plagues away. Whether you are a farmer, a tiller of the ground, or simply planting crops of a nonagricultural nature, you can rest assured God is working on your behalf.

Yet another way God opens the windows of heaven is by blessing us when we give. Generosity is God's antidote to greed. The heart and attitude of a blessed person is worth looking at. After all, do we not all want to be a blessed person? Blessed people are set apart in many ways because they have learned how to be blessed. We all have the opportunity to receive the blessing of God and be "under the shadow of the Almighty" (Psalm 91:1) if we so desire. The blessed person gives of his or her resources freely, cheerfully and out of genuine appreciation to God.

When we look upon the attitudes and heart of a blessed person, what will we discover? What is the heart like? What kind of attitude does one need to receive the blessing? What about the heart of a blessed person? What theme was so important to Jesus that He talked about it more than anything else? Was it heaven? Was it repentance? Was it prayer? Was it salvation? No. It was the subject of money. He knew that if He had our money, He would certainly have our hearts.

What about the attitude of a blessed person? Overall, the principal attitude must be that all money and all possessions belong to God. He trusts us with the care of these things until we prove ourselves unworthy of His trust. It is not our money, so it's not our problem to worry about it. It is our basic responsibility as good stewards to use it correctly.

> **Begin now to live a principled life. Determine at this moment to live the principle of open heavens!**

The Biblical Principle
of Kingdom Investing

Matthew 6:19-21

"Do not store up for yourselves treasures on earth, where moth and rust destroy, and where thieves break in and steal. But store up for yourselves treasures in heaven, where moth and rust do not destroy, and where thieves do not break in and steal. For where your treasure is, there your heart will be also."

Most of us understand what we classify as earthly treasures. This list includes earthly possessions such as cars, boats, clothes, houses, bank accounts, jewelry, portfolios, etc.

In Scripture, Jesus is warning us about protecting our hearts from the love of these things, all of which can seem so real, so lasting, so concrete, but in reality can disappear so quickly. *They can literally be here today and gone tomorrow.*

Death is the great equalizer, the constant leveler. Some of the ancient tombs discovered in the Middle East have been found packed with food and furniture, as well as slaves. Yet all of those buried remains, buried under sand for thousands of years, have done nothing for the one who spent a lifetime accumulating them.

Our stock portfolios are always in great risk to the ups and downs of the market, the wars and rumors of wars, the economy of the nation and world,in which we invest. Our bodies and our minds, which may seem so healthy and sharp, may be wasted by disease or crushed by a mishap tomorrow.

We invest in what we care about. If we invest our money with God, we will be interested in the ministry advance of our local church and will pray for the expansion of His kingdom locally and globally.

Note, in the Matthew 6 passage, Jesus is not saying to have nothing, enjoy nothing or that possessions are a sin. Christ is saying to us to not get too tied to these things. Be a conduit, not a dam. *It is not about what we have, but what has us.* If you center your life on things, if you base your living upon possessions, you will for sure be disappointed.

Don't base your life, your future, your well being or your happiness on the things you have accumulated. Instead, be sure you lay up for yourself the real treasures, the ones that will be of eternal value.

Notice the tone of this Scripture (Matthew 6:19-21). It doesn't seem to be a suggestion, rather a definite command of sorts. It is no secret that the rich attract a lot of interested people. While he has money, everyone wants to be near him. Should his riches disappear, so will his friends. Not much different from a beautiful, talented young actress, singer or musician. When her beauty fades, or talent diminishes, the world looks for another to admire.

Treasures on earth can become paths to building heavenly treasures if they are used and distributed for the Glory of God.

Many of the homes constructed in the ancient Middle East were made with sun-baked clay or loose stones. Although adequate for housing, it presented a comparatively easy way for thieves to dig under the wall, through the wall or by other means. No possessions were safe from those that would steal.

Of course, we know that rust can destroy even the best of tools and moths also attack things we consume. Literally, rust in its destructive path will eat into and can destroy nearly everything. Rust will eventually corrode all metal, including silver and gold. Figuratively speaking, rust can be anything that destroys you and your life. In short, all your treasures, whether physical or otherwise, can be destroyed.

The possessions we accumulate in this world are temporary at best. Each of the three metaphors found in Matthew 6:19-21 tells us together that life is short and futile. Anyone of these things, when expanded to include those things that can destroy from today's culture, clearly demonstrate to us the folly of putting our trust in earthly possessions. Bad investments, or good investments pilfered away by bad management or dishonest CEOs, can make our lifetime of savings disappear overnight.

It's not that saving or storing assets is in itself sinful. Paul notes in 2 Corinthians 12:14 that parents ought to save up for their children. When increase comes our way, we should use it, not only for our needs, but also for the good of others.

Treasures on earth can become paths to building heavenly treasures if they are used and distributed for the Glory of God. Jesus understood clearly that in the consumer culture of this world, a constant battleground for our affections, our hearts and our souls rage.

"Our callings are not simply secular means of making money or a living, but are God's means of utilizing our gifts and interests to His glory."
—*a paraphrase of Martin Luther (1483—1546)*

"Alas, how many, even among those who are called believers, have plenty of all the necessities of life, and yet complain of poverty!"
—*John Wesley (1703–1791)*

"Money never made a man happy yet, nor will it. There is nothing in its nature to produce happiness. The more a man has, the more he wants. Instead of its filling a vacuum, it makes one. If it satisfies one want, it doubles and trebles that want another way. That was a true proverb of the wise man, rely upon it; 'Better is little with the fear of the Lord, than great treasure, and trouble therewith.'"—*Benjamin Franklin (1706–1790)*

Begin now to live a principled life. Determine at this moment to live out the principle of kingdom investing!

The Biblical Principle
of First Things First

*P*ersonal prosperity will never come at the expense of ethical values and biblical principles. Settle it once and for all in your heart and mind. God values obedience and makes it a condition of His blessing. Until your personal life and financial life get in line with His morality and commandments, don't expect financial miracles to be the norm in your life. Those who have not learned this lesson often struggle for years with the burden of heavy debt.

An interesting group of Scriptures surround the story of rebuilding the ancient Temple. The main characters in this story are Joshua the high priest, Zerubbabel the governor of Judah and Haggai the prophet and the Israelites. It seems they had become so involved in their own personal lives and building their own houses, that they had neglected the building, finishing and operational needs of God's house.

God apparently finally had His fill of the people's inability to focus upon the principle of "first things first," and He sent word to the governor through Haggai the prophet. The message to be delivered was straightforward, direct, to the point and quite harsh. He stated their current condition, summarized the problem and stated the result. There is nothing ambiguous about the mind of God.

Haggai 1:5-10

"Look at the result: You plant much but harvest little. You have scarcely enough to eat or drink and not enough clothes to keep you warm. Your income disappears, as though you were putting it into pockets filled with holes! 'Think it over,' says the Lord Almighty. 'Consider how you have acted and what has happened as a result! Then go up into the mountains, bring down timber, and rebuild my Temple, and I will be pleased with it and appear there in my glory,' says the Lord. 'You hope for much but get so little. And when you bring it home, I blow it away—it doesn't last at all. Why? Because my Temple lies in ruins, and you don't care. Your only concern is your own fine homes. That is why I am holding back the rains from heaven and giving you such scant crops'" (*TLB*).

What are you doing in your personal financial life that is not pleasing to God? Why are you out of the flow of God's divine blessing? How many problems have you brought into your life because you have failed to line up with the principles of God's Word? Don't you think it is time for you to assess your current lifestyle and make the proper adjustments needed to bring your life back in line? It is never too late to begin again. God is awesome and full of mercy. But He does want your priorities to be in line with the Word. Get your financial priorities straight and watch the blessings of heaven begin to flow in your direction.

Begin now to live a principled life. Determine at this moment to live out the principle of first things first!

The Biblical Principle
of Being Proactive

Matthew 17:27

"Go to the lake and throw out your line. Take the first fish you catch; open its mouth."

Nothing will be thrown into our laps. No, financial prosperity is not an unconditional providential blessing, and yes, conditions are attached. We are to take action and be proactive. The abilities and giftings God provides motivate us to action. Sometimes it takes our persistence in doing the same things faithfully with the heart of a servant. Other times, it is time to try new things, new methods and seek new opportunities. Sometimes the steady plodding brings the success of the blessed life.

God allows us to possess certain things, but mere possession is not ownership. Those things you possess can be taken from you in an instant. The scores of dishonest accounting firms and corrupt corporate CEOs of our day have seen to that. Billions of honest dollars invested by millions of wage earners have disappeared. Wage earners have seen their retirement savings disappear in a matter of mere months. You can possess, but it is God who owns. You may earn a living, but it is God who gives to you the ability to earn. God is the one who gives to you the power to get wealth.

Let's note what Scriptures say about just how much you really own.

Deuteronomy 8:18

"But remember the LORD your God, for it is he who gives you the ability to produce wealth".

Psalm 24:1

"The earth is the LORD's, and everything in it, the world, and all who live in it."

Psalm 50:10, 11

"For every animal of the forest is mine, and the cattle on a thousand hills. I know every bird in the mountains, and the creatures of the field are mine."

Psalm 100:3

"Know that the LORD is God. It is he who made us, and we are his; we are his people, the sheep of his pasture."

Ezekiel 18:4

"For every living soul belongs to me."

Haggai 2:8

"'The silver is mine and the gold is mine,' declares the LORD Almighty."

Acts 17:28

"For in him we live and move and have our being."

Romans 12:1

"Therefore, I urge you, brothers, in view of God's mercy, to offer your bodies as living sacrifices, holy and pleasing to God."

Ecclesiastes 9:11

"The race is not to the swift or the battle to the strong, nor does food come to the wise or wealth to the brilliant or favor to the learned; but time and chance happen to them all."

Hebrews 12:1, 2

This verse tells us what to do and what to avoid:

"Let us throw off everything that hinders and the sin that so easily entangles, and let us run with perseverance the race marked out for us. Let us fix our eyes on Jesus, the author and perfecter of our faith."

Being a person of principle requires hard work, diligence and proactivity. Nothing will be handed to you without these requirements. The Bible says that if a person does not work, he should not eat. Now that's a pretty simple yet direct statement. Does God want to bless us supernaturally? Of course, He does. Will His blessing come to us if we are lazy, idle, slothful, passive and unwilling to roll up our sleeves and get to work? No, I don't believe so.

Proverbs 21:5

"Steady plodding brings prosperity; hasty speculation brings poverty" (*TLB*).

Proverbs 21:25, 26

"The sluggard's craving will be the death of him, because his hands refuse to work. All day long he craves for more, but the righteous give without sparing."

Taking action, being proactive, not giving up—all are principles for living the life of a blessed person.

Begin now to live a principled life. Determine at this moment to live the principle of being proactive!

The Biblical Principle
of Resisting Worldviews

*R*esisting the views of the world in handling our personal finances means we don't trust in riches, money or possessions. These things will surely pass away. But we do trust in God. He is our sole provider and should be in control of our lives.

We live in a culture that continuously encourages us to buy, buy, buy. From billboards to television commercials, from radio advertisements to magazine ads, we are told about everything we don't have, but must have right away. It takes a lot of stamina just to resist accepting what society tries to impose upon our thinking. The Bible cautions us in these matters and encourages us to withstand such pressure.

Romans 12:2

"Don't copy the behavior and customs of this world, but be a new and different person with a fresh newness in all you do and think. Then you will learn from your own experience how his ways will really satisfy you" (*TLB*).

Our culture and society have sold us a bill of goods. They teach us that to be happy we have to have certain things. We must refuse to accept the world's view of wealth, happiness and possessions. We do not have to have it all! We don't have to wear just the right clothes, drive that certain brand of car, have the latest model available, buy a bigger home, own six televisions, possess the latest digital camera and carry a dozen credit cards in our wallets to be fulfilled.

We must not allow the world to dictate its view of what possessions we should own. The world should not be allowed to design our lifestyle. The world should not tell us what success is and what the picture of affluence should look like. Success is doing what God desires.

Success and wealth look different from a Christian perspective. Wealth is having what you need. Wealth is more than money. It is having a local church that inspires you to draw close to God. It is having a loving spouse and the blessing of children. Wealth is enjoying great health and great relationships. Wealth is having good friends.

The world's view in our society is to look for ways to make a lot of money, very quickly, by doing little work. A constant lookout for get-rich schemes is prevalent.

Wealth is enjoying great health and great relationships.

The biblical principle centers on productivity, hard work, personal diligence and God's blessing. We are to use our God-given talents to partner with God's wisdom. If God chooses to bless us with wealth, then we properly use the riches God allows us to extend and further His kingdom.

Reject the worldview of materialism and self-centeredness at any cost. You won't benefit from having it all. If you have a family, trying to have it all will be a detriment to spiritual growth and may even cause major missteps in later years. Pray when tempted to jump at the latest scheme. If you have trouble resisting the constant bombardment of advertisements that make you want to go out and make an immediate purchase, shut off the television or turn down the radio.

There is another way: Be a good steward of God's gifts to you. Be careful what you do with your money, for someday you will have to account for how you used God's blessing. Every purchase you make should be a spiritual decision. After all, you are using His resources.

Begin now to live
a principled life. Determine at
this moment to live the principle
of resisting worldviews!

The Biblical Principle
of Temporary Possessions

1 Timothy 6:7

"For we brought nothing into the world, and we can take nothing out of it."

You will do well to remember that money and possessions are, at best, temporary. At most, money only lasts a lifetime. At worst, it doesn't last at all. It is very fleeting, only a vapor, just like our lives.

Psalm 39:4

"Show me, O LORD, my life's end and the number of my days; let me know how fleeting is my life."

Don't spend all your life trying to accumulate something that will never last. How much better it would be to spend your time investing in things of eternal nature. Being the recipient of God's provision and blessing and enjoying great wealth and prosperity is not meant for the purpose of accumulating earthly temporary gain. It is to be used to build a foundation for heavenly gain. Instead of hoarding it all for personal enjoyment, it is to be used to further the kingdom of God. Any prosperity you gain on this earth is because you have learned good stewardship principles. The biblical prosperity here in this life is but a foreshadow of things to come on the other side.

At the end of your life, will you look back and wish you would have owned a bigger home or a nicer car, or that you had spent more time with your family and friends? The only thing you can (and will) take out of this life is your soul. How much time do you spend daily pursuing eternal possessions instead of temporal ones?

On judgment day, will God be able to say to you, "Well done, My good and faithful servant"? Will He be pleased with the way you spent your days here on earth or will He be saddened by the amount of time you wasted on accumulating material possessions instead of eternal ones?

Possessions are temporary! Don't make the mistake of holding on to them too tightly. Job understood this when he said in chapter 1, verse 20, "Naked I came from my mother's womb, and naked I will depart. The LORD gave and the LORD has taken away; may the name of the LORD be praised."

It may be pleasant to accumulate many comforts of living, but just be sure you understand their temporary value and nature. To spend a lifetime gathering temporary possessions but neglecting the important treasures that last an eternity would be very foolish indeed. Don't get so focused on the here and now and in things of temporary value that you fail to think and see eternally. Treasure those things that have eternal and kingdom value. The only treasure worth possessing is kingdom or eternal treasure.

Matthew 6:19-21

"Do not store up for yourselves treasures on earth, where moth and rust destroy, and where thieves break in and steal. But store up for yourselves treasures in heaven, where moth and rust do not destroy, and where thieves do not break in and steal. For where your treasure is, there your heart will be also."

Psalm 89:47

"Remember how fleeting is my life. For what futility you have created all men!"

Proverbs 21:6

"A fortune made by a lying tongue is a fleeting vapor and a deadly snare."

Begin now to live
a principled life.
Determine at this moment
to live the principle
of temporary possessions!

The Biblical Principle
of Contentment

1 Timothy 6:8

"But if we have food and clothing, we will be content with that."

Millions of people today are on a quest to accumulate possessions and wealth. It is hard to be content with what we have when the world's entire system is geared toward making us unhappy with everything we have and wanting everything we don't have. From advertising to attitude, we face a discontented culture. How much money does it take to be content? Usually just a little bit more. Money cannot buy contentment or happiness. It is hard for us to be satisfied with what we do have, but we need to strive for contentment and contend for happiness.

"Contentment is a pearl of great price, and whoever procures it at the expense of ten thousand desires makes a wise and a happy purchase."—John Balguy

Making money is certainly not wrong, as long as it does not violate the laws of our land and the principles of God's Word. The all-for-me and none-for-others way of man's thinking is immoral. People of principle who subscribe to the values of the Bible will be good stewards if they obey the law of giving. They will find happiness in exact proportion to the degree in which they give. They will be content with life and all that it affords.

Money and happiness are not mutually exclusive. Benjamin Franklin noted, "Money never made a man happy yet, nor will it. There is nothing in its nature to produce happiness. The more a man has, the more he wants. Instead of filling a vacuum, it makes one." He also said, "Contentment makes poor men rich; discontentment makes rich men poor."

Being a good steward begins with the blessing of God, but the test and fruit of good stewardship is how we use those blessings. Are we a conduit or do we stop the stream of God's favor. Do we allow the river to flow, or do we dam up God's supply? To me it is a matter of management, not ownership. Are we to give only a little and hoard the rest for our own pleasure? I think not. God expects us to use what we need (He has promised to supply our need), then to multiply and return the rest. Stewardship is trust, knowing and disbursing His blessing. The blessing of stewardship is in giving.

Many wealthy people wish they had friends. Some of the most prominent people in the world are some of the saddest people on earth. Even their money cannot hide their unhappiness and displeasure with life. It is sad when people spend an entire lifetime trying to get rich, only to find that when they finally become rich, they are still unhappy, still dissatisfied with life and still sad.

Jesus let us know in Luke 12:15 that a person's life and happiness do not consist of things, possessions and money. In other words, all the possessions in the world will not bring contentment, nor will they buy happiness.

When the rich man in Luke 12:19 declared that after working hard for many years, accumulating great wealth and all the goods his world could offer him, he could now be free to take it easy by eating, drinking and being merry. He had dedicated his whole life to accumulating great possessions for such a time as this. Jesus called this man a fool because of his thinking. His thinking was wrong, his priorities were wrong, and because of wrong thinking, he was unable to be the kind of good steward he was required to be.

The Christian is not to love money. He is to love God. The Scripture is not much concerned about our having wealth, but is concerned with how it is obtained and how it is managed. God allows us to be partners with Him. God's role in the partnership is to meet our needs (Philippians 4:19). Our role in the partnership is to work (2 Thessalonians. 3:10). Our work is a means of worship and ministry. When we work, we meet the needs of our family and serve the Lord at the same time. We are also to work with proper motives (Colossians 3:23, 24).

The rich man, whom Jesus called a fool, was an example of a person who loved money more than life itself. But God had other plans for him. After calling the man a fool and after working selfishly for a lifetime just so he could retire in pleasure and ease, God said that tonight was his last evening on earth.

 The Christian is not to love money. He is to love God.

HARMFUL DESIRES
1 Timothy 6:9

"People who want to get rich fall into temptation and a trap and into many foolish and harmful desires that plunge men into ruin and destruction."

NOT LOVING MONEY
1 Timothy 6:10

"For the love of money is a root of all kinds of evil. Some people, eager for money, have wandered from the faith and pierced themselves with many griefs."

ALL ABOUT GREED
Luke 12:16-18

"The ground of a certain rich man produced a good crop. He thought to himself, *What shall I do? I have no place to store my crops*. Then he said, 'This is what I'll do. I will tear down my barns and build bigger ones, and there I will store all my grain and my goods.'"

In this passage Jesus is telling us that we should find contentment in what we have instead of living in the discontent of what we do not have. We are to be grateful for what we have been blessed with and stop always striving for more. "Now godliness with contentment is great gain" (1 Timothy 6:6 *NKJV*).

Genesis 2:15, 16

"The Lord God placed the man in the Garden of Eden as its gardener, to tend and care for it. But the Lord God gave the man this warning: 'You may eat any fruit in the garden except fruit from the Tree of Conscience—for its fruit will open your eyes to make you aware of right and wrong, good and bad. If you eat its fruit, you will be doomed to die.'"

Genesis 3:1-6

"The serpent was the craftiest of all the creatures the Lord God had made. So the serpent came to the woman. 'Really?' he asked. 'None of the fruit in the garden? God says you mustn't eat any of it?' 'Of course we may eat it,' the woman told him. 'It's only the fruit from the tree at the center of the garden that we are not to eat. God says we mustn't eat it or even touch it, or we will die.' 'That's a lie!' the serpent hissed. 'You'll not die! God knows very well that the instant you eat it you will become like him, for your eyes will be opened—you will be able to distinguish good from evil!' The woman was convinced. How lovely and fresh looking it was! And it would make her so wise! So she ate some of the fruit and gave some to her husband, and he ate it too."

Genesis 3:23

"So the Lord God banished him forever from the Garden of Eden, and sent him out to farm the ground from which he had been taken" (*TLB*).

Very little commentary is needed here. Adam and Eve had the privilege of living in a garden so beautiful that it was nearly indescribable. They could enjoy its beauty and bask in its atmosphere and eat of its fruit, save one tree. Yet they were not content and sought to have everything, when they actually needed nothing else. The result was personally devastating to them.

Begin now to live a principled life. Determine at this moment to live the principle of contentment!

The Biblical Principle of Proper Motives

*G*od is interested in your motives. Can you be trusted with prosperity? If you cannot be trusted now in poverty, why should you be given prosperity? Jesus said in Matthew 6:33, "But seek ye first the kingdom of God, and his righteousness; and all these things shall be added unto you" (*KJV*). How much money, health, wealth, position, prominence and influence can God trust you to handle? Have you been 100% trustworthy in the past with all that God has given to you? If not, why should He give you more?

Do you give a full day's work to your employer for a fair wage in return? If not, why should he trust you with a better job? Are you a good steward with the wage He has given to you? Are you judicious about how you spend your earnings? If not, why should you be trusted with a higher rate of pay if you are not a good financial manager with what you have already been given? Do you maintain your car, truck, home, etc, now? If you cannot be responsible now for taking care of the possessions God has already given you, why should He bless you with more?

If God were to look down upon you with the idea of blessing you beyond your expectations, but first checked your money motive, what would He find? Would you be the one He can trust with great wealth, knowing you would use it to bless the kingdom of God? Or would you be the one who would simply use it to gain more personal possessions and to live a life of personal fulfillment and easy living? The focus of many people is pleasure, sensual indulgence, money, selfishness, power and flattery. People who live this way do nothing of lasting or eternal value. They have no ultimate purpose in mind. As Christians, we need to have eternal values and purpose in mind.

Our motives and priorities must be God and His kingdom first, us last. Sometimes we get jealous of the success of others who are not Christians. They seem to be happy and rich and enjoying a life of luxury. A musician and prophet in Old Testament times by the name of Asaph said, "I was envious at the foolish, when I saw the prosperity of the wicked" (Psalm 73:3).

Ungodly men and women may achieve material prosperity apart from God, but they can never achieve the deep settled peace that comes from God. Riches gained without God are a snare and do not bring peace. Prosperity that comes from God brings not only an abundance of possessions, but also emotional peace, happiness and great joy.

Do you know why some wicked people are rich today? The Bible provides a simple explanation. The wicked who are rich are simply holding the wealth that someday God will give to His children.

"And the wealth of the sinner is laid up for the righteous" (Proverbs 13:22, *ASV*).

In the Old Testament, Solomon tells us in Proverbs 22:7 that the borrower is a servant to the lender. In the New Testament, Luke 16:13 says, "No servant can serve two masters. Either he will hate the one and love the other, or he will be devoted to the one and despise the other. You cannot serve both God and money." Both Scripture passages confirm each other. How can you properly serve God when you are a slave or servant to a creditor? When you want to follow God wholeheartedly but are a slave to debt, a conflict of interest arises. You need to be debt free to follow the will of God for your life. While your creditors are not concerned about God's will for you, they do want their money returned to them.

Your heart concerning the kingdom of God may be proper and principled, but if your motives and decisions are influenced at all by a love for money or the things money can buy, your thinking is tarnished. If your thinking remains tainted, it won't be long until your heart is also corrupted.

Begin now to live a principled life. Determine at this moment to live the principle of proper motives!

The Biblical Principle
of Financial Stewardship

Luke 16:11, 12

"So if you have not been trustworthy in handling worldly wealth, who will trust you with true riches? And if you have not been trustworthy with someone else's property, who will give you property of your own?"

Every human being alive must be a steward of personal resources of skill, knowledge, strength, possessions and influence. We don't need to necessarily aspire for more or feel discouraged about areas of what we may perceive as lack, we just need to use what we have. Hard work, efficient use of our available resources and a disciplined personal life will lead to prosperity and success. Os Guinness said, "Ownership is God's; stewardship is ours."

Matthew 25:24-28

"Then the man with the $1,000 came and said, 'Sir, I knew you were a hard man, and I was afraid you would rob me of what I earned, so I hid your money in the earth and here it is!' But his master replied, 'Wicked man! Lazy slave! Since you knew I would demand your profit, you should at least have put my money into the bank so I could have some interest. Take the money from this man and give it to the man with the $10,000'" (*TLB*).

In Matthew 25:14-30 the parable of the talents is recorded. This story tells of a certain man who distributed his wealth among three servants, giving to each according to his ability. As this parable would imply, our abilities vary individually, and it is wise for us to realize that this is true also in our ability to earn money.

The parable proceeds to tell how each man invested his seed money. The first two traded theirs, that is they used it, and in the process they doubled the amount they had originally. The last person, however, tried to hoard or keep his by doing nothing with it. In the end, each had to account for his actions.

The man with only two talents, through his small ability and industry, gained a 100% increase, and he was promoted. He was responsible only to use the ability he had to do the best he could do. What about the man who had one talent? According to the Bible, his complaining and whining attitude was not well received. His employer, though critical, was just in his actions. He told the slothful servant that he could have tried at the least to obtain help from others by placing the talent into the hands of those who knew what to do with it.

Instead, the man chose idleness. He was cast away and punished, not because he misused the talent or lost it or sold it, but because he did nothing with it. God expects us to be doing what we are able to do with what He has committed to us. If we apply ourselves and use the talents He has given us, He will bless us. If you are a good steward over a little, then God looks at you and thinks, *I can trust this person with more*.

Revelation 2:23

"I will repay each of you according to your deeds."

Begin now to live a principled life. Determine at this moment to live the principle of financial stewardship!

The Biblical Principle
of Financial Supply

Matthew 17:26

"So go down to the shore and throw in a line, and open the mouth of the first fish you catch. You will find a coin to cover the taxes for both of us; take it and pay them" (*TLB*).

One of the wonderful principles of the Bible is that of divine supply; God promises to supply our every need. Financial supply is a God-given gift. God gives us many gifts, but His greatest gift was His death on the cross, providing a living sacrifice for our sins. He has given us the gift of salvation. He gives us the gift of life, of family, of friends and of good health. The Bible says that He loves to give us good gifts.

Matthew 7:11

"If you, then, though you are evil, know how to give good gifts to your children, how much more will your Father in heaven give good gifts to those who ask him!"

If a gift is promised, but not yet given, why do some people borrow and go into debt just to obtain what God had intended to supply anyway? Is this because of our impatience or a lack of trust? Is it because we don't really have faith for God's abundant supply or don't agree with His timetable?

When two people marry in the traditional Christian wedding, the vow includes the statement, "until death do us part." Many good marriages break apart because of a great wall of debt. Unfortunately, in our current culture, this sacred vow might be more accurate had it said, "until debt do us part." Many statistics now conclude that the majority of all divorces are influenced by financial controversy and seemingly insurmountable debt. Debt can be avoided in most cases. Most borrowing and getting into debt is not the result of unplanned medical expenses, but rather deliberate choices to burden oneself with more financial obligation.

If you know that most borrowing is not necessary and most debt can be avoided, and that your heavenly Father will provide for your needs, why then do you want to put your financial life in jeopardy by taking on more debt? You can be sure of these things:

- God knows your need.
- He wants to provide for you.
- He desires to bless you with good gifts.

Everything we have is a gift from the Lord. He desires to bless and prosper you. Jeremiah 29:11 says, "For I know the plans I have for you," declares the LORD, "plans to prosper you and not to harm you, plans to give you hope and a future."

Along with these gifts comes personal responsibility. Jesus talked about stewardship a great deal. *Jesus dealt with money matters because money matters!*

Both Jesus and Satan know that "where your treasure is, there your heart will be also" (Matthew 6:21). That's why both are very interested in what we do with our money. *Our attitude toward money is a spiritual matter!* If our attitude is right, we will be good stewards of all God has allowed us to oversee, and by doing so, an unending supply of provision will come our way.

Begin now to live a
principled life. Determine at
this moment to live
the principle of financial supply!

The Biblical Principle of Seeking Counsel

2 Chronicles 18:4

"But Jehoshaphat also said to the king of Israel, 'First seek the counsel of the LORD.'"

Hosea 4:6

"My people are destroyed from lack of knowledge."

Families are faced with many financial challenges and decision-making opportunities. It is a good thing we are not able to see into the future or we might become very discouraged indeed. But such is life! We take the good with the bad, and somehow it all seems to come out okay.

Financial decisions are a regular part of life. We cannot get around them, but we can learn to handle them effectively. Satisfactory solutions must be found to complicated questions. What to do about housing? Should one rent or buy? How to get out of debt? How to stay out of debt? Is certain debt bad? Can debt ever be considered good? Various resources can be used to solve these problems and to achieve individual family goals.

Other questions include: How can we keep ahead of the bills when the family is growing and needing so many things? Can we afford to finance a new car? How do we know if we are saving enough money? These are important questions and each raises a particular concern. Be assured that not any one answer will suit all individuals and families.

The questions raised can be answered by tackling one challenge or problem at a time. Part of the answer is simply recognizing the problem and then solving it or answering each question one at a time. By doing so, people can be productive and cope with the difficult decisions better. An added plus is receiving the satisfaction that comes from being in control of your financial life.

Although the answers to these personal financial questions may differ from person to person, the method of arriving at the answers can be similar. Each question answered, and each financial problem solved can move your family and you one step closer to your goals. If you find that your goals and objectives are not being met, then possibly not all of the problems have been completely solved.

Isaiah 30:1

"Woe to the rebellious children," says the LORD, "Who take counsel, but not of Me, and who devise plans, but not of My Spirit" (*NKJV*).

Isaiah 16:3

"Give us counsel, render a decision."

Let's look at some steps to solving those financial challenges.

SEEKING IMPROVEMENT

Facing financial challenges begins with knowing that a situation can be better. The process starts by realizing the difference between what is and what ought to be, and then wanting to do something about it. If you don't know that a situation can be better, you will hardly be ready to solve a problem. You must be aware that challenges do in fact exist before they can be solved. Once the awareness is there, you can then seek the answer.

CLARIFYING GOALS

Facing financial challenges means having a clear definition and understanding of individual and family financial goals. Sit down as a family and put on paper those personal goals that you wish to accomplish. Prioritize them, rating their importance.

If you have children, perhaps you want each of them to have some exposure to music; if so, then music lessons might be a family goal. But you may have other family goals that do not include music. By listing those goals, you can measure any success in terms of the goals that are achieved. A clear definition of those goals is necessary before you can begin your journey.

DEFINING THE PROBLEM

Facing financial challenges means that once the goals are known, the problem needs to be defined. After you identify your goal, you are ready to state the challenge or obstacle that stands in the way of reaching it. More than one obstacle may become apparent. Possibly several solutions will have to be found. Financial challenges need to be defined carefully. If they are formulated only in vague and general terms, the solutions are apt to be vague and general, too. Problems can also be studied more easily if they are stated in relationship to your goals. Stating the problem helps keep the goal in focus and the problem in perspective.

As you attend to one goal, you'll find it related to other goals. In this way, an overall view is necessary; a snapshot is not enough. Seldom can a problem be considered individually. The solution to one puzzle may alter other solutions, or it may introduce new problems and obstacles. This process of problem solving goes on and on. It can never stop, and must be continual.

DETERMINING RESOURCES

Facing financial challenges means that after the challenge is stated, the available resources need to be determined. What resources are available or can be made available that might contribute to the solution of the challenge or problem? Resources are the tools that will help you reach your goals. Human resources will include your own personal skills, talents, knowledge, health and energy. Material resources include your money, house, household equipment (camera, mower, washer and dryer, sewing machine, computer), vehicles and so forth. Each of these things has potential to generate additional income to meet a specific family goal.

OUTLINING ALTERNATIVES

Facing financial challenges means that alternative solutions to the challenge need to be outlined. Once the…

a) financial challenge has been identified
b) the goals defined
c) resources evaluated

…then all the alternatives need to be outlined. This will provide an opportunity to select the most satisfying solution. This process may require additional information. After alternative solutions to a problem have been outlined, each choice must be evaluated in terms of its outcome.

The need for factual and instructive information becomes even greater when seeking solutions involving expensive purchases. In many cases special support may be needed, and assistance from experts may help. Until such information is obtained, an individual or family is not in a position to make those decisions or choose between solutions with confidence.

MAKING A DECISION

Facing financial challenges means that after the alternatives have been analyzed, it is time to make a decision. The moment comes to decide on adopting one of the possible solutions. The decision must be made and acted upon, and the results evaluated.

SUMMARY

Managing your finances involves financial problem solving by choosing among alternative solutions to each challenge. To start with, realize that a problem (such as managing your credit or getting out from under a heavy burden of debt) exists. In other words, something about the present practice or procedure isn't satisfactory and must be changed.

If it seems nothing is being accomplished, then the current circumstances are probably not acceptable. To know what needs to be accomplished, the goals must be defined. The real purpose for solving the problems confronting us is to achieve particular goals. In reaching those goals, we can state the challenge or problem that has become an obstacle. Then, after seeing more precisely the problem or challenge, we must determine what we have to work with by taking inventory of our resources.

Keeping our resources in mind, we are ready to outline the possible solutions to the problem (identify the alternatives) and how each solution is likely to work out. On the basis of our analysis of the possible outcomes, a decision can be made about a solution. The decision must then be acted upon, that is, it must be implemented. After a period of time, the results can be evaluated through various means of measurement.

Begin now to live a principled life. Determine at this moment to live the principle of seeking counsel!

The Biblical Principle
of Managing Possessions

*B*ecause we are not our own, we should dedicate to God all that we are, all that we own, and all that we will ever be. *You are God's, so all you have belongs to God. You simply manage your possessions for Him.* Your business belongs to God. When everything you have belongs to God, it takes off all of the pressure.

In many countries, citizens pride themselves on private property ownership. In reality, all the property, possessions, money and wealth belong to God. We are simply managers of what belongs to Him. All the land and all property still belong to the Creator.

The Bible offers many stories and illustrations of approval of wealth. But according to Scripture, riches are a gift and a special blessing. Wealth was given by God on many occasions to meet the needs of the poor, not just for having more. It is clear that accumulating wealth is meant for kingdom purposes. The rich are to be good stewards of their resources, for they have come from God.

1 Corinthians 6:19, 20

"You are not your own; you were bought at a price. Therefore honor God with your body."

When your possessions and business belong to God, you are not responsible for their ultimate success. Of course, you are required to be a good manager. Let's say you are a farmer and your farm belongs to God. If the weather is dry and it doesn't rain, you don't have to worry about it because it belongs to God. If your business is dedicated to God, it becomes His problem and not yours.

The apostle Paul realized that although everything in the universe belongs to God, if we team up with Him, He allows us to keep some of everything He provides.

Paul said that the soldiers in the army do not pay for their own expenses. The farmer who harvests the crop has a right to eat some of it. The one who plants the vineyard gets to enjoy some of its fruit.

Luke 1:52, 53

"He has brought down rulers from their thrones but has lifted up the humble. He has filled the hungry with good things but has sent the rich away empty."

Luke 1:53 profiles some rich people of Jesus' day. The rich hoarded all their possessions and treasures. They did not share their resources with the poor and needy. They believed God approved of them and their lifestyle so He gave them great wealth. Because of this erroneous attitude, they looked down upon the poor as being people that did not have the favor and blessing of God. They idolized their wealth and held it very close. Their very identity was defined in how much money they had and the possessions they gathered around them.

In Jesus' day, many common and ordinary people were very poor, but they were not poor because God did not love them. Nor were they poor because of their own personal failings or lack of intelligence. They were not lazy, they worked hard, yet were very poor. Many could not even provide the essentials for themselves and their families. They were vulnerable to the rich and powerful of their time. They had no way to improve their economic condition or their family social status.

Our stuff should never have a firm grip on us— not on our attitude, not on our character and not on our sense of self-worth.

Today, many people find their own sense of worth and identity in what they have, where they can travel to and what kind of possessions they have accumulated. We need to be wise and watch that our own sense of value comes solely from our inner spiritual character and not from what we have or what we possess.

Our *stuff* should never have a firm grip on us—not on our attitude, not on our character and not on our sense of self-worth. Our outward behavior should reflect our inner spirituality. Our actions should be an outgrowth of our character. We are not owners or possessors. We are but managers of the temporary allowances of God.

Begin now to live a principled life. Determine at this moment to live the principle of managing possessions!

The Biblical Principle of Appropriate Use

Is it wrong to have money? Does being spiritual mean you must give up all your possessions and live in poverty? Are possessions bad? Doesn't the Scripture say money is the root of all evil? Of course, the accurate and truthful answer to each of these questions is "no." The Bible does say in 1 Timothy 6:10 that the "love" of money is the root of all evil. God created the world. God created all the varied pleasures of life itself. First Timothy 4 lets us know that everything God created was good, and that nothing is to be rejected when it is received with thanksgiving. Satan did not, and cannot, create anything. All he can do is attempt to corrupt every good thing God has given to us.

Mark 10 tells us the story of the rich young ruler. Here was a decent person, one who had worked hard and who had become very wealthy. We are not told that he had any real problems with theft, murder, adultery, perjury or anything else. In fact, he admits to living by the Ten Commandments from a very young age. The rich young ruler wanted eternal or everlasting life. But when Jesus the Everlasting Life looked into his eyes and said to give all he had to the poor and follow Him, the cost seemed too high. Jesus did say that by doing so the young ruler would have treasure in heaven. But the young man went away sad.

What was the rich young ruler's situation? Was it that he had too much money and that people with great wealth cannot go to heaven? Of course not! His stumbling block was that his wealth had him. Possessions and money are not bad—in fact they are good when used as tools to support the kingdom of God. The young man suffered from foolish decision making. When the greatest opportunity of his life was staring him in the face, he chose to reject it in favor of his money. He had not learned the principle of appropriate use.

It is not all about having great wealth and using it the wrong way. Many Christians have very little money, yet have to overcome the same obstacle as the rich young ruler. When Jesus was warning the rich, He was not classifying people according to the amount of money they had. He was cautioning them about how attached they were to what they had. You can be overly attached to your money and possessions whether you have just a meager amount or great wealth. Will your money become your blessing or your curse? Can money buy happiness? Can it buy contentment? Can it buy peace of mind?

145

Contrast the man of wealth in Mark 10 with the founder of the Quaker Oats Company, who gave 70% of his income to God. Or contrast the Chicago seven to Abraham, the wealthy father of many nations. Abraham was not only a great man of faith, but also a very wealthy individual. Solomon was probably the richest man of his day. Barnabas, an early New Testament local church leader, was also wealthy but used his money and affluence to extend the kingdom of God.

James 5:1-3 speaks to the wealthy who use their money for personal gratification. James tells them they will weep and howl because of all the misery that is coming upon them. He boldly says that their gold and silver is plagued, and their precious metals will soon rust. James points out that it is foolish to value and esteem riches so highly that it causes corruption. It is harmless to possess riches, as long as the riches do not possess us.

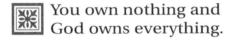 ## You own nothing and God owns everything.

Jesus recommended that we not stockpile our treasures in this life, at the expense of accumulating our treasures for the hereafter. In other words, if one is a long-term planner and visionary, it makes much more sense to accumulate wealth for the long haul in eternity. Time here on earth is the short haul; the temporary vapor of life. Life in eternity and life in heaven is the long-term commitment.

You own nothing and God owns everything. Whatever you have, God allowed you to accumulate. But when you die, how much of your money will you leave behind? All of it! When you die, how much of your money will you take with you? None of it!

Ultimately, you own nothing. You won't take your new BMW with you. You won't take those diamond rings or precious jewelry with you. You won't take your house with you. You won't take any property with you. You won't take any of the possessions with you that you have managed to accumulate here on earth. You won't take your body because you don't own it. When your spirit leaves your body, it will return to dust.

Begin now to live a principled life. Determine at this moment to live the principle of appropriate use!

The Biblical Principle
of Avoiding Overindulgence

*I*f you plan to become debt free and stay that way for life, we need to address the subject of personal pleasure and overindulgence.

Proverbs 21:17

"He who loves pleasure will become poor; whoever loves wine and oil will never be rich."

This verse tells us that loving pleasure and overindulgence squanders assets and prevents us from building proper financial resources.

Jesus said this in Luke 12:15, "Watch out! Be on your guard against all kinds of greed; a man's life does not consist in the abundance of his possessions."

In the United States, we live in a world filled with *things* and *stuff*. Revolving around things and stuff can be defined as materialism. Too often, our spending habits are built upon the foundation of materialism because we want things, and more things. We just can't seem to get enough *stuff*.

Now hear me out. Having things is not the problem. Having the money to be able to purchase things is not the problem, but *stuff* and *things* should not be bought just because you have the money. Of course, if you don't have the money, they should not even be considered. As biblical stewards, we are not to spend the Master's money on things we don't need. That would be very foolish.

So if having wealth is not the problem, and having possessions is not the problem, then what is the obstacle, the potential stumbling block? The spiritual problem comes with the love of things. When we can't get enough, when we must have more, this is where we stumble spiritually.

Many parents attempt to express their love for their children by overindulgence in gifts and money. Perhaps this is their way of making up for being absentee parents, workaholic parents or for a lack of spiritual guidance in the family. But this contradicts many other biblical principles. The Christian way is all about servanthood and sacrifice, not materialism and overindulgence.

One definition of materialism states:

"The tendency to give undue importance to material interests; devotion to the material nature and its wants." —*The American Heritage® Dictionary of the English Language, Fourth Edition*

Another definition of materialism:

"A desire for wealth and material possessions with little interest in ethical or spiritual matters." *Webster's Revised Unabridged Dictionary,* © *1996, 1998 MICRA, Inc.*

A. W. Tozer said, "Never own anything; get rid of the sense of possessing!"

"Materialism is a view of life that regards the possession of material things as the highest good, the *summum bonum*. It involves more than a mere appreciation of physical things. It goes beyond the simple enjoyment of material benefits. This view is both radical and an ism. It is radical because it makes material things the heart or 'root' (radix) of all human happiness. It is an ism because it turns the neutral word 'material' into a philosophy of life." —R. C. Sproul Jr., *Biblical Economics,* Tennessee: *Draught Horse Press,* 2002, p.23.

Here is a biblical story about a fool and his possessions. He was even called a fool by God!

Luke 12:16-21

"And he told them this parable: 'The ground of a certain rich man produced a good crop. He thought to himself, *What shall I do? I have no place to store my crops*. Then he said, 'This is what I'll do. I will tear down my barns and build bigger ones, and there I will store all my grain and my goods. And I'll say to myself, *You have plenty of good things laid up for many years. Take life easy; eat, drink and be merry.*' But God said to him, 'You fool! This very night your life will be demanded from you. Then who will get what you have prepared for yourself?' This is how it will be with anyone who stores up things for himself but is not rich toward God."

Well, what do YOU think? Was he a fool? Not many people have been so singled out by God. But before you jump on the bandwagon in agreement, read the story again. This story seems to be a picture of the American Dream! The rich man was probably a hard and productive worker. He built and saved and toiled for a lifetime. This is not unlike some people today. They purchase their first little house, and when they outgrow it, they sell it and buy a bigger one. And when they get a little equity in the place, they place it on the market and look for a bigger, better, nicer, newer house!

The man in Luke 12 was shrewd. He was a builder; he was an investor. There is no evidence that he was dishonest, no evidence that he broke the law and no evidence that he evaded paying taxes. None whatsoever. Some people today are just like him. They write bestselling books, give expensive seminars, have university buildings named after them and are proclaimed publicly as entrepreneurs—the individuals that make America great! They work hard, invest well and retire early.

Yet, in Luke 12 Jesus called this man a fool! Wow! Why?

It must be known that our spiritual prosperity is infinitely more important than our material prosperity.

Is it wrong to be successful? Is it wrong to have wealth? Does this mean that Christians should all be poor? No! Abraham, Isaac, Jacob, Joseph, David, Solomon, Daniel, Joseph of Arimathea and Cornelius were all wealthy. Some of them, in fact, were extremely wealthy.

So what is the difference between the man called a fool by God and these great Old Testament patriarchs and New Testament characters? The difference is this: This man's outlook on life was totally self-centered. Everything he did was for himself. Every event, every purchase, every sale, everything was all about his personal ease and happiness. In his mind, HE, not God, was the sole owner of his life and his possessions. And his priorities—they were so badly skewed that he deserved the tag "fool."

He used his wealth for himself rather than for the kingdom of God. His security was all wrapped up in his ability, his money and his possessions. He was headed for a retirement life of ease, but one without God. A retirement of self-serving gratification, not a retirement of servanthood.

Yes, it's true that the Abrahams, Isaacs, Jacobs, Josephs, Davids, Solomons and Daniels of the Bible were rich. But here is the difference between them and the Luke 12 fool. They had wealth, but each of them was totally devoted to God.

Is it wrong to enjoy the blessing of God? Of course not, but the blessing of God does mean we must have our priorities right in life. First, God must be recognized as the source of all things. Second, He must be credited with full ownership of all we possess. Third, it must be known that our spiritual prosperity is infinitely more important than our material prosperity.

3 John 2

"Beloved, I pray that you may prosper in all things and be in health, just as your soul prospers" (*NKJV*).

Joshua 1:8

"Do not let this Book of the Law depart from your mouth; meditate on it day and night, so that you may be careful to do everything written in it. Then you will be prosperous and successful."

Begin now to live a principled life. Determine at this moment to live the principle of avoiding overindulgence!

The Biblical Principle
of Financial Diligence

Proverbs 10:4, 5

"Lazy hands make a man poor, but diligent hands bring wealth. He who gathers crops in summer is a wise son, but he who sleeps during harvest is a disgraceful son."

Becoming debt free and remaining debt free requires financial diligence. Nothing can be accomplished without meticulousness in your economic life. As the Scripture says, lazy hands lead to poverty, but attentiveness to good work habits and good financial habits can lead to prosperity and success.

Some people today would rather ask for a handout go to work. You see them waiting at the freeway exits holding signs that read "Will work for food." After offering one person a day's work in exchange for wages, his response was nothing more than profanity and gestures. The integrity of this person was certainly lacking and his honesty brought into full question.

A person's usefulness is determined to a great degree by his motivation to work. Idleness is not looked upon kindly in biblical passages nor within our society today.

The Bible is clear about the principle of working diligently. It says that a lazy person who conveniently excuses himself from working with a little sleep, a little slumber and a little folding of the hands to rest will come to naught. His life will be one of poverty, bankruptcy and uselessness. He is one who consoles himself with rest, unconcerned that others are getting the job done.

The person who does not work diligently is nothing short of lazy. However, the person who gets up early, gets right to work and prepares for the future will someday be honored for it. Proverbs 22:29 points this out by saying, "Do you see a man who excels in his work? He will stand before kings" (*NKJV*).

Hebrews 6:10, 11

"God is not unjust; he will not forget your work and the love you have shown him as you have helped his people and continue to help them. We want each of you to show this same diligence to the very end, in order to make your hope sure."

From this Scripture, we can clearly see that diligence produces the fruit of what you hope for. If you commit to working diligently, God says He will not forget what you have done and will, in turn, reward you.

Colossians 3:23

"Whatever you do, work at it with all your heart, as working for the Lord, not for men."

This passage tells believers they must be diligent and focused on whatever God is asking them to do. That not only applies to a job, but also to finances. Finances are, of course, directly linked to your job—that's what brings in the cash! Diligence and hard work are simply part of the Christian walk.

Begin now to live a principled life. Determine at this moment to live the principle of financial diligence!

The Biblical Principle
of Fiscal Planning

Proverbs 21:5

"The plans of the diligent lead surely to advantage, but everyone who is hasty comes surely to poverty" (*NASB*).

The shrewd person looks ahead and plans for the future. He manages money so as to provide benefit not only for the present, but also for future financial reward. William Jennings Bryan (1860–1925) noted, "Destiny is not a matter of chance, it is a matter of choice."

What is involved in the planning process? Planning is outlining a course of action now in order to achieve a financial goal, thus fulfilling a desired objective. It is predetermining today a course of action for tomorrow. It is throwing a net over tomorrow and making something happen. It is being tomorrow minded rather than yesterday minded.

The only way to reach a financial goal is to work at it. The most important step in reaching the goal is to develop a plan to achieve it. That's why it is important to plan ahead for your retirement and your financial future. The idea of planning ahead and building a solid financial strategy for success can sometimes be intimidating and feel a little overwhelming, but once you get started it will become easier for you.

With a little planning and a better understanding of what your investment options are, you too can successfully manage your money and pursue your financial goals. So what is planning? Planning is knowing where you are today, outlining the steps it will take to reach your financial goals, developing a sound plan, and continuing to follow the pattern you outlined by pursuing your goals. Planning involves measurement and feedback. Planning is being decisive and doing work today designed to cause specified occurrences tomorrow.

"I urge you to plan your work and then work your plan. I urge you to let no obstacle get in your way of accomplishing your plan. Either go around it, over it, or through it. But don't turn around and go back. You do not retreat. You do not quit."—*Alan N. Canton*

The principle of financial planning is important. Take time to plan for your financial future. Good planning is an essential step toward meeting your financial goals. Plans must be flexible. They must be evaluated. They must be revised from time to time. Don't delay, get started today!

Begin now to live a principled life. Determine at this moment to live the principle of fiscal planning!

The Biblical Principle
of Tomorrow Thinking

2 Chronicles 26:5

"As long as he sought the LORD, God gave him success."

Proverbs 21:5

"The *plans* of the diligent lead surely to advantage, but everyone who is hasty comes surely to poverty" (*NASB*).

RETIREMENT PLANNING

Financial security does not just happen. It takes a lot of planning, a heavy dose of commitment and money. It is a fact, according to government statistics, that less than half of Americans have put aside money specifically for retirement. One third of those who have 401(k) coverage available to them do not participate in the plan. You can't retire with security unless your really prepare for it. This means facing up to reality and beginning to take action for tomorrow as well as today. Putting away money for retirement is like giving yourself a raise. It's money that gives you freedom when you want it and when you deserve it.

Increasing numbers of people are finding that retirement is staring them in the face before they are ready to leave the workforce. The jobs they had counted on to sustain them in their later years may have been a victim of company layoffs. Many are facing employment that pays less, but more significant, the loss of pension or retirement plans they thought would be theirs. It is important to invest personal money and adequately prepare for the golden years.

Retirement planning is taking on greater importance these days, as more and more people face involuntary termination because of changes in corporate downsizing and the American economy.

Know your retirement needs. Retirement living is expensive. How much are you saving for the future? Most financial planners recommend you save 10–15% of your income. But many of us fall short of that goal. How much will you need to retire? How much will you need to save by the time you are 62, 65 or 66? Experts estimate you will need at least 70% of your pre-retirement income to maintain your standard of living. If you are not making a moderately good living now, you may need as much as 90% of your current income to live comfortably in your retirement years.

Know your future financial needs. According to the government figures on aging, only one-third of people currently employed have attempted to learn how much they must save to achieve a comfortable retirement. Of those who have investigated it, still 42% remain unsure how much money they will need to save to retire. How much money do you need for retirement?

The answer depends on the lifestyle you foresee during retirement. It depends on how long you live and how long your family members historically have lived. The answer to this also depends on your retirement goals. Do you plan to travel around the world? Do you plan to live just as you do now? How much money will you be leaving to your heirs? Some expenses will go down as a result of your age. You won't be paying Social Security taxes, work expenses or contributing to retirement plans. However, some expenses, such as health care and travel, may increase dramatically.

Know your housing needs. Most older people prefer to remain in their own homes during their later years, even if it means some remodeling to accommodate their health concerns. Even when frail and vulnerable, or when afflicted with a chronic illness, people want to stay in familiar surroundings. This can mean hiring expensive healthcare professionals to come into their homes to provide proper care. Often this is not possible when people have failed to save enough to meet such needs. Adequate income and assets are critically important to enable well being in virtually all dimensions of life in our later years.

Know your health needs. A wealth of information is available about maintaining physical and mental health, as well as achieving an adequate level of economic security to remain as independent as possible. You can live an active and productive life and enjoy retirement. The longevity of life provides new opportunities for our retirement years. The aging of the American population presents both new challenges and new opportunities. Of course, this also heaps more responsibility upon us to prepare for that lengthened life span. As a result, our retirement plans must address special needs.

SAVING FOR RETIREMENT— YOUNG AND OLD

Whether you are close to retirement or many years away, it is never too early or too late to plan for retirement. You control your financial future by identifying your retirement needs, setting money aside and making wise investment decisions now. Tell some young family to start now to prepare for retirement and they stare in disbelief. They think they are still young and have lots of time before they need to save for retirement.

The earlier a family starts, the more they will be able to salt away some great savings. That is because time is money and the power of compound interest is enormous. Assume you want to build a $100,000 nest egg by age 65 and that you can earn 10% on your money. You need to contribute only $16 per month if you start saving at age 25. If you wait till you're 35, you need to contribute $44 per month. The necessary contribution rises to $131 per month if you wait till 45, and skyrockets to $484 per month if you wait till 55.

Here is another example. Suppose you are a young person 20 years old. You start saving or investing just $21.60 each week and attain an average of 10% on your investment over a 45-year period. By the time you reach the retirement age of 65, your account would be worth $1,000,802.11. More than one million dollars! This shows the power of investing just a little bit over the long haul.

INVESTMENT DETAIL

- Interest Rate Compounded Continuously
- Weekly Payment Made at Beginning of the Period
- 45 Years/2,340 Weekly Payments of $21.60
- Interest Rate of 10%
- Total Contributions: $50,544

The chart below shows some variations to the above.

INVESTMENT DETAIL

- Interest Rate Compounded Continuously
- Weekly Payment Made at Beginning of the Period
- 45 Years/2340 Weekly Payments of $25.00
- Interest Rate of 10%

On the other hand, some older couples excuse their lack of saving by thinking they are too old to start saving for retirement. Although it is true you can't make up for lost time and opportunity, it's never too late to start saving. Someone who takes early retirement at age 55 may still be going strong 30 years later. You'll have to contribute more to your retirement savings account than if you started it decades ago, but the time to start saving seriously is now.

No one actively plans to fail in providing for a comfortable old age. We simply fail to plan. Our grandparents faced different problems with money than we do. They were frightened by bank failures and the depression and tended to put their money into just three places—a home, a bank and insurance. Today we have to be prepared for the havoc that inflation can play on our investments over the long term, as well as corporate fraud or an up and down economy. No one actively plans to fail in providing for a comfortable old age. We simply fail to plan.

Begin now to live a principled life. Determine at this moment to live the principle of tomorrow thinking!

AGE AT BEGINNING OF INVESTMENT	INVESTMENT VALUE AT AGE 55	INVESTMENT VALUE AT AGE 60	INVESTMENT VALUE AT AGE 65	WEEKLY CONTRIBUTION
20	$417,902	$697,446	$1,158,336	$25.00
25	$248,351	$417,902	$697,446	$25.00
30	$145,512	$248,351	$417,902	$25.00
35	$83,138	$145,512	$248,351	$25.00
40	$45,305	$83,138	$145,512	$25.00
45	$22,359	$45,305	$83,138	$25.00
50	$8,441	$22,359	$45,305	$25.00

The Biblical Principle
of Economic Rewards

Jeremiah 17:10

"I the LORD search the heart and examine the mind, to reward a man according to his conduct, according to what his deeds deserve."

Matthew 16:27

"He will reward each person according to what he has done."

All actions have their reward. Whether good or bad, temporary or eternal, rewards come as a result of our action. Often we predetermine our reward by predetermining our actions. But, of course, it all takes action on our part. How about your language skills? Could they use some improvement? Do you wish you had a bigger vocabulary but can never find the time to do a lot of studying?

Suppose you could carve 10 minutes out of every day (during TV commercials?) and you used that time to learn a new word. In 25 years you would have learned 9,125 words! This would be a nice reward indeed! The point is a simple one. The small changes we make in our lives can have a significant effect if maintained over a long period of time.

Sometimes our rewards come as a result of our actions that begin with New Year's resolutions. Most resolutions are started in the first few months of the year. We might want to lose weight, eat healthy, exercise or even get out of debt. Those are all worthwhile goals.

Most of us get frustrated trying to reach something that's too big. We just can't picture ourselves being 40 or 50 pounds lighter. In fact we won't lose that much weight in a short time even if we go on an all-out crash diet. The majority of people put the pounds right back on after they finish their diets.

Those who are successful follow a different approach. They change their lifestyle just a little bit, but only as much change as they're willing to accept on an ongoing basis. Maybe they cut out one soda per day—or add 15 minutes of exercise per day, something they can sustain for years to come.

Will they lose the 40 pounds? Not all at once. But they will begin to lose a pound or two each month. After a couple of years they will have achieved their goal and also given themselves a healthier lifestyle.

What is the lesson to be learned here? There are two. The first is that you don't need to be afraid to dream big. You can accomplish big things without doing anything heroic or noteworthy.

FINANCIAL REWARDS

The second lesson? Take small and determined steps toward your goal. Save a few dollars each and every week. Not a lot one week and none the next, but a few dollars each week.

Make regular progress to your ultimate destination a habit. If you fail one day, get right back on track. You won't go far in any one day, but you will cover a lot of ground over time.

On the other hand, you can decide that you don't want to make the small changes. Maybe you will be the one in 37 million who hits the lottery. But it's much more likely that you'll just be swimming upstream your whole life.

 All actions have their reward.

So how does that apply to our financial lives? Let's take a look at another natural occurrence. One thing we notice in nature is that many things start small and take time to grow. But they can grow to a large size if enough time passes.

Trees are an excellent example. They start from a seed, acorn or sapling and can grow to be hundreds of feet high.

The same thing can happen with our finances. Consider borrowing money. Suppose you spent $10 more than you make each week. And you continue to do that every week for 50 years. Remember that $10 isn't a large amount to borrow each week. But if you do that continually and

pay only a fairly good rate of interest (10% annually) you'll owe more than $762,000 after 50 years.

Of course, it works the same in the other direction. If you saved $10 a week you'd be a millionaire in the 52nd year of your program. So it really doesn't take a big shift to move you from serious debt to being comfortable financially.

Okay, I can hear some of you saying that you'd have a tough time saving $10 per week. Could you save 72 cents a day? That's $5 a week. In just 30 years you'd have a bit less than $50,000. Again, a small change in direction can make a major difference.

SAVING REWARDS

You can receive financial rewards by saving and by personal discipline! It isn't easy to save! It takes a commitment to start saving and sticking to it. Something else will always be waiting to take your money. But no one else will save for you, so you have to do it for yourself.

You may have heard that "a penny saved is a penny earned." But actually a penny saved is more than a penny earned. This is especially true if you invest it in an IRA or retirement plan. If your pennies earn a 7% interest rate, then the following applies:

- In 10 years, 1,000 pennies, or $10 a week, would grow to $7,185.
- In 20 years, 1,000 pennies, or $10 a week, would grow to $21,318.
- In 30 years, 1,000 pennies, or $10 a week, would grow to $49,120.

A financial reward is waiting for you when you save. But, of course, your prearranged action predetermines the extent of that financial reward. How much and when you begin makes a difference in the amount of the reward.

When should you begin? As early as you can. If you start at 25, and put away $25 a month, you could reach $300,000 by age 65. If you wait until 45, that $300,000 at 65 may cost $300 a month.

Remember the rule of 72. This tells you how long it will take to double your money at a given rate of interest. You simply divide 72 by the interest your money is earning. At 6%, your savings will double in 12 years. At 9%, it will double in eight years.

Year after year, any money you invest may earn interest, dividends or capital gains. When you reinvest those earnings, they help generate additional earnings; those additional earnings help generate more earnings, and so on. This is called compounding. For example, if an investment returns 8% a year and its earnings are reinvested annually:

- After one year, your total return will be 8%.
- After five years, your cumulative total return will be 47%.
- After ten years, your cumulative total return will be 116%.

Remember that the financial reward may not be of the greatest importance to all. Other rewards can play an even greater role.

Thomas Edison was one such person in which another reward was greater. He said, "One might think that the money value of an invention constitutes its reward to the man who loves his work. But speaking for myself, I can honestly say this is not so. . . . I continue to find my greatest pleasure, and so my reward, in the work that precedes what the world calls success." (1847–1931)

John Ruskin weighed in with this word, "The highest reward for a person's toil is not what they get for it, but what they become by it." (1819–1900)

Begin now to live a principled life. Determine at this moment to live the principle of economic rewards!

The Biblical Principle
of Being Debt Free

Romans 13:7, 8

"Pay everyone whatever he ought to have: pay your taxes and import duties gladly, obey those over you, and give honor and respect to all those to whom it is due. Pay all your debts except the debt of love for others——never finish paying that!" (*TLB*).

These Scriptures are clear about the benefits of being a lender as opposed to being the borrower. Clearly, being the lender is preferred. Of course, you can never enjoy being in that position unless you have become debt free yourself.

Shakespeare said, "Neither a borrower or lender be, For loan oft loses both itself and friend, and borrowing dulls the edge of husbandry." (1564–1616)

The relative ease of obtaining credit enables consumers to get goods and services when cash is not readily available. It also allows them to buy things on sale, make purchases when prices are low, and pay for items at the same time they are using and enjoying them.

Unfortunately, problems and financial risks occur because consumers and creditors abuse credit. Careless use of credit can lead to financial difficulty, family problems, repossession of property, garnishment of wages and even bankruptcy. The bottom line is this: If you don't borrow money, you can't get into debt.

Options are available to help you manage financial difficulties when bills stack up and you cannot pay them. This topic discusses how to spot potential debt problems, how to set up a debt-payment plan and court provisions for handling credit obligations.

Many people find themselves deep in debt at least once in their lifetimes. It is not necessarily brought on by a desire to spend oneself into oblivion, but rather by a lack of family financial planning. In this section, I list 15 steps one can follow to get out of debt. This should help fight the debt mountain.

Some of my friends who are snow skiers can't understand why I am not excited about joining them on ski trips to Mt. Hood. I grew up in the Midwest, where 20 degrees below zero and annual snowfalls of well over 100 inches took all the excitement and anticipation out of the winter months.

Yet my friends continue to tell me that gliding down the slopes is exhilarating and that there's nothing like it.

Skiing into debt is also exciting. However, the price of escaping from the debt is greater than most people realize. Simply stopping the intake of new debt is not enough. A multiple financial reverse is involved. Look at what must happen to work out of the debt trap.

- Stop spending more than is earned.
- Spend considerably less than before.
- Pay the oldest debt.
- Pay the interest on the debt.

The bottom line is this: If you don't borrow money, you can't get into debt.

Your journey to financial freedom will be an individual one. Your own circumstances will have a lot to say about your plan. The following steps are a guide to map your own course.

- Decide to change.
- Determine not to overspend.
- Spend much less than you make.
- Do not add any new debts.
- Pay with cash.
- Determine what you owe.
- Prioritize your debt.
- Determine how much you can pay.
- Create a payoff plan.
- Communicate with your creditors.
- Establish a repayment timeline.
- Reduce your timeline with all extra monies.

- Stay focused on your plan.
- Stay with your plan.
- Seek professional counsel as needed.

Begin now to live a principled life. Determine at this moment to live the principle of being debt free!

The Biblical Principle
of Not Borrowing Money

Proverbs 22:7

"Just as the rich rule the poor, so the borrower is servant to the lender" (*TLB*).

This Scripture and others like it show us who is really calling the shots when it comes to money. The "haves" rule the "have nots" (i.e. the borrower is the servant to the lender). Yet in spite of this biblical reality, the debt-ridden consumer continues to borrow even more money without regard to the consequences.

There is a great danger in our society of getting trapped by debt. With this principle I want to address a number of borrowing and credit issues. Perhaps the greatest need in families today is understanding the consequences of being trapped by debt with limited income and in a financial position where it seems like it will be impossible to recover.

Any person can find a wealth of information that focuses on borrowing, easy credit and debt issues, but the problem I have found in counseling is failing to get a person(s) to recognize the seriousness of their actions before they make wrong decisions. All to often, people only want help after their situation has become nearly hopeless. Just know that borrowing can be very hazardous to your financial health and possibly to your mental health, spiritual health and the health of your relationships.

Much of borrowing done by a person today is for short-term loans. But for the most part this kind of credit goes to purchase things that generally have no asset value associated with them. Usually this has more to do with our wants and desires than our actual needs. Unfortunately, long after the item purchased is consumed, the debt repayment goes on.

Mark Twain had a couple of significant things to say about credit. "Beautiful credit! The foundation of modern society. Who shall say that this is not the golden age of mutual trust, of unlimited reliance upon human promises? That is a peculiar condition of society which enables a whole nation to instantly recognize point and meaning in the familiar newspaper anecdote, which puts into the mouth of a distinguished speculator in lands and mines this remark: 'I wasn't worth a cent two years ago, and now I owe two millions of dollars.'"

Too often families are quick to borrow instead of trusting the Lord to meet their needs. After all, does not Scripture tell us that our God is a providing God; that He will take care of us by meeting out needs? What if we turn to credit and take on new debt, when all along God wanted to show Himself strong on our behalf? Before you run to the bank for a loan, before you pull out the charge card, before you rush to meet your own needs, give time for the provision of God to work.

Philippians 4:17-19

"Not that I am looking for a gift, but I am looking for what may be credited to your account. I have received full payment and even more; I am amply supplied, now that I have received from Epaphroditus the gifts you sent. They are a fragrant offering, an acceptable sacrifice, pleasing to God. And my God will meet all your needs according to his glorious riches in Christ Jesus."

Because we have been taught from childhood to make our own way, to make decisions, and to move quickly and decisively, we hurry to fix our own problems. While we are not to be slow to work, we should be slow in waiting on God. We should be slow in always making our own way independently of seeking the wisdom of God.

Isaiah 55:7-9

"Let the wicked forsake his way and the evil man his thoughts. Let him turn to the LORD, and He will have mercy on him, and to our God, for He will freely pardon. . . . For my thoughts are not your thoughts, neither are your ways my ways," declares the LORD. "As the heavens are higher than the earth, so are my ways higher than your ways and my thoughts than your thoughts."

BORROW MONEY AS A LAST RESORT

Loan consolidation, home equity loans, or refinancing your home are ways to avoid repossession or loss of income through wage garnishment. These options may reduce the amount of your monthly payment. However, the cost for borrowing is usually increased, because the borrowing time is extended and you may be borrowing at a higher interest rate. If you can manage to pay your debts without loan consolidation, home equity loans, or refinancing, you probably will save yourself extra expense.

The use of these options generally does not improve poor money management habits, and the reduced monthly payment may encourage you to acquire more debts.

GETTING INTO DEBT IS SIMPLE

The road into the misuse of credit is wide, broad, simple, easy, accessible, effortless, uncomplicated, painless, spacious, available and trouble free. However, there is no quick and easy way out from under a heavy debt load. *With debt, in essence, you slide in and climb out*—easy to get in, difficult to get out. If you have ever been heavily in debt and burdened down with monthly payments so steep that you could barely keep your head above water and then had to slowly and methodically climb out, you know what I am talking about. It is an uphill struggle. There is no easy way out. I cannot wave a magic wand and help you undo in 12 months what it took 12 years to accomplish.

THE LIFESTYLE OF DEBT

What about a lifestyle of debt? Is a Christian to borrow? Is debt okay? Some would believe it is wrong for a Christian to have any debt. Some will say it is all right to borrow for a house, but never borrow for anything that would depreciate. While I am not in that camp, I do believe that one of the greatest challenges and hindrances to reaching the world for Christ is that people who live in a society where there is the possibility of making significant amounts of money all to often spend their way into enormous debt. In doing so, there is little left over above their tithing to give to their local church, missions and evangelism projects. If you have to borrow, learn to give while borrowing.

BORROW MONEY WITH THE RIGHT INTENTIONS

It is not wrong to borrow money, but it is wrong to take on debt without the ability to pay it back or with the intention of never repaying what is owed. What is meant in Romans 13:8 when it says not to owe anything to anyone?

"Obey the laws, then, for two reasons: first, to keep from being punished, and second, just because you know you should. Pay your taxes too, for these same two reasons. For government workers need to be paid so that they can keep on doing God's work, serving you. Pay everyone whatever he ought to have: pay your taxes and import duties gladly, obey those over you, and give honor and respect to all those to whom it is due. Pay all your debts except the debt of love for others—never finish paying that! For if you love them, you will be obeying all of God's laws, fulfilling all his requirements" (Romans 13:5-8, *TLB*).

These verses simply mean that you should obey the laws, pay your taxes and repay all of your debts. That just makes good sense. But more than repaying your debts at some future date, you are to pay your creditors on time with interest owed. A person who borrows but does not repay is called wicked, meaning wrong, sinful, immoral, evil and depraved.

Psalm 37:21

"The wicked borrow and do not repay, but the righteous give generously."

LIVE A SELF-CONTROLLED LIFESTYLE

If a person or family will live a restrained lifestyle, they will be able to live on thousands of dollars less each year. You should incur debt only when it makes good economic sense. The expense of borrowing should be less than the economic benefit you will receive.

Don't underestimate the interest of God to help you in every way. Over and over the Scriptures indicate that you are to live a controlled and temperate lifestyle.

"Now the overseer must be above reproach . . . temperate, self-controlled, respectable" (1 Timothy 3:2).

"Thus says the LORD, your Redeemer, the Holy One of Israel: 'I am the LORD your God, who teaches you to profit, who leads you by the way you should go'" (Isaiah 48:17, *NKJV*).

THE PROBLEM OF EASY CREDIT

The problem with easy credit is that banking institutions are always willing to give you more money than you have the ability to repay. If you need to borrow $1,000 for an unexpected need because you have not set aside dollars for that purpose, the lending institutions will try to give you several thousand more than you actually need. While at first blush that may give you great pride and confidence thinking that someone really believes in you, in reality the only way a bank makes money is to make loans.

If you receive $7,000 or $8,000 and you only needed $1,000, rest assured you will find a way to spend the extra. It will disappear without you knowing where it went. The less you borrow the less you pay back and the more you have available to give to missions and the needs of others. Credit should always be the exception and not the rule.

One of the problems with obtaining credit is that you are presuming nothing is going to change for the worse in the future. You are assuming you and your spouse will have adequate income for repayment, that your jobs are secure and that your income stream will be the same or more in later years.

There is a danger in making assumptions. It could be that your intended source of repayment changes. Jobs are lost, the value of stocks and bonds can decline or even disappear, assets may not appreciate as quickly as anticipated or they might even lose their value.

"Now listen, you who say, 'Today or tomorrow we will go to this or that city, spend a year there, carry on business and make money.' Why, you do not even know what will happen tomorrow. What is your life? You are a mist that appears for a little while and then vanishes. Instead, you ought to say, 'If it is the Lord's will, we will live and do this or that'" (James 4:13-15).

THE BONDAGE OF DEBT

Show me a person deep in debt and I'll show you a person who feels in bondage. You are so burdened down with the heavy load of debt, it is like becoming a servant to your creditors. You work all day for days on end just to meet your payment obligations to your debtors. You gladly volunteer for all the overtime you can get, work a part-time job in the evenings or on weekends, all for the purpose of getting a larger paycheck so you can turn it over to someone else. Well, all this is not breaking news. You knew about it long before you borrowed the money. You read about it in Scripture.

"The rich rule over the poor, and the borrower is servant to the lender" (Proverbs 22:7).

IS CREDIT DEBT DANGEROUS?

Americans are 2 trillion dollars in debt. Credit, the ability to borrow money, can be very dangerous. In short, it's spending money today that will be tomorrow's income. Most economists would say that credit is an important part of the ability of individuals, families, cities and ultimately nations to function in a financial world. Credit consists of unpaid balances on auto loans, credit cards, student loans and generally any non-mortgage debt.

One of the real dangers of excessive borrowing is that it creates high monthly payments, which often strains even well planned budgets. The pace of borrowing often exceeds the family's growth in income and leads to a form of "credit debt bondage." The interest expense of credit debt is often very high. Banks and other lending institutions often will loan to people with a higher credit risk, but do so at the expense of the borrower.

When employed by a major national bank as a Vice President and Business Banking Officer,

I learned of a huge profit opportunity for the company. Often those that did not qualify for the terms of a regular loan could still get money, but at an interest rate several points higher than normal. Of course, individuals, families and businesses would quickly agree because, in reality, they needed the money at any cost.

People that have high monthly credit payments often sacrifice their other financial goals just to make their payments. This is a very serious offense. By not investing in a house, savings account or other forms of investment, they seriously put their future retirement in question.

Excessive debt cannot be ignored. It will not go away. You can ignore past due bills, but you do so at the risk of finding yourself in even worse circumstances. A chain of events is triggered when you do not pay your bills. Creditors can take action against you, the past due bills can be turned over to a debt collector, your property can be repossessed, your wages garnished, and so on.

While debt bondage is the result of unwise decisions and excess credit purchases, there is no easy way out. The reason people find themselves in this position is that they spend more than they earned and the only way out is to spend less and pay the difference on their debt balance. The only way out of this dangerous situation is to be in control of their spending and put themselves on a budget, which is just a written plan that provides oversight and guidance to their spending habits.

SECRETS OF BORROWING LESS

It is always wise to borrow less than more. Cultivate the mind-set that you will borrow only for absolute necessities, and that you will repay the loan at the earliest possible date. Paying back a larger amount than the required fixed payment will help you retire the debt early. For what things should you not be getting a loan and for what would you borrow? In general, it all depends on your ability to repay the loan within a practical period of time.

While you could obtain credit to purchase an asset with reasonable potential to gain in value, you should not borrow for something that will continue to lose its value from the moment you buy it. Another sensible cause to borrow money would be for something obtained that would bring you income opportunity. If you have a skill or a trade and a particular tool or machine that would generate additional income, then credit might be a possibility to explore.

PLEDGE YOURSELF TO DELAYED GRATIFICATION

Don't get in the habit of buying something before you need it or because you think you might use it at some future date. Indulgence because you think you "owe it to yourself" or "it will help your self-esteem" is a bad habit.

You can develop habits that will ensure you will enjoy financial success, regardless of how much or how little your income. Many earn very little over a lifetime, yet manage to save enough for a debt-free and secure retirement.

CREDIT CARD DEBT AND INTEREST

Your current credit card debt represents more than just the fact that you owe money. It represents the fact that you are spending more money than you are making. It represents the fact that you are out of touch with your financial future. It represents the fact that you need to attend to this now—or it will likely get worse before it gets better.

A few years ago I was preparing my taxes and had been waiting for my interest statement paid to the only Visa card I have. In that particular year, I charged $26,000 on my credit card and I wanted to know my interest amount. So I called the card issuer and was told I had paid zero interest that year. In disbelief, I went back through each statement and found it was true.

The lesson here; if you are going to have a credit card, use it for convenience and pay it off in full at the time of each statement. If you cannot do that, you have no business carrying a card with you—pay cash instead.

Record nickels and dimes spent for the past 90 days and the next 90 days. If you don't know where the money went, how can you get out of debt? Close your eyes and visualize a stress-free, debt-free lifestyle. You are on vacation, but you have paid it all in advance. It is not more income you need; it is less spending.

Scripture says the poor will always be with us, but it does not say none of them will be Christians. A friend of mine, who is very brilliant individual, once made a statement that seemed very odd to me. He said, "I cannot understand why God has not made me rich yet." I have no magic formulas, but this one: Live within, not above, your income!

I have a friend who had purchased a couple of fine houses, but then sold them to pay off his debt, only to get into debt all over again. It is more important that I teach you why you should stay out of debt than to teach you how to get out of debt.

Let me settle something for you right now. You will never win the lottery so quit spending money on tickets. Quit spending money as if you were about to win the lottery. *God's ways are not about windfall income like the lottery.* His ways are about thriftiness, staying out of debt, working hard and serving Him. How do we get out of debt? Just the way we got into debt—one step at a time.

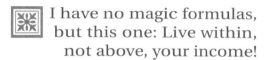 I have no magic formulas, but this one: Live within, not above, your income!

If you give a man a fish, you can feed him for a day. If you teach him to fish, you can feed him for life. It's not going to help you one bit if I major on how to get out of debt. The real help comes if I can change your attitude that causes you to move from a lifestyle of debt to the freedom of being debt free and becoming financially independent.

Deuteronomy 28:43-45

"The alien who lives among you will rise above you higher and higher, but you will sink lower and lower. He will lend to you, but you will not lend to him. He will be the head, but you will be the tail."

HOW CAN I GET HELP?

First go to God in repentance and ask forgiveness for mishandling that which He has entrusted to you. Remember that in your borrowing, you promised to repay. In essence, you made a vow when you incurred debt. Borrowing or lending, for that matter, is not necessarily wrong or prohibited in Scripture, but it is discouraged in a number of Scriptures. When you get into trouble because of your own unwise choices and bad decisions, while God will help you find a way out, it will not be at the expense of defrauding those to whom you go. Forgiveness is always available, but the consequences of our wrong actions remain.

Luke 11:9, 10

"So I say to you: Ask and it will be given to you; seek and you will find; knock and the door will be opened to you. For everyone who asks receives; he who seeks finds; and to him who knocks, the door will be opened."

In order to borrow at competitive rates it is important to be a credit-worthy person. Everyone knows that potential lenders look closely at your credit record, but did you also know that landlords and insurance companies do, too? Here are some tips for building up a clean credit record—and making sure it stays that way.

You probably already know that your credit report is all-important when it comes to qualifying for any type of loan, including a mortgage, an auto loan, or a low-rate credit card. But you may not realize that having a lousy credit rating (or credit score, which I'll talk about in a minute) can impede you when it comes to getting a job, renting an apartment or even getting a decent rate on auto insurance.

Landlords, employers and insurance companies have all discovered that someone who pays bills on time is likely to be responsible enough to pay them as well, and responsible enough to drive safely on the roads. That means it's in your best interest to keep your credit report—and your credit score—in its best possible condition.

Now you probably know that your credit report is essentially your credit history. It details what sort of loans are outstanding, how long you've had them, whether you pay your bills on time and so on (the information is not just from credit card companies, but all your creditors, including utilities, landlords, hospitals, banks, etc.).

Your credit score, however, is more complicated. It's a computer-based determination of the risk you pose to each of your creditors. In fact, it's calculated differently for each lender, using those particular parts of your credit report that are thought to be the most telling.

According to Fair, Isaac & Co., a leading supplier of credit data, these scores include up to 100 factors, including the number of times you've paid bills 60 days late, the size of your credit line (particularly the part that isn't being used), the number of recent inquiries into your credit history (an indication that you're looking for more credit) and any bankruptcies, liens and foreclosures.

Unfortunately, while you can, and should, take an annual look at your credit report, you can't see your credit score. It's available only to lenders and they pay handsomely for it. But you improve your score (and your overall credit history) with some fairly simple maneuvers, which I will cover later.

Begin now to live a principled life. Determine at this moment to live the principle of not borrowing money!

The Biblical Principle
of Financial Discipline

Hebrews 12:11

"No discipline seems pleasant at the time, but painful. Later on, however, it produces a harvest of . . . peace for those who have been trained by it."

Financial discipline is the ability to handle money in a responsible manner. The Bible indicates that control of finances in one's possession is a direct indication of the control exercised in spiritual matters. If a person cannot handle God's blessing of finance, it is likely he cannot handle too much time on his hands, promotion on the job, authority on the job, authority in the church, and probably a whole host of other spiritual and natural issues. The "unjust steward" of Luke 16 had other personal problems besides just being a bad manager for his lord. His dishonesty became very apparent when he was about to lose his job. The handling of a person's financial affairs is similar to his/her other values. The value system of one's heart is exposed by his relationship to money and material things. The rich young ruler is another illustration of that fact (see Matthew 19:16-22).

The biblical principle of financial discipline cannot be ignored. Ignoring that principle allowed you to get into debt in the first place. While staying out of debt is not so easy, getting out of debt once you are in debt is very difficult. Benjamin Franklin said, "Creditors have better memories than debtors."

Before you can become debt free, you must assess just where you are. How much in debt are you? What kind of debt do you have? What can you do to perform a financial checkup? What information will you need to gather? Are you headed for serious financial trouble? All these questions need to be answered before you can get on the right road to financial recovery. Two Chinese proverbs are applicable here: "A good debt is not as good as no debt," and "Free from debt is free from care."

CHECK YOUR FINANCIAL WELL-BEING

So what's the quickest way to check your financial well being? If you don't like accounting, math and bank statements, you've probably never really taken your financial temperature. But is there a fast and painless way to get a feel for whether you're in financial trouble? Yes, there are a couple of techniques that you can use. Obviously, they're not going to give you as much information as if you took the time to do a personal balance sheet and budget, but they will let you know if you're heading for serious financial trouble. Let's spend some time giving you a financial checkup to see the condition of your financial health.

CHECKBOOK

One way is to look at your checkbook. If I were to ask to see all your cancelled checks and credit card statements for the past 12 months, what would that tell me about you and your spending habits?

One biographer said that when he started to do research on a person, the first thing he wanted to know was how that person spent money. He felt that if he could look at the checkbook, he'd learn more about that person than if he went to interview friends and relatives.

We can learn a lot about ourselves in the same way. What's the biggest check you wrote last month? If you still have a mortgage, that should be it. If the biggest check went somewhere else, you might want to ask yourself "why?"

Paying for college is expensive and may demand a rather high monthly payment. But if your car payment is as high you could be heading for trouble financially.

Maybe you don't have a mortgage payment. Perhaps you're elderly and have already paid it off. If so, the biggest check each month should be written to your retirement saving account. Or are you taking that money and using it to pay for a boat or other luxury instead?

Look at the other big checks you write. How many of them are to pay monthly bills for things you bought long ago? Are you still paying for the furniture that's been in your living room for three years? What about TVs, stereos and electronics? Making monthly payments on those types of items is a danger sign.

Now let's do a little rough math. Look at your deposits for the month. Then compare those big unavoidable monthly bills, you know, your mortgage, car payments and utilities. Do those payments consume more than two-thirds of your deposits? If so, you are already in dangerous territory. A closer look is in order.

Don't forget about the little checks either. Are you writing a lot of small checks to credit card companies? How are you recording your credit card purchases? Are you deducting from your check register each time you make a credit card purchase?

Maybe you're spending too much time in the mall. What about checks for cash or ATM transactions? Are you always just a little short of cash? If so, it may be time to look at some of that "miscellaneous" spending. Those 5- and 10-dollar lunches can add up over time.

What about your credit card bills? Are you among the 30% who pay off all their purchases every month? If so, you probably have your spending under control.

CREDIT CARD STATEMENTS

Look at your credit card statements. Can you remember what you bought with each charge? If you can't remember what you bought, there's a good chance you didn't need it.

Think about all the ones you do remember. Were you buying things you really needed? Or was it for something you just wanted at the time? Have you used all those things since you bought them?

Here's a quick test for you. Are you just paying the minimum each month on your credit card account? Flash the warning lights! Look at it this way. For every $1,000 you owe on your account you may be paying up to $200 each year in interest payments.

FEELINGS ABOUT MONEY

If you have a credit card balance of $5,000, that comes to about $100 in interest every month that doesn't bring any food, clothing or anything else into your house. Do your own math to see how much is flying out your window every month in interest. Wouldn't you rather have no credit card balance? Wouldn't you rather be debt free?

Finally, how do you feel about money? Some people look at money as a vehicle to have some fun and base their happiness on the amount of fun money can bring to them. They think they can buy things and happiness will follow. Those are usually the people with large credit card bills.

Others view money as a measure of their success. They need to earn more than their neighbor to feel "content-satisfied-justified-fulfilled." Their income (and what they buy with it) determines how happy they are. They're always on a quest for "more," so they can't be happy with what they have. It's a great formula for a lifetime of unhappiness.

> Begin now to live a
> principled life. Determine at
> this moment to live the principle
> of financial discipline!

The Biblical Principle
of Financial Danger

2 Peter 2:19

"By what a man is overcome, by this he is enslaved" *(NASB)*.

This is a danger that comes with being a slave to anything, and money is no exception. You can be a slave to money when you have it in excess and you are still wanting more. Equally as dangerous is when you have no money and have become a slave to a burden of heavy debt. The principle of financial danger is simply this: Do not become a slave to debt. There is serious danger in doing so.

Financial stewardship includes how we handle our money and our debt. Money is very important to us and sustains our livelihood. If spent in the right way, on the right things and in the right places, it can do us a lot of good. But more important is the fact that what we are is far more important than what we possess.

Debt is a serious financial and spiritual problem. Usually it means we have slipped into a lifestyle of poor stewardship. Every person must fulfill a fiduciary responsibility. This is a relationship of trust and confidence in our obligation to our family, friends, God and fellow man. Our life's stewardship should reflect God's interest in all He has entrusted to us.

Financial danger comes when you continue to borrow without the means to repay in a timely manner. The only problem with borrowing money is that you have to pay it back. No pressure on a marriage is quite like the burden of debt. The pressure to repay debt can feel like the powerful tentacles of a giant sea monster pulling you down into the suffocating deep. Robert Frost once said, "A bank is a place where they lend you an umbrella in fair weather and ask for it back when it begins to rain."

Debt is nothing more than borrowing from your future income to buy now what you cannot afford to purchase with your current income. Don't let debt break your back; get a handle on your spending.

Fortunately, potential debt problems can be spotted before they reach the serious stage. By knowing what danger signals to look for, you can take steps to prevent a problem before it occurs.

I have prepared a checklist below. If any of these danger signals look familiar, you may be headed for financial trouble.

DANGER SIGNALS OF TOO MUCH DEBT

- You think of credit as cash, not debt.
- Your debts are greater than your assets.
- You owe more than seven creditors.
- You are an impulsive or compulsive shopper.
- You and your spouse are dishonest with each other about your use of credit.
- You don't know how much your monthly living expenses are or the amount of your total debt.
- Your expected increase in income is already committed to paying off debts.
- You depend on extra income, such as earnings by a second person or overtime by the breadwinner, to help you make ends meet.
- You have less than two month's take-home pay in cash or savings where you can get to it quickly.
- You have to pay back several installment payments that will take more than 12 months to pay off.
- You have more than 15 or 20% of your take-home pay committed to credit payments other than your home mortgage.
- You get behind in utility or rent payments.
- You have to consolidate several loans into one or reduce monthly payments by extending current loans to pay your debts.
- You cannot afford to pay for regular living expenses or credit payments.
- Creditors are sending overdue notices.
- The portion of your income used to pay debts is rising.
- This month's credit balances are larger than last month's.
- You are usually late paying some of your bills.
- You borrow for items you once bought with cash.
- You don't have enough savings to meet expenses for at least three months.
- You don't know how much installment debt you owe and you are afraid to add it up.
- You have borrowed money from a new source to pay off an older, perhaps even overdue, debt.
- You have borrowed money to pay for regular household expenses such as rent, food, clothing, gas or insurance.
- You have reached your credit limits.
- You hurry to the bank on payday to cover checks already written.
- You no longer can contribute to a savings account or have no savings at all.
- You pay bills with money earmarked for other financial obligations.
- You pay minimum amounts or less on your outstanding debt.
- You use a cash advance from one credit card to make payments on others.
- You have applied for more credit cards to increase borrowing.
- You have drawn from savings to pay regular bills.
- Your liquid assets total less than your short-term debt.

. . . and on and on!

This causes you to . . .

a) Take out a loan.
b) Withdraw savings.
c) Skip payments.
d) Pay only the minimum amount due on your charge accounts.

1. If you identified with at least four of the above statements, examine your budget and look for ways to tighten your belt.

2. If you identified with five or more, you are probably headed for financial trouble.

3. If you identified with seven or more, then your financial health is in trouble and you are in financial danger!

Debt is nothing more than borrowing from your future income to buy now what you cannot afford to purchase with your current income.

At some point, most everyone applies for some form of credit, whether it's for a new house, a new car or bank credit cards. Very few people can afford to pay cash for every single purchase.

This is where banks come in. Many businesses will not accept a personal check from a person who does not have a credit card. It is also difficult and sometimes impossible to rent a car without a credit card. The credit card has fast become a major identification tool.

Your credit rating is very important and must be protected at all costs. Whether good or bad, your credit standing is no secret. Whenever you apply for any type of credit you will be investigated. Your payment habits go on file at the credit bureau. Your credit file shows your credit history, income level, and your habits and tendencies with regards to payments. Delinquent entries on your credit report may very well result in denial of credit.

Not only is having credit a necessity, but it's also just as important to maintain a good credit rating. However, each year, millions of well-intentioned people find themselves in financial crunches that severely jeopardize their credit standing.

These are well-meaning people, just like you, who might have been laid off, lost income through illness, and/or hospitalization, job loss, or more commonly, simply overextended themselves. The reasons why you are now in a financial bind are not particularly important at this point. Your aim now is to get out of debt and reestablish your credit.

How can you tell whether or not you have a credit and/or debt problem? Well, you have already seen one long list, but here are a few more:

First of all, ask yourself these questions:

- Are you paying high interest rates?
- Are you being charged late fees?
- Are you getting calls from creditors?
- Can you afford the monthly payments, but not the past due amount?
- Are you making monthly payments, but your balance never seems to go down?
- Do you worry about paying your bills?
- Would reducing your payment help?
- Are you able to only make minimum payments and your balance is not going down but UP, UP and UP?
- Are you racking up credit card debts faster than you can pay them?
- Do you feel like sinking in quicksand, and you sincerely want to get out of it once and for all?
- Are you always short on cash because you have to cover the past due bills?
- Are you incurring penalties because you cannot meet the minimum payment or are not paying your bills on time?

If you answered "yes" to any of these questions, you have a problem.

Purposely I gave you two opportunities to determine whether or not you have a debt problem. Some of the nicest people have the worst problem handling debt and credit matters, but unfortunately by the time they realize it, it's too late.

Begin now to live a principled life. Determine at this moment to live the principle of financial danger!

The Biblical Principle
of Lifestyle Change

2 Samuel 14:20

"Your servant . . . did this to change the present situation."

Getting out of debt is an attitude before it is an action. When so many people get into debt so quickly, a mistake usually happens when there is a desire to maintain a certain standard of lifestyle. Sometimes this occurs due to our particular culture of overindulgence and excess, or simply because some young people want to have now everything their parents have but have taken a lifetime to accumulate. Sometimes to reverse this lifestyle of debt, a change in lifestyle has to occur. The current situation and attitude must change.

What are some of the mistakes families make when managing their finances? Hundreds of wrong choices could be listed, including those that result from making decisions without knowledge or without taking the time to clearly think them through. Some mistakes are the result of character issues such as wrong values, selfishness, irresponsibility and lack of integrity. Other mistakes simply are the result of hastiness, lack of education, wrong priorities and so on.

Some are simply wrong choices made out of greed. How much is enough money? Usually just a little bit more. This kind of thinking gets people into trouble and is an indication that lifestyle changes need to occur. There are only five things you can do with money. Give it, save it, invest it, lend it and spend it. Notice where spending comes in that lineup: last. Spending should never be the first thing you do with your money. Because the proper management of money is specific and orderly, to short-circuit the system by spending it first results in fiscal disorder and finally financial chaos.

It's not what you make, it's what you spend. Here's a plan for people who have a spending habit that has gotten them into trouble. Get a plan, get out of debt, stop spending money you don't have and then when you are in complete control of your money, go ahead and start saving for specific needs or for a home. But you first need a plan, a written plan, a budget. A written plan stands firm whether you're on an emotional roller coaster or an even keel. Your attitude toward spending should be *"no debt no matter what."*

The following is a list of 10 financial principles penned more than 100 years ago by President Abraham Lincoln. I think you will find these truths to be as trustworthy today as when they were written. Part of the beauty of these remarks is that they are short, to the point and easily understood by anyone.

1. You cannot bring about prosperity by discouraging thrift.

2. You cannot help small men by tearing down big men.

3. You cannot strengthen the weak by weakening the strong.

4. You cannot lift the wage earner by pulling down the wage payer.

5. You cannot help the poor man by destroying the rich.

6. You cannot keep out of trouble by spending more than your income.

7. You cannot further the brotherhood of man by inciting class hatred.

8. You cannot establish security on borrowed money.

9. You cannot build character and courage by taking away men's initiative and independence.

10. You cannot help men permanently by doing for them what they could and should do for themselves.

LIFESTYLE CHANGE MEANS DOING WITHOUT THE NONESSENTIALS

In his book *Who Moved My Cheese*? Dr. Spencer Johnson says, "When you change what you believe, you change what you do."

You CAN do . . . WITHOUT these things:

- Restaurants
- Movies
- Massages and manicures
- Starbucks and other gourmet drinks
- New clothes/shoes
- Hobby acquisitions and/or expenses
- Lodging expenses at the beach, mountains or other destinations
- Unnecessary vehicles (all new vehicles)
- Cable TV
- Sports events
- Call waiting, call forwarding, conference calling
- Cell phones
- At home Internet service (go to your local library instead—it's free!)
- Name-brand clothing and goods such as Steve Madden, Ralph Lauren, MAC, etc.
- Magazine subscriptions
- PDAs and other expensive electronic equipment
- The newest CDs and DVDs (at least wait until they are on sale to buy them)
- Supplies for your pets that are not necessary (toys, name-brand food, etc.)

LIFESTYLE CHANGE MEANS PAYING WITH CASH

Albert Einstein noted, "In the middle of difficulty lies opportunity." Yes, it is a huge challenge for those who have been charging most of their lives and are in the habit of pulling out the plastic to pay for goods and services. Plastic—ATM card, debit cards and credit cards—are all stand-ins for money. They are not the real thing, they are just representatives and often poor representations when they often represent debt.

FIVE REASONS TO PAY CASH!

- Paying cash means making some lifestyle changes and sacrifices, but it will keep you from drowning in a sea of red ink on your journey to financial freedom.

- Paying cash keeps you focused.

- Paying cash promotes contentment because it adds meaning and value to the things you do buy.

- Paying cash lets you own things, not merely acquire them.

- Paying cash makes spending difficult and uncomfortable—and that is exactly the way it should be!

LIFESTYLE CHANGE MEANS COMMITTING TO GODLY PRINCIPLES

Certain principles, if followed, will lead to a peaceful and prosperous life.

Psalms 128:1, 2

"Blessings on all who reverence and trust the Lord—on all who obey him! Their reward shall be prosperity and happiness" (*TLB*).

You must never keep it all. The first thing you must do when money flows into your life is give some of it away.

You must never spend it all. After tithing your income, always pay yourself before anyone else. Always. Not only must you set aside a portion of all the money you earn, but you have to put that money to work for you. Merely saving is not enough.

God is your source. Your employer, your spouse, your investments, your trust account, your parents or any other entity are not the source of your money. God, who gave you the talents, intelligence and ability to think and work, is the source. Your responsibility is to be a good steward of all that you receive.

Employers, investments, spouses and parents are only the conduits in the delivery system. Taking hold of this truth will bring a sense of peace and calm to your life. No longer will you worry about a drop in the stock market, or the plunging of real estate values. No longer will you lay awake worrying about losing your job.

The way your money is delivered may change radically and frequently, but the source never changes. It is the same yesterday, today and forever.

What you receive is what you deserve. God promises to supply all your needs and He says if you delight yourself in Him, He will also give you your desires. He is not ignorant of your needs or your desires. He never falls asleep on the job or issues a due date. All He asks is that you obey His laws and trust His word. Those who do, and go on to demonstrate that they can be trusted with more, are blessed beyond what they deserve or could possibly imagine.

Debt is like cancer. At first it is not life threatening because it involves only a cell or two. But it never stays tiny. It begins to grow and then it takes over. It becomes the master; you become its slave. Never believe that a little debt, manageable as it may seem, is okay. It is not. Neither is a little cancer.

LIFESTYLE CHANGE MEANS LEARNING SOME TIMELY PRINCIPLES

- A good rule for borrowing is: Never borrow to buy depreciating items.

- Americans are blessed with a lot of cash flowing through our hands. Bring a halt to some of the flow.

- Attack the problem aggressively with a plan. Your credit problems didn't just suddenly appear. It took a lot of steps to get into trouble, and getting out will mean taking as much time, if not more, to draw up a financial recovery plan.

- Debt is incurred because I want something before I have the money to pay for it.

- Debt is nothing more than borrowing from future income to buy now what we cannot afford with current income.

- Getting out of debt is an attitude before it is an action.

- How do you get out of debt? Same as you got into debt—one small step at a time.

- If money isn't working for you, it's working against you—you just don't know it yet.

- If you are not content where you are, you will not be content where you want to go.

- If you don't borrow money, you can't get into debt.

- It's not what you make, it's what you spend.

- Keep track of every penny.

- Make impulse buying difficult. Leave your checkbook and credit cards at home.

- The fear of doing without in the future causes many Christians to rob God's work of the very funds He has provided.

- The only problem with borrowing money is that you have to pay it back.

- The purpose of budgeting is to free you, not confine you.

- We buy things we don't need with money we don't have to impress people we don't like.

- When you find yourself in a hole, the first thing to do is stop digging.

Begin now to live a principled life. Determine at this moment to live the principle of lifestyle change!

The Biblical Principle
of Counting the Cost

Luke 14:28-30

"But don't begin until you count the cost. For who would begin construction of a building without first getting estimates and then checking to see if he has enough money to pay the bills? Otherwise he might complete only the foundation before running out of funds. And then how everyone would laugh! 'See that fellow there?' they would mock. 'He started that building and ran out of money before it was finished!'" (*TLB*).

Counting the cost, or budgeting, is scriptural. Proverbs 27:23 says, "Know well the condition of your flocks, and pay attention to your herds" (*NASB*). Scriptural guidelines for budgeting can be found throughout God's Word. For instance, if you don't happen to have any herds and flocks, God is probably saying, "Know well the condition of your clothing budget, your housing budget and your food budget."

Like it or not, money is an important part of our lives. While it is true that "money cannot buy happiness," it is also true that when it comes to spending more than we earn, the lack of money can contribute to much unhappiness. If properly managed, money can enhance family relationships and can be a springboard for family discussions that will help the entire family pull together for common goals. Not properly managed, money can potentially become a real curse.

Budgets aren't records of expenses; they are forecasts of expenses. Preparing a meaningful budget (as opposed to a wishful one) depends largely on that first step—keeping accurate records.

Counting the cost will help you become debt free. If your goal is to achieve and maintain a debt-free position and to use your resources in a manner that is right, you need a written budget. Trying to go without one is like trying to find your way out of a wilderness area without a map—you don't know where you are, where you are going or what lies ahead. You might get lucky and get rescued, you might wander around a long time before you get out or you might not make it out at all.

Even if you have a budget, you still need to review it once or twice a year to make sure your spending habits are on track, to adapt to any significant changes in your life and to make sure you are achieving the goals you established.

Budgeting will free you, not confine you. God expects us to be participants in planning budgets, not observers. As Proverbs 16:9 says, "The mind of man plans his way, but the Lord directs his steps" (*NASB*).

Budgeting is a means to count the cost. Budgeting is a tool for managing money. It is a financial plan. A financial plan is a necessary tool in managing money. A financial plan helps in making realistic decisions. Decisions must be made within some kind of framework or design. That framework or design provides guideposts that mark the limitations or boundaries within which the family must operate.

An individual struggling with a load of debt is obviously under more strain than a debt-free person. How many times have you said to yourself, "I need to get out of debt and control my spending"?

Granted, the Bible talks about preplanning in areas of finance, but just how does this help? It helps in this way: Budgeting stops unnecessary spending. Do you find yourself constantly pushing yourself or your family to new heights of debt because you want to keep up with the neighbors or your friends? If the answer is yes, you are probably one who shops and buys impulsively, spending money in excess. You probably spend irrationally, and when it comes to special sales at your favorite retail stores, you can always find a reason why you must buy it now.

Budgeting helps you break bad habits. Most of us have taken many years to establish our spending habits, accumulate our debts and dig ourselves into financial holes. Habits are indeed hard to break. It is not so easy or logical that we should be able to snap our fingers and get out of debt, and onto sound financial footing by next week. Not even next month. Not even next year.

How do we get out of debt? Just the way we got into debt—one step at a time.

Regardless of your past habits of money mismanagement, a sound plan, carefully thought out, can bring financial success in the future. A budget is simply an organized way to manage your finances.

Counting the cost helps you keep the money you earn. You work hard to earn the money you receive. But once you have your paycheck in hand, do you use it wisely and efficiently? Without a spending plan it is difficult, if not impossible, to use the money in an efficient, strategic manner. Without a budget, most of us will just muddle through life, trying very hard to stay one step ahead of our bills. If a budget makes you cringe, just think of the entire process in this way. First of all, you are simply summarizing how you already spend your income and second, you are simply outlining some basic guidelines for your future spending. It becomes your own personal tool to develop awareness of how you are spending, where you are spending, and on what things you are spending your money.

Therefore, as we apply practical concepts in handling our money, God provides godly wisdom. It should free you from worrying about whether the annual insurance payment will be made, whether you put money aside for the taxes on your home, and whether enough money will be available to buy the clothes your children need. If you're not willing to live on a budget, you will not be able to help them live on a budget either. So a budget can be a good teaching tool, as well as a good measure of self-discipline.

Begin now to live a principled life. Determine at this moment to live the principle of counting the cost!

The Biblical Principle of Refusing to Be a Cosigner

Proverbs 17:18

"A man lacking in judgment strikes hands in pledge and puts up security for his neighbor."

SCRIPTURAL INSIGHT

This Scripture clearly warns us of the danger involved in providing collateral, security or surety for another person. One very quick way of going into debt is by cosigning someone else's loan. People who cosign think they are doing a relative or friend a favor. The potential cost of their signature is usually not explained very carefully to them.

When you cosign a note, you are taking on someone else's debt. Rarely do you know just how much and what kind of debt that person may have. Debt is an excess of liabilities over assets. Of course, this means that if you are a cosigner of debt, your assets may be called upon to pay off the debt of another person without assets.

A home, if financed conservatively, may usually be sold for more than is owed by the mortgager. A car, or furniture, or most any depreciating item purchased on time cannot usually be sold for sufficient money to pay off the lender. This is often the kind of debt for which cosigners are asked to be involved.

A better name for cosigning may just be "borrowing a signature" or lending a signature. The concept is really that of "co-borrowing" instead of just cosigning. Cosigning conveys the idea that the action is simply a five-minute exercise of goodwill. Co-borrowing conveys a longer-term relationship! When you view the action with "co-borrowing" in mind, your signature could actually mean everything you own—your home, bank account, stocks, bonds, possessions, your good name and good credit history.

YOU ARE LOANING THE MONEY

Let me explain what you are doing if you cosign a note. You are loaning the money you borrowed to a person who was too great a risk for the professional lender. You are involving yourself in a business transaction that the expert money manager would not touch. If the professionals are afraid that the risk is just too great to extend the loan, why would you want to put your personal credit and accumulated assets at risk? It just does not seem like a wise thing to do.

TRUSTING THAT THE LOAN WILL BE PAID

You are hoping that your friend or relative will pay back the loan. There's a good chance that it will *not* happen. When your friend or relative defaults, then you have the "privilege" of paying back the money. My advice is to never cosign a note unless you can afford to give the money away!

COSIGNING FOR YOUR CHILDREN—A BAD IDEA

You may argue that you need to cosign a loan for an offspring so that he or she can establish good credit. While it does seem admirable for parents to help their children get established, think about what your potential action is saying to them. If you are cosigning so they can get their first credit card, you are sending the message that it's okay to buy things on credit that you could not afford to purchase with cash. You are telling them that when they have no sufficient means to save the money first, then go ahead and plunge into debt. You are sending the message that impulse buying is okay. You are authorizing them to buy now, pay later; pay interest through debt servicing instead of gain interest through savings and investments.

Young adults should understand that it is not wise to go into debt for things that often depreciate rapidly and do not retain their initial value.

They should be taught to save first and plan for their spending at a later date. Young people do not appreciate the value of a dollar, nor have they had the exposure and experience to make wise money decisions. They need to learn and practice the habit of financial discipline. If you offer to cosign for them, they may only learn financial smarts by graduating from the school of hard knocks—and you, as the parent, may learn a hard lesson also.

YOU BECOME THE BORROWER

When you cosign a loan, know that you are now being asked to guarantee the full amount of the debt. The lender has refused to make the loan to the person for whom you are cosigning. His decision has been based on facts that reveal the risk is too great to loan the money to your friend or relative.

Be sure you have plenty of money to pay the loan should your friend default. If the borrower misses a payment, the creditor is going to be looking your way within days. You will have to come up with the funds. You are just as much a borrower as the other party. Do you really want to accept this full responsibility? Be sure you can afford to pay any and all debt payments, and even the full balance of the loan if need be.

When you sign the note, the money is really being loaned to you. The reason you have been asked to sign is that your collateral, your character, your credit and your capacity are sufficient for the loan officer to feel good about the security on the loan. Your signature is the loaner's security.

YOU RISK RUINING YOUR CREDIT RATING

When you cosign a loan, your credit is affected immediately. Does this shock you? You see, it doesn't matter that the loan may eventually be paid in full by the initial borrower. Your credit will be affected the minute you sign the paperwork.

How does that happen, you ask? It happens because the loan details get reported to the credit agencies on a regular basis and this goes on your personal credit record also because you are a co-borrower. The federal *Equal Credit Opportunity Act* requires lenders to report information about co-borrowers equally.

Even if you never have to pay on the loan, your liability for the loan may keep you from obtaining other personal credit that you desire. Lenders will consider the fact of the cosigned loan as part of your accumulated debt responsibility. Because of this, lenders may not extend to you additional credit. This additional debt load you assume as a cosigner weakens your ability to borrow for your own personal needs.

A VACUUM OF INFORMATION

You may not be notified should the borrower miss a payment. Payment after loan payment may be missed, and as a cosigner you may never know. That is until the loan is in default and the collateral has been repossessed. By that time, it may be too late for you to save your personal credit rating and protect your good name. Don't assume this involves only vehicle payments. Don't get involved in renting an apartment either. You could not only be liable for rent and utilities payments, but you may also be responsible for any damage deemed to have been done to the living quarters.

LOAN DEFAULT CONSEQUENCE

What happens if the person with whom you cosigned a note refuses to pay or misses a payment? In most states in this country, should a friend, relative or acquaintance miss just one payment, the lender can immediately go to you the cosigner and immediately collect from you WITHOUT FIRST looking to the borrower of the money.

The lender may or may not look to the original borrower to get the money. There is a very good chance that they will look first to you, the cosigner of the loan. "Why?" you ask. The reason the original borrower of the money was not credit worthy and represented a great risk to the lender is how you came into the picture in the first place. You, as a cosigner, actually made it happen. You made the loan possible.

THE ODDS ARE AGAINST YOU

Statistics show that the cosigner winds up paying for nearly three out of four cosigned loans that end up in default. The lender can go directly to the cosigner, bypassing the original applicant immediately. Furthermore, all the typical methods available to the lender for debt collection can be directed solely toward the cosigner. They may include some of all the following: adding late charges, collection costs, legal fees, suing you, garnishing your wages, listing the default on your credit record, etc. Remember that the cosigner of the loan is really nothing more than a "co-borrower." He assumes all the responsibilities involved in the loan, but instead of receiving the loan receives nothing. All the risk, but none of the reward!

ASSET REPOSSESSION

There is always the possibility that what you cosign could be repossessed, leaving you still on the hook for most of the outstanding loan. Ask any credit union or bank how they come out financially when goods are repossessed. Repossession is usually a financial disaster for both the borrower and the lender.

Say, for example, you signed an auto loan in the amount of $25,000. After taxes, licensing, etc., maybe another $1,000 or so comes into play. What if the person with whom you agreed to cosign defaults after just three months?

Assuming you have no extra cash flow to take over the vehicle, and the bank has to foreclose on the loan, what happens now? The bank will simply turn the vehicle over to a third party who will wholesale out the car for perhaps $15,000, and add fees, expenses and other costs onto the balance.

MORE THAN YOU THOUGHT IS OWED

In the event of loan default, all that extra expense, transaction fees, legal fees, etc., will be added on to your bill as a cosigner. You could increase your debt obligation to nearly $30,000 less the proceeds from the sale of the vehicle. In this scenario, you could easily end up owing nearly $15,000 with no vehicle to show for it. This is how quickly a friendly cosigning gesture of your kindness can turn sour in a heartbeat. Not only would you be liable, but you could also lose any personal assets you have.

FRIENDSHIP AND RELATIONSHIPS

One of the reasons a person considers helping a friend or relative is to be a nice person. But ask yourself this: How long is the friendship going to continue if you are always asking whether or not the person has made the loan payment? Even if you don't ask, every time you talk or are together, you will be wondering whether or not he is up to date on his loan payments. When a friend comes to you asking for your signature, why not take the time to pass along the following wisdom to him or her?

Let them know that a good rule for borrowing is this: *Never borrow to buy depreciating items.* Such things as new cars, furniture, clothes, appliances, boats and luxury items should not be purchased until cash is available.

PEACE OF MIND

Are you able to sleep well at night and wake up the next morning fully rested? If so, you might want to ensure that you continue in good health by not cosigning a loan. If you lose the ability to get a good night's rest by helping out a friend, you might consider rethinking what you are about to do. This might be an excellent reason, and reason enough, to turn down a cosigning opportunity.

I AM DETERMINED TO BECOME A COSIGNER

While I believe that biblical concepts and practical horse sense suggest strongly that you do not do so, and that cosigning anything is a huge mistake you most likely will regret, if you so insist, here are a few guidelines.

- Be aware that you are borrowing the money.
- Be sure you can afford to repay the loan.
- Before you pledge any of your personal assets to secure the loan, make sure you fully understand the potential consequences.

- Know that you are assuming full responsibility of the entire debt.

- Don't be pressured into cosigning anything without first understanding the full scope of the paperwork.

- Negotiate all terms favorable to you before agreeing to sign.

- Ask for copies of all paperwork, including the loan contract, the Truth-in-Lending Disclosure Statement, and warranties and other important documents.

- Require the lender to provide you with written notification within two weeks if the borrower ever misses a payment or violates any other terms of the contract. Get this lending agreement in writing.

- Ask the lender to provide in writing all the extra costs to you should you end up paying the loan.

- If property is being purchase with the loan, be sure your name is listed on the deed of trust.

- If a vehicle is being purchased with the loan, be sure your name is also listed on the title.

- Be sure the asset is fully insured should something happen to it during the life of the loan. Be sure you obtain proof that the insurance premiums have been paid.

- Once you cosign a loan you are responsible for 100% of the entire loan (not just 50% of it).

- Beware of all the risks involved and take steps to minimize them.

Begin now to live a principled life. Determine at this moment to live the principle of refusing to be a cosigner!

The Biblical Principle
of a Good Name

Proverbs 22:1

"A good name is more desirable than great riches; to be esteemed is better than silver or gold."

Proverbs 3:4

"Then you will win favor and a good name in the sight of God and man."

It is biblical to have a good name, an honest report and a history of integrity. This means maintaining a lifestyle that produces uprightness and results in a good credit report. Your good name, in a financial sense, is often reflected in your credit report. It reports how well you have met your financial obligations. Remember that money matters to God because money matters.

Socrates speaks to this issue when he said, "Regard your good name as the richest jewel you can possibly be possessed of—for credit is like fire; when once you have kindled it you may easily preserve it, but if you once extinguish it, you will find it an arduous task to rekindle it again. The way to gain a good reputation is to endeavor to be what you desire to appear."

While I despise the snares of borrowing and credit terms, you do need to know this: Your credit can determine more than whether or not you have a good name. It may determine what type of car you drive (although this rapidly depreciating form of transportation should not be purchased with credit), what you can buy and even where you can live. It is important to maintain the best credit report possible. Each person should check his or her credit report and make sure it is correct.

Having a good financial name is about understanding the world of credit. To understand the credit process you first need to understand what information is contained in a credit report. Although the style, format and coding may be different depending on which credit reporting bureau is used, the typical consumer's credit report includes the four following types of information:

Identifying information: includes your name, nicknames, current and previous addresses, Social Security number, date of birth and current and previous employers. This information comes from any credit application you have completed, and its accuracy depends on your filling out forms clearly, completely and consistently each time you apply for credit.

Credit information: includes specific information about each account, including the date opened, credit limit or loan amount, balance, monthly payment and payment pattern during the past several years. The report also states whether anyone else besides you (i.e., a spouse or cosigner) is responsible for paying the account. This information comes from companies that do business with you.

All lenders make a judgment about your character, capacity and collateral.

Public record information: includes federal district bankruptcy records; state and county court records, tax liens and monetary judgments; and, in some states, overdue child support payments. This information comes from public records.

Inquiries: includes the names of those who have obtained a copy of your credit report for any reason. This information comes from the credit reporting agency, and it remains available for as long as two years, as per federal law.

HOW IS CREDIT INFORMATION USED?

A credit bureau score is one type of credit score. It is calculated from the information on your credit bureau file at the time the information was requested. Consequently, a credit score is like a snapshot: It sums up, at one given point in time, what your past and current credit usage say about your future credit performance.

Credit scoring helps lenders apply one set of rules to everybody. The sophistication of today's models allow for certain behavior patterns. As a result, a 20-year-old's credit history would not be compared to a 45-year-old's credit history. One reason these scoring models are so widely used is that they can differentiate between the credit patterns of individuals.

ONLY DATA IS ANALYZED

Scoring models and other tools analyze data only—using this data to predict future credit performance.

A scoring model contains a list of questions and answers, with points given for each answer. Information proven to be predictive of future credit performance is used in a model.

Here are a few examples of what a typical model will (and will not) consider: Information from your credit application such as how long you've lived at your address, what is your job or profession, how much you owe.

It will also consider information pulled from your credit bureau report, such as the number of late payments, the amount of outstanding credit, the amount of credit being used, the amount of time credit has been established. Credit scoring systems do not consider race, religion, gender, marital status, birthplace or current address.

CHECK YOUR CREDIT REPORT

You can order a copy of your credit report from any one of the three major credit bureaus. If you live in Colorado, Georgia, Maryland, Massachusetts, New Jersey or Vermont, or if you've been denied credit before, you can get one copy free each year.

If you don't live in those states, they'll cost you up to $15 each. It makes sense to check it about once a year, or three to four months prior to the time you know you'll be applying for a major loan, which will give you time to clean it up.

MISTAKES HAPPEN

Once you receive it, read it over. Look for accounts that don't belong to you, mistakes made not by you but by your bank or creditors, as well as for any companies that have been looking into your report without your permission.

Report all of them immediately. Once you've found a mistake on one credit bureau's report, you'll need to request the other two and repeat the process to make sure they're all in sync.

FRAUDULENT CREDIT CLEANING COMPANIES

Finally, many people want to know if the agencies that promise to clean up your credit rating are legitimate. The answer is a resounding no. What these organizations often practice is fraud—they swap your Social Security number or other identifying details with those of someone with cleaner credit or no credit at all to allow you to start from scratch.

Such schemes also rarely work. It's a harsh fact of life that bankruptcies and other blemishes on your credit report stay there for up to eight years without being erased. What you can do, however, is explain your lapses in good behavior right on your report.

If the credit bureau refuses to remove a mistake on your report, or if you have a good reason (like illness) for your behavior, you can write a 100-word explanation that becomes part of your report.

Lenders who get the full report are likely to take it into account—after all, they're in the business of trying to make as many loans as possible.

WHY DO I HAVE CREDIT PROBLEMS?

Why is it that some lenders say "no" when others say "yes"? Here is why—all lenders make a judgment about

- *character* (your willingness to repay)
- *capacity* (your ability to pay)
- *collateral* (the value of what you are buying)

before deciding whether or not to grant you a fixed loan or line of credit.

Several tools aid lenders in making this judgment, including automated credit or risk scores. In some cases, these scores replace human decision-making. As a result, separate lenders can look at the same loan and view the same credit risk differently.

If your loan application was met with "no" at one lender, there may be another lender out there whose credit risk criteria is different. If so, they may have a loan for you. But be prepared to sign on the dotted line for a "higher than usual" interest rate. The more of a risk you present to the lender, the higher the annual interest rate.

WHAT IS "LESS THAN PERFECT" CREDIT?

How you used your credit in the past and the reasons for your past financial difficulties are two factors that figure in your ability to get a loan. The first step is to understand whether or not you are considered a credit risk. Most lenders will consider you a higher credit risk only if your credit report states you have more late and slow payments than stated in the categories given below:

Revolving credit (i.e., credit cards): No payments 60 days or more past due and no more than two payments 30 days past due.

Installment credit (i.e., car loans): No payments 60 days or more past due and no more than one payment 30 days past due.

Housing debt (i.e., mortgages and rent): No payments past due. This can be proven by providing (borrower's) canceled checks for the past 12 months or a loan-payment history from the mortgage servicer.

In all categories, all late payments must be explained. Contrary to popular belief, good credit does not necessarily mean perfect credit. If your credit reports show any 60 to 90 day late payments you may need to seek out a lender that specializes in less than perfect credit.

Begin now to live a principled life. Determine at this moment to live the principle of a good name!

Section Five

The Practical Application

Make a Decision to Change

*B*eing in debt requires change. Make a decision to change your attitude, lifestyle, spending habits and invest in a new you. When your debts are high and your monthly income is not enough to cover the payments, there are ways to solve your debt problem. However, the road to financial recovery takes a total commitment.

When you make a decision to change, it must be firmly rooted in the knowledge of what got you there in the first place. You must know why you work your entire week just to serve a lender. It's really nothing new; the Bible clearly summed up this same situation many years ago. Proverbs 22:7 says, "The rich rule over the poor, and the borrower is servant to the lender."

Debt can be presumptuous. You can assume that after borrowing the money, or signing on the dotted line for that large purchase you really could not afford, everything somehow will all work out. The problem is that this presumption is kind of like driving down the freeway the wrong way with your eyes closed. You are hoping you don't get hit by a tractor trailer coming in your direction, and somehow you will avoid a head-on collision, but the reality is you really have your eyes closed. Unpleasant things happen when your head is buried in the sand or your eyes are closed and you are unable to clearly see your way.

Debt also can be a failure to trust God. After all, many biblical references point out that God is a giver, beginning as the giver of life itself. God gave us all of creation. He gave us life. He gave us His life so we could have eternal life. He gives us what we need. He is the ultimate giver. So why do you mistrust what His Word says about meeting your need?

Debt also can be overcome. Will it be easy? Of course not! Will it be difficult? You can count on it! But it can be overcome. It matters not how much debt you currently have, how little income you currently have or what others say about your situation. The bottom line is this: If you want to get free from the burden of your debt and if you want to be free of stress and worry, you absolutely can get there someday. But it does take courage. It does take commitment. It does take planning. It does take a budget. It will take change and it will take action on your part. Not just action for a day, a week or a month. It will take consistent, continual, reliable, unswerving, unshakable and steadfast personal, hands-on engagement. But it can be done. You can become debt free!

You must decide you want to be debt free. Discipline yourself and take the necessary action to begin to pay back your debts, not take on new debt, and have the commitment to stay with the plan until you are truly debt free. Only you can determine if you are willing to make the necessary sacrifices to achieve this goal.

Getting out of debt is like getting through boot camp. It's a lot of hard work and some days you want to quit. But when graduation day arrives, memories of pain and trouble will pale in the light of the pride and accomplishment you will feel. You made it! You didn't quit.

Like boot camp, getting debt free is not the end; rather, it's the beginning of a whole new adventure. To drop out at graduation and go back to your old way of living would be to turn your back on everything for which you have been preparing. It would be like closing the door on your dreams of financial freedom. It would diminish the importance of what you accomplished. Who would be so foolish as to do the difficult work and then not stick around to enjoy the reward? So get started, get a plan and let's move on it.

**Your future is bright.
You CAN make it!
Make a decision to change now!**

Determine Not to Overspend

Most people know how much they earn, but don't know how much they spend. It's easy to go on a spending binge and spend, spend, spend. Overspending and self-indulgence are problems for many people today. They don't purposely overspend; they just are not disciplined to be thrifty. To overspend means to spend at a high rate, to blow money, to squander, to waste and to exhaust available supply. It means to consume more than is necessary, to expend more than one can afford. One person jokingly said, "We didn't overspend our budget; it's just that our capital allocation fell short of our expenditures." When you overspend it creates a fundamental weakness in your family economic foundation.

Isaiah 55:2 says, "Why spend your money on food that doesn't give you strength? Why pay for groceries that do you no good?" (*TLB*).

Your monthly spending should be preplanned, preallocated and predetermined. You need to tell your money what to do instead of it telling you where it will go.

John Maxwell said: "Where there is no hope in the future, there is no power in the present." —*Famous Quotes Search powered by FreeFind*

You must keep your total monthly spending less than your total monthly after-tax income. Having a budget and determining to live by it will keep you from overspending. People overspend for a variety of reasons. Many people justify their excess spending because they feel they must keep up a particular image. Their lifestyle is one of living above their means. Others spend out of impulse. They shop continuously, always on the lookout for that special thing they simply must have. Still others cannot refuse a sale, a bargain, a discount . . . even if it means going into more debt for something they just won't use or certainly don't need. Then there are those who are so selfish that they must have instant gratification; they see or hear an advertisement and something within says "you deserve this . . . go out and buy it for yourself." Regardless of why you overspend the way that you do, it is now time to deny your wants and wishes. Simply look into the mirror and firmly say, "no!"

"To become financially independent you must turn part of your income into capital; turn capital into enterprise; turn enterprise into profit; turn profit into investment; and turn investment into financial independence." —Jim Rohn, *Famous Quotes Search powered by FreeFind*

You simply cannot spend when you don't have the cash. You can't drive a Jaguar on a Kia budget. If you *underearn* you shouldn't *overspend*! Use of credit cards encourages overspending and living

NUMBER OF DAYS	GOURMET COFFEE AND PASTRY	P.M. BEVERAGE & SNACK	ANNUAL EXPENSE
1 day per week	$5.85	$2.15	$400.00
5 days per week	$29.25	$10.75	$2,000.00

above your means. In any given month, if you overspend in one area, you must underspend in another area. This may mean the delay of some other planned spending.

One seemingly insignificant way we overspend is in our morning pastries and gourmet coffee and afternoon beverages and snacks. This can easily amount to $8.00 each day. If you were to spend $8.00 each day on these things, note your annual cost of 50 weeks per working year.

Eating at home is a good way to keep spending down. If you were to keep track of all of the money you spend on eating in restaurants, buying beverages, etc., you would be alarmed at the annual total cost.

Another simple and practical way to save cash is by not eating lunch out every day. Not only will you save some substantial money, but you will also not be using the credit card to incur debt. The following chart shows the weekly and annual cost of lunch and the various combinations of eating out versus bringing/making your own lunch.

The dollar figure I have used for eating out is $7.00 per meal. It is fairly difficult to eat lunch anywhere for less, especially if you add the cost of a drink to the meal. Bringing/making your own lunch is much cheaper. I have used a dollar figure of $1.00 per meal. The weekly expense has been multiplied by 50 weeks each year, leaving two weeks for vacation. We realize some additional holidays are involved, but usually these days are spent eating out or adding more expense in food costs.

So how does one keep from overspending? The best and most effective way is to get in the habit of paying cash. Ditch the credit cards, installment loans, lines of credit and purchase only with cash. Leave your home without cards and just enough cash to put gas in your tank and a small allocation for lunch if you haven't prepared a sack lunch. The big obstacle here is impulse buying. When you purchase with credit, you think you have more money than you really do. When you purchase with cash, you feel every dollar that leaves your pocket. When you are conscious of every dollar spent, you will spend less.

NUMBER OF DAYS EATING OUT FOR LUNCH	NUMBER OF DAYS MAKING YOUR LUNCH	TOTAL LUNCH EXPENSE	ANNUAL LUNCH EXPENSE
5 days per week	0 days per week	$35.00	$1,750.00
4 days per week	1 day per week	$29.00	$1,450.00
3 days per week	2 days per week	$23.00	$1,150.00
2 days per week	3 days per week	$17.00	$850.00
1 day per week	4 days per week	$11.00	$550.00
0 days per week	5 days per week	$5.00	$250.00

Do Not Add New Debts

*I*f you are going to rescue your life and liberate your future by breaking free from your bondage of debt, not only will you be repaying current debt, but you must also not add any new debt. You must decide once and for all that you will not take on new debt and not become a slave to your old habits. Also decide that you will not (this is very important!) borrow new money for any reason or purchase additional merchandise on credit.

When it comes to personal finances, the Bible clearly teaches that debt is a big fat negative and it is to be avoided, if at all possible. You may ignore biblical teaching on the subject of debt and personal finance, but that doesn't change what the Scriptures say about it. Don't hide your head in the sand and ignore the current state of your finances.

Ignoring the obvious isn't going to make it go away, no matter how you try to justify it or how you may want to argue your position. Imagining that your debt isn't there will just get you deeper and deeper into trouble. Stop the arguments, stop the defenses and stop pretending it isn't really there.

Acknowledge your debt problem and determine to do something about it. Make tough financial decisions on purpose. The key is to recognize the problem before it gets out of hand. If your positive cash flow continually falls below your expenditures, you are already in trouble.

AVOID EXPENSIVE ITEMS

If you have an appetite for expensive things, it has to end. You cannot go finance a new car without knowing just how much that vehicle will cost after you make all payments of principle and interest. The $30,000 car ends up costing $40,000 (because of the interest added on), but is worth only $10,000 after you finally get it paid off. In the end, you will experience a net loss of $30,000.

Even worse to consider is, if you had opted to drive a beater for a few years and saved the payments you would have made, how much money would you have now after the bank pays YOU the interest? What if you invested half that money you saved and purchased a two-year-old model of the car of your choice? The result would be this: You would have $20,000 invested, and the car of your dreams after someone else already paid for the first two years of depreciation.

CHECK INTEREST RATES

Be concerned with the cost of interest. Pay attention to the amount of interest you are paying each month. Forget the payment; check your interest charges. This alone should make you stop spending. Just two kinds of people come to mind when we are talking about interest—those who understand it and receive it and those who aren't very smart because they pay it. Of course, I am referring to those who could refrain from adding more debts, but choose to continue to plunge deeper each month. Pay current debts on time to avoid additional interest and late charges. Credit card companies and banks make most of their income on extra fees and charges most people never know about until they get dinged with them. Others get dinged for the fees, and make their regular payments without even realizing extra charges were deducted out of their payment.

DESTROY CREDIT CARDS

Now would be an excellent time to have a credit card destruction ceremony in your home. It's time for plastic surgery. Gather your family, take a large pair of scissors, and deliberately cut each credit card into tiny pieces. Make a list of all charge accounts. Write each store and tell them to close your account.

People who stay in debt are those who have no financial clue. They do not have a monthly budget and they do not live below their means. Usually, they live above their means. They do not budget, nor do they know the amount of their debt. They do not understand the cost of debt. They do not save for expenses that will come at an unexpected or inopportune time. They have no plan for the future and usually live from paycheck to paycheck.

DO NOT BORROW

You cannot work your way out of debt if you continue to borrow for new purchases. The key to your success in avoiding new debt is to learn to do without. As with all journeys of faith, the first step can sometimes be the hardest. It requires a reality check, a change in behavior and a walk in unfamiliar territory. This new ground you will be covering is the walk of both acknowledgment and denial. You are acknowledging mistakes, bad habits and a personal debt problem as well as denying yourself the freedom to spend, spend and spend. Deny yourself! Exercise self-discipline! You will be amazed that you don't really need all of the so-called necessities.

Have a credit card destruction ceremony in your home. It's time for plastic surgery.

Look at your situation and make tough decisions now. Get that second job. Sell that second car. Cut out weekly entertainment and outings to fine restaurants. Yes, it will be hard for now and for some time, but down the road, life will be much simpler and you will be living in an easier world of personal finance.

Determine to get started right away. This means no new debt starting right now. Don't cram in a few more things right away before you get started. If you don't start immediately, you might change your mind and lose the will to begin. Beginning is often the hardest part. If you don't begin now, what will suddenly change in your life that will finally help you decide to begin? Are you tired of being in debt? Aren't you tired of embarrassing telephone calls and the unending stream of credit collectors on your back? What about all the unpaid bills and the extra cash you never have?

Isn't it about time to do something about your debt problem? You can stop adding new debt, stop making any more credit card purchases and begin your journey toward debt reduction, debt riddance and financial independence. Regain the self-respect you once had. Feel better about yourself and your choices. Choose to focus on a better financial life filled with peace of mind and a loving, prosperous, fulfilling life.

Your future is bright.
You CAN make it!
Do not add new debts
from now on!

Break Free from
the Spending Habit

*T*o become debt free and to remain debt free, break free from those unproductive spending habits. When you get sick and tired of being strapped financially, then perhaps you will finally do something to change your current behavior. Break free from those bad spending habits and those no-good all-day shopping trips. Now that I have your attention again, know that the Bible does not teach, as some propose, that all debt is wicked and sinful. However, having said that, it does teach how really awful debt is and how undesirable it really is. Debt should always be a short-term situation and a last resort. Debt was never meant to be a way of life.

The only way to get out of debt is to stop getting into debt! The only way to stop getting into debt is not to take on more debt. And the only way not to take on more debt is to break free from your long-lived, unproductive spending habits.

If you do not have the discipline or ability to pay your credit card balance in full each month, you should get rid of it, or them. Cut up the cards, put them in the deep freeze, hide them in the garage, or whatever you need to do to curtail and eliminate unnecessary spending. Remember, if you are spending more than you are earning, you are going into greater debt. If you keep spending in this fashion, your are headed for a debt burden snowball—once it starts rolling, it's hard to get it under control again. At this point you will be rolling toward sure disaster.

If you have more than one credit card, get rid of the one charging the highest interest rate. If you pay your outstanding balance in full each month, as I do, get rid of the card that charges an annual account fee of $25 to $50. I have done just that.

A few years ago both my spouse and I signed up for the "Universal Card" by AT&T. By signing up when the card first was offered, AT&T agreed not to charge any annual fee for life. We maintain separate accounts with AT&T, so that if something happens to one of us, the other still has a lifetime of credit without any annual fee. You may say, "Well, what's $50?" My response is, "waiting for your ship to come in" probably never will happen, so every dollar saved is a dollar earned. The road to financial independence comes by making hundreds of small prudent decisions over a lifetime, each seemingly insignificant, but collectively making the difference between financial dependence and financial independence.

One way to break free from the spending habit is to look at the credit in terms of total outstanding balances instead of minimum monthly payments. Each month, pay off all new charges on your cards, plus interest and a portion of the previous balance. You'll reduce each month's debt balance below the previous month's. It should get easier as you go.

The road to financial freedom comes by making hundreds of small prudent decisions over a lifetime.

Credit cards are not an extension of your paycheck. You end up having less money, not more. Never get a cash advance with a credit card. I have had a Citibank Premium Visa card for at least 15 years. The normal interest rate is charged only when they must pay for your purchases. Cash advances are charged to your account immediately when you acquire the monies, and the interest rate on the cash advance is at least 3% higher than the normal rate.

Many checking accounts offer dangerous overdraft features. These accounts make it easy to borrow money by writing checks even without adequate funds in the account. All these "easy credit" methods will get you into debt trouble and keep you there if you don't make up your mind once and for all to break free from your spending habits.

Your future is bright.
You CAN make it! Break free
from your spending habits now!

Pay-as-You-Go

*G*et in the habit of paying-as-you-go. Paying cash for an item gives a person that sense of confidence and well being and keeps debts at a lower balance than the previous month. If you do charge for an item with the intention of paying it off when the bill comes due, keep a written tally of your purchase.

I keep a notebook on my desk on which I write the name of the store where new charges are made, the amount of the charge, the purpose of the purchase and a running balance of all new charges made since the last credit card statement. In this way, I am informed continuously what that new statement is going to say when it arrives in the mail. There are no surprises!

In addition to a budget, prepare a personal balance sheet. It can be handwritten very simply. If you have a PC, many software programs are available for both personal budgets and Statements of Financial Condition, commonly known as balance sheets.

I personally like a program called "Microsoft Money." For under $75, you can plug in the information and let the software do its work. If you list the information by hand, list all your assets in one column and all your liabilities in another. Subtract total liabilities from total assets and this will give your net worth.

Some people owe more than they own. If you find yourself in the financial position of owing more then your assets, or having more monthly bills to pay than your income permits, then it is clear that borrowing has gotten out of hand. If you do not have money to pay when a debt is due, communicate with the creditor to work out a solution with his or her agreement. It is your responsibility to take the initiative. If you are open and honest with the creditor, most will work with you.

Don't wait for your creditors to come to you if you are going to miss a payment or you have run short of cash. Be up front about it and get them on the telephone! Don't wait for collection agencies to call; call them as soon as you realize you can't make a payment on time. Be honest about the situation and what you can afford to pay each month.

Your future is bright.
You CAN make it! Pay as you go from now on!

Manage Your Cash Flow

*I*f you are like many people, you'll find that from time to time, cash flow seems to come to a screeching halt just before payday. In some cases, it seems to dwindle just after the paycheck arrives. That which was a mighty river on payday, overnight seems to become a dried up little creek. Are you anything like that? Do you regularly find yourself in a cash crunch just before payday? Do you find yourself juggling money between savings and checking because you can't maintain an adequate checking account balance? Perhaps you let one bill payment each month slide into next month. Or, even if your bills seem to be under control, you find it impossible to save any money. Sound familiar? If so, welcome to life.

MANAGING CASH FLOW BY FINDING MISSING MONEY

Everybody needs some kind of system to account for spending and cash flow. Spending needs to be controlled. But first you'll have to find that missing money—the income that somehow flies out of your grasp. Ultimately, it's not what you earn that gives you financial security, but what you save. Many are still trying to learn how to live within their means, instead of living above their means. Yet to save more money and spend it wisely, you must first know where your money goes. And that means keeping records.

You may think the records you already keep are evidence enough. Check stubs, receipts and charge account statements do paint the big picture of your rent or mortgage, utilities, car payments, furniture and other major purchases, but the clues you really need are smaller. What about all your pocket money? How were those $50 withdrawals from automated teller machines spent? And the $45 department store charges? What do these sums tell you about your spending patterns?

It's a lot easier to tell others how to budget than it is to discipline yourself! Recognize that it's easy to stumble, to make a wrong choice and to fall flat on your personal discipline. But don't make that your last chapter! Get up, start over, get some discipline into your life and get back on track! There is always hope if you don't give up. So don't give up!

MANAGING CASH FLOW BY RECORDING SPENDING

What about that pocket money that seems to elude your financial oversight? If you're like many people today, you don't know because you don't accurately keep track of spending. Yet, doing so is surprisingly easy. With that accomplished, you'll be able to analyze your spending patterns, solve "The Case of Your Missing Money" and draw up a realistic form for accounting for the missing money.

All you really need is about $10 worth of materials. First, buy a daily journal. Special daily expense logs are tailored for business use, but for our purposes a 49-cent spiral-bound notebook small enough to fit in to your pocket or purse works fine. Second, buy a simple ledger book or columnar pad with one wide column on the left and at least six narrower columns ruled for entering figures. These plus a pocket calculator and a sharp pencil and you're ready to hunt for the missing money.

SETTING UP EXPENSE CATEGORIES

The initial step is to set up expense categories. They should be narrow rather than broad; the purpose of keeping records is to develop a detailed picture of monthly spending. Catch-all categories such as "household expenses" aren't useful—what you want to discover is just what those household expenses consist of (groceries, furnishings, linens, home maintenance, gardening supplies and the like). Later on you can consolidate. For now, instead of "clothes," use "his clothes," "her clothes" and "kids' clothes."

On the first ledger sheet, list spending categories down the left-hand column. Every family's spending habits will vary to some degree, but many categories are common to all households. Use a worksheet as guide, adding as many categories as you want. Each column of figures will represent one month's spending, so label them accordingly.

Expenses fall into two types: fixed and variable. Fixed expenses—such as rent or mortgages, loan payments, insurance premiums and tuition are constant amounts at regular intervals. Utility bills paid on a level-payment plan are fixed expenses, while those based on each month's usage are variable.

Don't forget to set up an expense category for savings. The primary purpose of your record keeping is to increase savings, but you can get a jump on it now. Savings should be considered a fixed expense—10% or more of your income, if possible. Think of it as paying yourself first.

Fixed expenses will be recorded directly in the ledger. You can do the same with variable items that are paid in one monthly sum. Use the daily journal to list out-of-pocket expenses down to the penny or nickel. It feels odd at first, but quickly becomes a habit.

In the journal, label a page for each category of expenses and record every outlay under the appropriate category. This means every purchase of clothing, groceries, furniture or bark mulch; each dinner out; gasoline, oil and other auto expenses; haircuts and dry cleaning; books, CDs and DVDs; stamps, magazine subscriptions and newspapers; baby-sitting; daily commuting expenses; and so on.

KEEPING GOOD SPENDING RECORDS

You needn't pull the journal out of pocket or purse every half-hour. Take a few minutes each evening to write down the day's expenses while they're still fresh in your mind. Receipts can help jog your memory, but remember to separate the expenses into their proper categories. The supermarket receipt, for example, may reflect not only groceries but also lawn chairs, medicine and other items.

TOTALING THE SPENDING

At the end of the month, sit down with your daily journal and checkbook. First, total the outlays for each category in your journal. Then allocate each check you've written into one or more categories, using credit card statements and receipts as reminders. Finally, combine the journal and checkbook numbers and record the month's total spending by category in your ledger.

Remember, a $100 check to *Visa* tells you nothing. Break it down into $62 for children's clothing, $17 for yard supplies and $21 for a gift. If you keep your daily journal in good order, recording total monthly expenses should take just half an hour or so.

You now have an accurate picture of one month's spending. It's early yet for analysis, but if outgo exceeded income, zero in on discretionary spending such as clothing, entertainment, gifts and purchases for the home. What can you cut down on next month?

> There is always hope if you don't give up. So don't give up!

STAYING WITH THE PROCESS

Now repeat the process. One month's records tell you little about spending patterns over time. To gain a full understanding of your spending patterns you need a long perspective. Three months is good. Six months is better. Over and above fixed expenses and some fairly steady variable expenses, your outlays will fluctuate, perhaps widely, from month to month. Seasonal expenses include vacation, Christmas, birthdays and anniversaries. Some fixed expenses are spaced over long intervals—insurance premiums, taxes and car-registration fees, to name a few. Then come unexpected expenses, such as big medical bills, car repairs and new appliances. All are as much a part of your overall spending profile as groceries, utilities and mortgage payments.

RECORD KEEPING BASICS

Income—In this category, income is anything used to pay expenses and could include bonuses, investment gains, gifts or inheritance. Record savings withdrawn to pay expenses as income, and classify money put into your savings account as an expense.

Salary—It's simpler to include only your take-home pay as salary. That way you can skip expense categories for income taxes, social security, 401(k) contributions and the like. A self-employed person, however, records gross income and all such expenses.

Accuracy—Be accurate, but don't go overboard. Amounts need not add up to the penny, and if you forget an outlay, it's not the end of the world. Aim for 99% accuracy—for $2,500 in monthly expenses to match $2,500 in income plus or minus $25. Round monthly subtotals and totals to the nearest dollar, too. Getting rid of those extra digits will make the numbers easier to analyze later.

Continuity—This system is built on the cash method of accounting—income and expenses are recorded when they are received and paid, not when they come due. So if you defer one regular monthly expense into the next month, record it in the month it was actually paid. Likewise, if you pay off a charge card bill in installments, record only the amount paid each month, remembering to allocate charges to the proper expense categories, such as "night out" or "his clothes."

Once you complete months of meticulous record keeping, you will know within a few dollars how much you spent each month and on what. If you stick with it, keeping track of spending will become second nature.

More important, over time you will develop a realistic gut feeling about spending—a realization that when one category of expenses is higher than usual, economies are in order elsewhere. This sounds simplistic, and it is, but if you have chronic money problems, a realistic gut feeling about spending may be precisely what you lack.

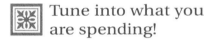 Tune into what you are spending!

TRACKING THE LITTLE STUFF

Keeping track of those nickels and dimes turns casual spending into a conscious, ordered process by linking the act of spending money with the act of recording the outlay. Now instead of thinking about each purchase only once, you think about it twice. This simple exercise builds discipline in spending money.

After three to six months of recording monthly expenses, your ledger page will become a spreadsheet, which will become a mathematical model of your finances over time. You can follow rows across the page to see how particular categories vary. You can calculate average amounts for variable expenses—in effect turning them

into fixed expenses, which are much easier to use for planning.

At this point, a home computer becomes a powerful planning and budgeting tool. By using a spreadsheet program or money management program, you can ask your financial model "what if" questions, instantly manipulating income and spending categories to analyze different approaches.

Some great money management programs for your computer include *Microsoft Money Manager* and *Quicken* or *Microsoft Excel* for spreadsheets. You can do the same with paper and pencil, of course. We will provide detailed budgeting in the next couple of chapters.

You'll find yourself setting goals, establishing priorities and beginning to sketch the framework of a realistic personal financial plan. Now you're ready to budget for keeps.

MANAGING CASH FLOW BY RIGHT SPENDING

Some financial advisers recommend a rigid approach to spending: a certain percentage of income for housing, so much for food, this much for installment debt and so on. Others take a simpler and more flexible approach, dividing expenses into needs and wants.

Your first priority is to tithe the tenth (10%) that belongs to God. Tithe to your local house of worship. This is the place you receive your spiritual care. Next, put away 10% for savings and investing. Take care of yourself by setting goals, then treating those payments as fixed expenses. Suppose you have two children to put through college and you want a comfortable retirement. The first checks you write each month should be to your IRA, 401(k) and college savings plans.

Then come your living expenses. Roughly 70% of your money is already spoken for by needs such as rent or mortgage, utilities and taxes. Those are pretty much fixed expenses, although you can reduce taxes with proper planning.

Those are needs; then you can worry about the wants.

Once needs are met, about 10% is left for debt reduction and other wants, and that's where you begin making choices. You can buy new cars or used ones. Food is very discretionary—you can choose to eat very well or just a basic menu. And clothes—you need appropriate clothing for work, but after that there is a lot of leeway. Every type of expense requires similar thinking. For instance, some heavy readers stock up on books and subscriptions, but you can use the library instead and save money.

Many people underestimate (or overspend on) gifts. There are many more occasions to give than just Christmas and birthdays. All those baby showers, Mother's Day presents and graduation gifts can add up. Take a hard look at what you spend for gifts.

MANAGING CASH FLOW BY WATCHING THE CASH

Tune into what you are spending! Write it down. Don't make it a guessing game. Most people do not even know how to tell whether they can afford something. Everyone, not just those who think they are short of money, should use a ledger detailing all cash flow.

Tune into what you are spending! Virtually every business uses a system to define the inflow and outgo of cash, and so can you. No matter how much money you think you have, it's a useful exercise to determine where it comes from and where it all should go.

Your future is bright.
You CAN make it!
Manage your cash flow now!

Follow a Budget

*I*t will be impossible for you to get out of debt and stay out of debt without developing a written budget. A written budget helps you preplan for your expenses in advance, before your income arrives. By planning in advance and following your predetermined budget, you will not spend money on things not already in your budget.

The most important part of making a budget work is not how the budget is set up. The most important part of the budget process is you! You are the only one who can make it work.

Many people say, "I just don't know where it all goes," or "I just can't seem to make ends meet." Form a habit of writing down your expenses. Keep track of your outgo. It's surprising what you find when you put it all down on paper.

By putting it on paper, you can . . .

- Review past spending and saving.
- Regularly record all expenses.
- Intelligently explore all expenditures, and their options.
- Control what you spend.
- Project future spending and saving.
- Enjoy including family members in the process.
- Manage your money, rather than allowing it to manage you.

If you want to become wealthy, you have to save and invest. No, not by buying lottery tickets or hoping your ship will finally come in. The first step to riches begins with learning how to budget. You can't save or invest until you know both what you spend and just how much is available for you to set aside in savings. That knowledge comes with a plan and a budget.

Take control of your income and outgo. It can be fun and will certainly be a challenge. Set up a workable budget that every member of the family (if you are married) understands and supports. Your family and/or friends can become a team pulling together for a common goal. That goal may mean sacrificing now to provide for a college education for the children (if you are a parent) later. But it will be worth it when you achieve that goal. If you have been in debt more years than you care to remember, you can look forward to the wonderful, amazing feeling you have when you make the last payment on those debts.

Be in control of your financial future. The key to a budget that works is not some sophisticated, elaborate budget process—just old-fashioned hard work. You are the single most important key. Take the opportunity to be in control of your money, rather than having your money control you.

Altering a lifestyle isn't easy. But that's what making a budget work usually requires, if you really want to get out of a rut. If you are tired of being broke all the time—if you are tired of being dissatisfied with your finances—then set up that budget and make it work for you!

DETERMINE TO GET STARTED NOW

First, categorize and list all regular expenses. This will give you a financial snapshot of where your money is going. Because everyone handles his or her money differently, there isn't one method of categorizing that is exclusively right. Design a system that fits your personality, can be applied consistently and tells you what you need to know. If you're a generalist, don't attempt a detailed system with lots of categories.

On the other hand, if you're a person who likes detail, don't adopt a system that's too general. Use more detailed tracking for those categories that cause you the most problems and stress. Some need to watch their expenditures in the area of sporting goods and tools, while others need to focus on clothing expenditures.

Next, add up your total income and expenses. If your total income exceeds your total expenses, you've just cleared an important hurdle leading toward "no debt." However, if your expenses exceed your income, analyze each budget category, consider whether something is a desire or a

necessity, and reduce your expenses. Pay special attention to those areas that consume much more income than they should. If not controlled, they can lead to financial disaster.

The most common surprise lurks in the "miscellaneous" category, which often becomes a catchall for everything from restaurants to espresso, film and greeting cards. Once monitored, people often discover they're spending $50 a month on lattes and vending machines, or $260 a month for fast-food meals. Beginning budgeters often find that car payments and insurance are sinking them, and they may be better off driving a smaller or older car.

Try to analyze your expenses better. Determine what percentage of your net income is spent per month in each category. To calculate that percentage, simply divide each expense by your net income. (Example: If your total housing costs are $1,000 per month and your net income is $3,000 per month, you're spending . . . $1,000/$3,000 = 33% of your income on housing.) Try to keep your housing expense percentage under 25%.

Designing a budget is more than number crunching and statistical analysis. After all, money is just a tool to help you accomplish something you want. As you work through this process, don't allow yourself to get so wrapped up in the numbers and money concerns and forget the big picture—everything we have is on loan from God, to use to His honor and glory.

Take the opportunity to do a little dreaming also. That might include buying a house, saving for your children's education (if you have dependents), giving to the church or a charity, taking a vacation, paying off a debt or buying a newer car. If you're married, you need to talk this over with your spouse. Regardless of your marital status, ask for God's guidance (Jeremiah 17:7, 8; James 4:10).

So take a little time to ask, listen and dream. Then establish a few short- and long-term goals, set priorities and adjust your budget accordingly. If you're already into deficit spending, ask God's guidance in making cuts as well.

THE BASICS—MAKING YOUR BUDGET WORK

Make columns for housing and utilities, groceries, meals out, transportation, medical and dental, clothing, insurance, debts, family vacation, recreation and all other categories of expenses that apply to your family. You now have the basic tools necessary to set up a working budget. If you haven't selected a format, here's a simple way to start. Write your categories down the left-hand side of a piece of paper, then draw 15 vertical columns to the right of them. Label the tops of those columns in this way:

Column 1:   *"amount budgeted"* per month
Columns 2-13: month (January through December)
               As the year progresses, you will record your actual costs for each category in these columns.
Column 14:   "total" cost for the year
Column 15:   "average" monthly cost for the year

This format is designed to be a starting place. A more detailed budget, allowing you to keep track of balances in each category, is suggested. At the end of this section I have printed for your use my personal budget design. Use it all or just review it for ideas as you fashion a budget design that works best for you.

Now you know: This month you spent $35 on coffee and bagels, $85 on lunches, $450 on groceries—whatever. You're not looking so much for precise targets here. Instead, this exercise will give you an expected spending range. That way, before the next month starts (and while your fiscal reality is fresh) you can sit down and make a spending plan.

> A budget is a powerful method of gaining control, planning, communicating and fulfilling your dreams.

Once you've discovered how much you have coming in, you get to decide what to spend it on. That's the key phrase: you decide. You are controlling the money, not the other way around. Start by determining how much to sock away in savings and what to pay against your credit card debt. Then allocate leftover cash for everything else. By laying out your budget this way, you'll see opportunities to cut spending you may not have noticed before.

For example, maybe you'll find you can save $30 a month by eating out less, $50 by buying fewer clothes, $20 by carpooling and $25 by sharing a baby-sitter. Add these up and you'll have an extra $1,500 by the start of the new year. Invest that money—conservatively, no less—and you'll have nearly $29,000 in 10 years; $125,000 in 20 years; all thanks to some very simple cutbacks.

Here are two areas to watch carefully. First, some people find it particularly hard to stick to a budget when they're addicted to credit cards. That kind of plastic is too free, flexible and—ultimately—expensive. So try to kick that habit and switch to debit cards instead. Second, it's crucial to build some free money into your budget each month—even if it's just a few dollars. That way, if there's a CD you just must have, or a night you feel like going out with the girls (or guys), you can do it without feeling like a failure.

Once you see how you have been spending your money, set up a workable plan for changing your spending patterns and habits, if necessary, to accomplish your new long-, medium- and short-range goals.

SOME BUDGETING TIPS

A budget is a powerful method of gaining control, planning, communicating and fulfilling your dreams. At the very least, a budget should allow you to find extra spending money in your paycheck every month. Everyone can successfully reap the benefits of budgeting; just take it step by step. The payoff is big. It is a great life-changing experience to get and maintain control of your finances. The effects permeate to every aspect of your life.

If you are new to budgeting, don't overwhelm yourself and categorize your expenses into too many little categories. Start with a few big buckets at first, until you get the rhythm, then fine-tune your budget.

Make this a household activity by involving all members, and make sure there is some fun in it for everyone. If you never go any further than spending some time tracking your expenses for a few weeks, at least do that. The insights you'll gain from paying attention to your habits will go a long way!

- Be patient. Consider the first three months as a test period. You may have to adjust your budgeted amounts in some categories.

- Invest or save any windfall income. At the very least, treat it with care. Example: tax refunds, dividends and bonuses.

- If you have a quarterly, semiannual or annual payment, such as auto licenses, insurance or taxes, calculate how much those cost you on a monthly basis. Then save that amount each month, so when the bill arrives, it doesn't throw your budget into a tailspin.

- Don't forget to pay yourself. If possible, make sure you save something each month that can go toward an investment.

- Don't try to keep track of every penny (nickels and dimes, yes!). It will drive you and everyone else nuts.

- Make impulse buying difficult. Leave your checkbook and credit cards at home.

- Make sure you set aside some money for having fun.

- Have some fun money for each family member.

- Budget for a fun item (vacation, toy).

- Don't overcategorize (too many "expense" categories).

- Don't divide a couple's paychecks functionally (using her check for certain categories and his for others).

- Use an interest-bearing checking account.

- Make savings an "expense" item.

- Create an "expense" item to pay off credit card balances.

- Pay off the highest-interest rate cards first.

- Don't use credit cards again until the balance is paid off.

- After a loan is paid off, keep paying the loan amount to yourself (make a vacation fund, or car fund).

- Reconcile your budget at least once a month when reconciling your checking statement.

- Get utilities or banks to change the due dates of bills to make your work easier.

Remember, just the act of identifying your expenses is extremely valuable. This simple form of budgeting can work even for those who are very young and have little income or perhaps have only the allowance given by their parents.

HOW TO ORGANIZE YOUR MONTHLY, QUARTERLY AND ANNUAL BILLS

- Paying your bills promptly will help you avoid late fees and save you money.

- Following basic steps will help you get rid of procrastination and keep your finances in good order.

- Set aside a special place to put your bills when they arrive, such as a special slot on your desk, a special section in a drawer or a bill "inbox." Always remember to put your bills in this special place immediately upon their arrival.

- Set aside two times a month, two weeks apart, to pay bills. The middle and end of the month are good times.

- Call the companies that send you bills and have them revise your payment due dates to correspond with one of the two times monthly you plan to pay your bills.

- Mark your calendar to remind you of bill-paying dates, then pay on schedule.

- Pay your bills with checks or money orders, then note on the receipt portion of the bills your check number and the date and amount you paid.

- File these receipts away and keep them for up to seven years.

- Place the outgoing envelopes containing your payments next to your car or house keys, so that you remember to take them with you and mail them immediately.

- Be sure to continue your bill-paying efforts all the way to the mailbox. Nothing is more frustrating than to write your bills on time, then find them not mailed in the backseat of your car a week later.

Some credit card companies, mortgage lenders and automobile financing companies move due dates around. Check the due dates for such bills as soon as they arrive in the mail.

Utility and phone companies are usually a little more flexible and will wait for a few days before they send a reminder notice or charge a late fee. Credit card companies, mortgage and automobile lenders, oil companies and landlords are not as forgiving. Many banks allow you to set up automatic bill payment with your checking account. Call your bank to find out if it offers such a service. But be careful –unpaid bills can lead to disconnected utilities, a bad credit rating and debt.

BUDGETING

The word *budget* sounds boring. It even can sound a little intimidating! The very word seems to spell work, details, recordkeeping—bringing up all sorts of unpleasant visual pictures. But it really isn't all that bad. Budgets are a way of life for all companies and families who need to get control of their finances. Families who have everything under control and who are financially free still need a budget.

Because we live in a "now" world, we are used to having everything done yesterday or today at the very latest. But some things are not this easy. Getting out of debt falls into this category. Creating a practical long-range plan is important. Budgeting opens the door to financial security. A budget is a money plan. With it, you can organize and control your financial resources, set and realize goals, and decide in advance how your money will work for you. Budgeting is a great way to assess your financial needs. It will give you an overall picture of where your money is coming from, when it is coming in, and how you are spending the money you earn.

Many people think that preparing a budget is complicated or that it takes too much time. Even if you are financially free of all debt, budgeting is still an essential part of your financial life. A budget can be as simple as it is powerful. The basic idea behind budgeting is to save money up front for both known and unknown expenses. A budget is the key to making everything else work. It's your game plan, your strategy. And it has to be proactive. Knowing where you stand financially and how to control your finances is a valuable life skill.

Budgeting gives your family a spending plan. A budget is simply a family spending plan—a money makeover, if you will. You've heard of personal and physical makeovers. You know that if you diet (and don't cheat) and get on an exercise plan (and stick to it), the pounds are going to come off. You will feel better about yourself and more in control of your physical health. Budgets are like your own personal or family business on a smaller scale. It paints the picture of all your income, minus all your expenses, and tells you what is leftover. It becomes a guideline to all your spending. When you budget your income and

expenses and see the result, you may either have to raise your income or reduce your spending.

Here's how it translates financially: If you make a budget (and stick to it) and put money away for short and long-term goals (regularly), you'll feel better about your financial health—and more in control of your financial future.

 A budget is simply a family spending plan—a money makeover, if you will.

Fortunately, you don't need an MBA to get your finances in shape. You don't need hours of extra time. A few basic steps will get you where you need to go. Budgeting will help you get in shape financially. When people ask about getting their finances in shape, they typically have very similar goals. They want to save more for emergencies today. They want to invest more for college and retirement tomorrow. They want to get out of debt. They want security for themselves and their families in case disaster strikes. And they want to know how to learn about their money—because they know that when it comes right down to it, they are responsible.

Budgeting is a team effort. Furthermore, a budget can be used to develop good communication between a husband and wife. It's one of those subjects you can discuss and then come to a reasonable agreement. A budget is really very simple. You have a given amount of money to spend. A budget helps you decide how you're going to spend it. No more will you be so quick to raise your debt to higher heights. You will be less inclined toward indiscriminate spending, arbitrary purchases and impulse buying. You will stay out of the stores that provide you with the greatest opportunities for temptation.

Budgeting will make you disciplined. The best way to start a budget is to keep tabs on all the money—all of it that comes in and goes out for a month. That means not only logging the checks you write to the electric and phone companies and everyone else, but also keeping track of the cash you spend. One way to get disciplined is to keep all your receipts, then jot down what you spent at the end of each day.

A budget for family spending gives order to family money. The dictionary defines *order* as meaning a regular arrangement, a method or system (*Webster's Unabridged Dictionary 1913*). This definition suggests that order means "harmonious relationships between parts or members." In other words, balance.

When talking about order in the use of money, each of these ideas is implied: a regular arrangement, a method or system, and balance. The dictionary definition of a budget is "a plan for the coordination of resources and expenditures."

Obtaining satisfaction from the use of one's money calls for some regular arrangement for managing it. A budget should exist to guide whatever method or system we adopt for paying bills, saving, providing for daily living needs and accomplishing goals.

A regular and systematic arrangement saves time and reveals what financial resources are available.

Budgeting gives you financial balance and order. Order also suggests balance. No one area of our financial lives should outweigh other areas to the point of weakening them or putting them out of focus. Order helps keep entertain-ment, for example, in line with the total budget so that essentials such as food and shelter are adequately covered.

A budget systematizes one's money affairs and aids in accomplishing goals. A budget, or plan, is a tool that is used in managing money. However, the budget does not do the managing; this is what people do.

A budget begins with a statement of family income. A statement of your income tells you exactly what financial resources are available. It tells you what money you will receive weekly, monthly and annually.

It should indicate any income you receive in addition to your earnings, such as interest on savings, or the benefit payments a family member may receive. Once you know your total income, you know one of the limits within which to do your financial planning.

A budget informs you of the fixed expenses to which the family is committed. Rent or mortgage payments, insurance premiums, contributions to church and charity, installment payments on any debt the family owes, taxes and all other payments made on a regular basis and in fixed amounts should be included in the budget.

A listing of these fixed expenses shows what you already have promised to pay and provides another set of limits within which to do further planning. Now you are in a position to plan more realistically and to use your resources to a greater advantage.

A budget provides for the necessary variable expenses. Expenditures for food, clothing, personal allowances, household, automobile expenses, dry-cleaning, laundry, recreation and other needs that can be controlled to a certain extent. A budget is simply a forecast of your earnings and expenses over a given period of time. This then is available as a guide for your future spending patterns.

A budget will help you with the big-ticket purchases. When the need arises to buy things of great expense, a budget will help you in the advanced planning stages, before the need arises. Perhaps this would be for the new house or new car. It might be the children's education, a remodeled room in the house, a shed in the backyard, or a fence around the property. Or perhaps it will be new blinds for the windows, new carpet on the floor, a range or refrigerator.

How about special goals? Next year's vacation, painting the kitchen, new furniture or drapes for the living room must be provided for systematically. If the amount of money needed for a special goal or coming event can be determined in advance, it may be practical to include a regular payment for this event in the "fixed expenses" category. Then the money will be on hand when it is needed.

A budget is the most fundamental and most effective financial management tool available to anyone, whether you are earning thousands of dollars a year, or hundreds of thousands of dollars.

Saving for what you want takes time, planning and some deliberate thought. If it is not thought out ahead of time, it is easy just to pull out the plastic, put it on a credit account and overspend, until we reach the critical stage of too much debt.

Budgeting helps you prepare in advance.

Sometimes people become discouraged with budgeting because an emergency arises and there is no money. The roof leaks, the front tire blows out, layoffs occur at work or some other minor or major disaster wrecks the family budget. A budget helps you cope with unexpected expenses. This is why it is important to build an emergency fund to help you during unexpected times.

PLANNING FOR EMERGENCIES

The more modest the income, the more important the budget. People living on a low income have less flexibility in their spending patterns. These emergencies cannot be determined in advance, but provision can be made for them in the budget.

How can one provide for such emergencies? What if, during a recessionary economy, sales are slow at the plant or office and the company is forced to arrange for layoffs to keep its budget on course for the year? Provision for emergencies such as a temporary work layoff should be made in advance, certainly not after the fact.

If an individual waits for this to happen, by then it is too late to do anything about it. At that point, one becomes a victim of circumstances out of his or her control.

It is important to find some extra money each week to put away for unexpected expenses. There are really only two ways to do that. You must either raise your level of income or reduce your current expenses.

Here is an idea. When working overtime on the job, set aside 75% of the extra income into a special "emergency savings account." Another idea that deserves some thought is to set aside in your special savings account any company bonus dollars paid in cash. This should be done until four to six months' income has been accumulated. After this, you can consider other timely investments with the extra cash. Resist the urge to spend the extra money. In the long run you'll be glad you did!

ATTAINING SPECIAL GOALS

Budgeting helps you attain special goals. Find out exactly where you are right now. Get all your financial bills and statements in order. It may not be very pleasant to find out how deeply you are in debt, but you might as well face it. Otherwise, you'll continue in the same old rut, digging ever deeper. Once you have noted all your debts, put down what income you realistically can expect to receive. Let's hope you have more income than outgo! If you find that that is not the case, get in the habit of living below your means.

If you are typical, you'll find your debts cannot be paid off right away. That's where budgeting comes in. Having a budget to many people is distasteful. It's like having to go on a diet, or like being a child told to go to your room. It seems like punishment for alleged wrong doing.

Budgeting gives you another chance. Having a budget is what you should have been doing all along. So don't look at it as unpleasant. Setting up a budget is like getting a new lease on life. It's a way to start over. It's a way to make a success out of your finances. Remember, your plan probably will have to be long range.

The chances are your home mortgage will be the greatest debt you have to pay. At least let's hope that is the case! Generally that is a fixed sum of money. So if you have 10 years, or even 20 or 30 years yet to pay, your long-range budget should be set up as long as you have one outstanding debt.

PLANNING REALISTIC PAYMENTS

Next, take your debts one by one and lay out a realistic payment plan. Your automobile may take another two years to pay. During that time, be sure to maintain your vehicle properly so it can last several additional years.

If you unwisely went into debt for furniture, clothing and other items, then they too will have to be paid each month—you may have charged enough that your long-range plan may take two, three or even four years. But do formulate a plan. It is never too late to start, and better now than never.

Make up your mind not to create any new debts while paying off the old ones. That is not going to be easy. It may take more family self-discipline than you have ever had to use before. Those debts will all have to be paid. There is no use putting it off any longer.

CUSTOMIZING A BUDGET

A budget should be tailor made for you. Each person or family has different needs. No one budget is suitable for everyone. The single person with no family has different needs than the single parent with three kids. Money management for the 61-year-old couple planning for retirement will be very different from the 21-year-old newlyweds. And the couple with no children certainly has different expenses than the parents of children. Even greater expenses occur when the children reach college age.

Each of us has different goals, and therefore a different plan and a different budget is needed. It must be customized for each individual circumstance. Each budget is neither right nor wrong, just different. Budgeting makes your money do what you want it to. Too many people have given in to their desires and extended themselves beyond safety in money management. You simply cannot spend more than you have coming in.

For most people with families, typical long-range goals are saving for a college education for the children, a paid-off home mortgage and sufficient funds for retirement. Mid-range goals include furnishing the home, purchasing and maintaining an automobile and perhaps a special vacation. Shorter-range expenses are for clothing, food and recreation.

Write down your own list of goals: long, medium and short range. But as you set down your goals and develop your budget, keep these points in mind:

- All goals must be based realistically on your projected budget.
- Provide for the basics first, then the comforts and finally the luxuries.
- Set up a plan for paying off debts already accumulated.
- Plan for savings, no matter how small. Increase your savings allocation as your old debts are reduced.
- Control your spending according to your budget.
- Never give in to temptations to depart from the budget.
- If you stumble, don't give up; regroup and get on task again.

Budgeting is an effective management tool. A budget is the most fundamental and most effective financial management tool available to anyone, whether you are earning thousands of dollars a year, or hundreds of thousands of dollars. It is extremely important to know how much money you have to spend and where you are spending it. A budget is the first and most important step toward maximizing the power of your money.

Budgeting gives you a financial outline. A carpenter never starts work on a new house without a blueprint. An aerospace firm never begins construction on a new rocket booster without a detailed set of design specifications. Yet many of us find ourselves in the circumstance of getting out on our own and making, spending and investing money without a plan to guide us. Budgeting is about planning. Planning is crucial to produce a desired result.

Budgeting allows you to know what is going on. Personal budgeting allows you to know exactly how much money you have, even down to the penny, if you so desire. Furthermore, a budget is a self-education tool that shows you how your funds are allocated, how they are working for you, what your plans are for them and how far along you are toward reaching your goals. "Knowledge is power," as the oft-quoted saying goes, and knowing about your money is the first step toward controlling it.

Budgeting gives you financial control. A budget is the key to enabling you to take charge of your finances. With a budget, you have the tools to decide what is going to happen to your hard-earned money, and when. It bears repeating: You can be in control of your money, instead of letting it control you!

SPENDING/BUDGETING WORKSHEET

My Spending	Monthly	Yearly	Budget	Actual	Diff (+ or -)
ALLOWANCES					
Parents					
Children					
CHARITY					
My Local Home Church (10-15%)					
Local Church Special Project #1					
Local Church Special Project #2					
Charity #3					
Charity #4					
Other					
DEBT REPAYMENT					
Student Loan					
Home Equity Loan					
Credit Card #1					
Credit Card #2					
Personal Line of Credit					
ENTERTAINMENT					
Movies/Videos/Sporting Events					
Recreation/Parks					
Weekend Trips					
Vacations					
Other #1					
FOOD					
Groceries					
Restaurants					
School Lunches					
Work Lunches					
HOUSING					
Mortgage or Rent					
Real Estate Taxes					
Gas					
Electric					
Water					
Sewer					
Phone - Landline					
Phone - Internet					
Phone - Cell/Pager					
Cable/Satellite					
Garbage/Sanitation					
Home Repairs					
Home/Appliance Maintenance					
Yard Upkeep					
Other #1					

My Spending	Monthly	Yearly	Budget	Actual	Diff (+ or -)
KIDS' SPECIAL EXPENSES					
School					
Lessons #1					
Lessons #2					
Camp					
Sports #1					
INSURANCE					
Vehicle #1					
Vehicle #2					
Vehicle #3					
Life #1					
Life #2					
Life #3					
Life #4					
House #1					
House #2					
Disability #1					
Disability #2					
Long Term Care					
MEDICAL/DENTAL					
Premiums					
Co-payments					
Prescriptions					
Vitamins					
PERSONAL					
Haircut/Beauty					
Dry Cleaning/Laundry					
Clothes					
Gifts					
Subscriptions					
SAVINGS PROGRAM					
Emergency Fund					
401(k)/Retirement					
College Fund					
Investment Fund					
Christmas/Birthday					
Other #1					
TRANSPORTATION					
Car Loan/Lease Payment					
Gasoline					
License Plates					
Maintenance					
Repairs					
Other #1					
OTHER					
Misc. #1					
Misc. #2					

Budgeting provides organization. Even in its simplest form, a budget divides funds into categories of expenditures and savings. Beyond that, however, budgets can provide further organization by automatically providing records of all your monetary transactions. They can also provide the foundation for a simple filing system to organize bills, receipts and financial statements.

Budgeting encourages communication. If you are married, have a family or share money with anyone, having a budget you create together is a key to resolving personal differences about money handling. The budget is a communication tool to discuss the priorities for where your money should be spent and enables all involved parties to run the system.

> You can be in control of your money, instead of letting it control you!

A budget allows you to take advantage of opportunities. Knowing the exact state of your personal monetary affairs, and being in control, allows you to take advantage of opportunities you might otherwise miss. Have you ever wondered if you could afford something? With a budget, you will never have to wonder again—you will know.

Budgeting offers you extra time. All your financial transactions are automatically organized for tax time, for creditor questions, in fact, for any query about how and when you spent money. Being armed with such information saves time digging through old records.

Budgeting brings you extra money. This might be everyone's favorite. A budget will

almost certainly produce extra money for you to do with as you wish. Hidden fees and lost interest paid to outsiders can be eliminated. Unnecessary expenditures, once identified, can be stripped. Savings, no matter how small, can be accumulated and made to work for you.

WHY BUDGETS FAIL

Don't you just hate to fail, especially when you've invested time and effort into a project? It happens all the time, especially for those who are starting to take control of their finances. Watch for these common errors.

1. UNREALISTIC GOALS

It's easy to fall into our first failure trap. In some ways it's hard to avoid it. That's because it's built right into the process. Our first step in starting a budget is to add up all our income and all our expenses. Then we try to juggle the two until we get the income equal to the expenses. It's a game of getting the math to work out.

What's wrong with that? Well, quite often, we take the list of expenses and pick a number that just seems right. For instance, we might decide that we can live on a grocery budget of $200 per month. But, if that target is just a guess, it's probably the wrong number. And, if we reduced it to get the expenses below our income, it's probably too low.

So now we put the budget into practice. Then we are near the end of the first month. There's a week left, and we've already spent our budgeted $200. Out comes the credit card, and we begin to curse our budget.

What has really happened here? We set up an unrealistic target—and missed it. Now that doesn't mean our budget won't work. It just means we need to set a more realistic target.

We're in a better position now to accomplish that because we have a better idea of what we actually do spend on groceries. No more guesses. This is no time to quit. Rather, it's an opportunity to make adjustments and keep moving toward our goal of having control of our finances.

2. QUITTING TOO SOON

The second common cause of failure, quitting too soon, is similar. Say you've been trying to use a budget for a couple of months. You've done all the math and kept track of both the money coming into your home and where you spend it. You've worked hard on this.

Yet you always seem to get to the end of your money before the month is over. Frustration sets in. The temptation is to throw in the towel and give up. A perfectly understandable response, but it's the wrong answer. Look at it this way. Suppose you were driving to Disney World and about halfway there you realized you had made a wrong turn and had driven 50 miles off your planned route. Would you quit and go home? Of course not!

So why should we give up on a budget just because everything doesn't work perfectly the first few months? Do the same thing you'd do on your vacation.

Look at your budget map and adjust your route to find the best way to reach your destination. Make the adjustment and move forward.

3. MISUNDERSTANDING WHAT A BUDGET REALLY IS

Another cause for budget failure is not understanding what a budget really is. Too many people think a budget is something to keep them from spending money. However, that is wrong. It's not a straightjacket.

A budget is a tool to provide information to manage finances. The knowledge gained by tracking income and expenses will help you get the most for your money. A budget can help you find money so you can spend where it will give you the most enjoyment.

Fortunately, all three problems can be corrected by using the budget as a management tool. Each month your budget will show what you planned and actually earned and spent. That's valuable information. The trick is to see where the actual numbers varied from the expected numbers.

Once you've found a big difference, you can begin to analyze why it happened. Was there a big one-time expense this month? Maybe you committed the first mistake and just guessed at what you'd spend. It could be that you've been spending carelessly on groceries. If that's the case, you'll look to find some savings this month.

Each month, work on the biggest differences until the whole process runs smoothly. Just take on one or two at a time. Month by month, you should get closer to actually having control of your finances. After a while it's just a matter of checking to make sure everything is roughly on target and making minor midcourse corrections.

Now that's not to say it's easy to resolve those differences. Sometimes it's not. But it's always easier to work when you have some clues to help point you in the right direction. The information your budget provides helps you know where to look for possible savings. That is often the difference between frustration and success.

It's always a shame when you work hard and don't receive any benefit from your work. Don't let that happen to your budget. It takes much less effort to fix a budget than to start one. You've already put in the hardest work, so take the time to reap the benefits. You deserve it.

4. Family or Spousal Strife

Genesis 2:24 says that God created a husband and a wife to be one. That means a budget must work for two people and not just for one.

A common error in budgeting is to try to overcorrect previous bad habits. Crash budgets may work on paper, but not where people are involved. The husband may deem some purchases for the wife to be unnecessary, while in fact he considers his fishing supply expenditures a necessity.

In some cases, the husband can plan a budget that works well for him, but in doing so he eliminates his wife's discretionary spending, while sacrificing none of his own. If this fits your situation perfectly, here is a Scripture for you. "The way of a fool is right in his own eyes, but a wise man is he who listens to counsel" (Proverbs 12:15). Lesson learned? The primary counselor of any husband should be his wife.

5. Going to Extremes

Some couples become legalistic and try to control their spending right down to the nickel. Unfortunately, many times it's the husband or the wife trying to control the other's spending.

The other extreme is that people don't maintain the discipline necessary to stay on their budgets. Many couples say, "We don't want to think about it. It's too depressing." However, thinking about how you're spending your money before you have problems is not nearly as depressing as to

think about it afterward when you're trying to climb out of a deep financial hole.

6. The More-Money-In, More-Money-Out Syndrome

This means you spend more, simply because you have more. This is particularly dangerous if the extra money is temporary income, or income generated by the wife, which could be stopped by pregnancy, a job layoff, a husband's job transfer, or a variety of other things. It is preferable not to include the wife's income in your monthly budget. Save her money and use it for one-time purchases such as a car, a down payment on a home or vacations.

7. Thinking "A Little Debt Won't Hurt"

Generally, the so-called "little debts" come from taking a "needed" vacation that is more expensive than you can afford, or from gifts you just had to buy, or a car you had to have. You get the idea. A little debt will hurt, because once you've developed a cycle of debt, it grows and grows. Eventually you find yourself borrowing money just to make payments on the money you borrowed. So limit your debt right from the start.

8. Using Automatic Checking Account Overdrafts

An automatic overdraft allows you to write a check for more than you have in your account, which becomes a loan from the bank. Many couples run up thousands of dollars in debt on overdrafts before they realize it. This does two things: It encourages you to be lazy and not keep good records, and it builds debt that is difficult to reduce.

9. Misuse of Automatic Teller Machines (ATMs)

Many people fail to log ATM withdrawals in their checkbooks, and end up writing bad checks. It's also easy to develop the habit of using the cash withdrawal to buffer your budget when you have spent what you originally allocated.

10. Refusing to Balance Your Checkbook

Make an absolute commitment to do this monthly, down to the penny. It's not difficult to do, and any bank has a convenient form that shows you how to do it.

11. Discouragement

Remember, if your budget doesn't work the first month you try it, don't become discouraged. Developing a realistic budget takes time.

Habits change slowly, especially spending habits. It may take six months or more before your budget begins to work well. At times your resolve will be tested by everything from a clogged sewer line to a broken arm.

Stick with it. Remember, once you have entrusted your finances to God's principles, He will be faithful to provide for your needs. Using a budget is a sign you want to employ God's wisdom in your finances. As He says in His Word, "By wisdom a house is built, and by understanding it is established" (Proverbs 24:3).

12. Wrong Thinking

"I don't have enough money to budget!" Anyone with any amount of income can create a simple budget that works. The belief that a person doesn't have enough money to be on a budget indicates the person does not understand the concept of budgeting. Everyone, especially every Christian, should operate with a budget to be the best possible steward for God.

Beware of an attitude that results in the *more-money-in, more-money-out* syndrome. Many people who think they don't make enough money to be on a budget believe that making more money will solve their financial problems. However, without a control vehicle (budget), the more money you take in, the more money will go out.

If you learn to manage your budget now, on a limited income, then managing your budget in the future will be much easier. Whether you make a little or a lot, living within your means on a budget can keep you on the path to a rewarding financial future.

13. Not Teaching Your Children

If you have children, this simple form of budget can work even for those who are very young and have little income or perhaps have only the allowance given by their parents.

"Instruct them to do good, to be rich in good works, to be generous and ready to share, storing up for themselves the treasure of a good foundation for the future, so that they may take hold of that which is life indeed" (1 Timothy 6:18, 19).

Your future is bright.
You CAN make it!
Begin to follow a budget now!

Generate a Financial Assessment

*L*ist all you owe. It may be difficult to believe, but most people don't have a good grasp of what they owe. A listing of all your debts, with the monthly payment required and the annual percentage rate of interest, can be most helpful. I enjoy using a financial spreadsheet program such as Microsoft Excel for this task. The headings on the "What We Owe" list would look like this: "Who We Owe"; "Total Amount Due"; "Monthly Payment"; "Interest Rate"; and "What Percent of Your Total Debt" the individual debt represents.

List all you own. Now list "What We Own." This list would include most of the things bought with borrowed money. Such items as automobiles, furniture, appliances, home and luxury objects might be some of what you own. Be sure to include everything—musical instruments, collections, guns, sports equipment, etc.

Determine your net worth. Calculate your net worth by subtracting your liabilities (credit card balances, auto loans and mortgages) from your assets (savings, investments and property). Early in the year is an excellent time to do this. Then you should review and update your net worth worksheet about twice a year.

Evaluate your monthly income sources. Record any money that you've earned (paycheck, bonuses, freelance income, tips, etc.) or received from investments, savings and investments (money not available to spend).

Record your monthly expenses. Fixed expenses: mortgage or rent payments, auto and educational loans, and insurance. Variable expenses: utility bills, clothing, transportation, entertainment and dining.

Put it all together. Subtract your total expenses from your total income.

Track your cash flow. Use a small notebook to record the amount and category (food, clothing, etc.) of each purchase, no matter how small. Include check and credit card purchases as well. Do this every day for three months. Total each category at the end of the month. The information will be used to help you adjust your spending.

Keep a written account of your progress. Set financial goals. This will help increase your savings and give you peace of mind and less stress about money issues.

Your future is bright. You CAN make it!
Generate a financial assessment now!

STATEMENT OF FINANCIAL CONDITION

(Personal Balance Sheet)

Prepared by the _____ Family as of (mm/dd/yy)

ASSETS (What You Own)		
CURRENT ASSETS		
Cash – (checking accounts)		
Cash – (savings accounts, money markets, CDs)		
Personal Property – Market Value (auto, jewelry, etc)		
Other Assets (itemize)		
TOTAL CURRENT ASSETS		$
LONG-TERM ASSETS		
Certificates of deposit		
Debt Owed to You (notes, contracts)		
Life Insurance (cash values)		
Partial Interest in Real Estate		
Real Estate (net market value)		
Retirement Accounts (IRAs, SEPs, 401(k)s, etc.)		
Securities (stocks, bonds, mutual funds, etc.)		
Vehicles (market value)		
Other Long-Term Assets (itemize)		
TOTAL LONG-TERM ASSETS		$
TOTAL ASSETS		$
LIABILITIES (What You Owe)		
CURRENT LIABILITIES		
Charge Accounts (itemize)		
Credit Cards (itemize)		
Current Monthly Unpaid Bills		
Personal Debts (short-term)		
Unpaid Taxes and Interest		
Unsecured Loans (short-term)		
Other Short-Term Debts (itemize)		
TOTAL CURRENT LIABILITIES		$
LONG-TERM LIABILITIES		
Home Equity Loans		
Loans – (You Owe)		
Mortgages on Real Estate $		
Notes Cosigned, etc.		
Student Loans		
Taxes – (You Owe)		
Other Long-Term Liabilities		
TOTAL LONG-TERM LIABILITIES		$
TOTAL LIABILITIES		$
NET WORTH (owner's equity)		
(Total Assets – Total Liabilities)		$

Determine What You Owe

*T*he first step in getting out of debt is to find out to whom you owe and how much you owe. Using your credit statements as a reference, list the following information about each debt:

If you find yourself with more bills than your monthly income can cover, you may need some help. For sure you need to develop a debt-management plan. Completing this plan takes patience, but it works if you really want to get out of debt. To set up a debt-management plan, follow these steps:

- Name of creditor.
- Creditor's address.
- Creditor's telephone number.
- Your account number.
- Collateral (property or any other asset that secures a debt).
- Balance owed.
- Remaining number of payments.

- Monthly payment.
- Payment due date.
- Amount last paid.
- Date last paid.
- Type of legal action taken (e.g., garnishment or repossession).
- Collection agency or attorney.

1. Find out whom you owe and how much you owe.
2. Decide how much you can pay back and when you can pay it back.
3. Set up a plan for paying back your debts.
4. Discuss your plan with your creditors.
5. Control spending by sticking with your debt-payment plan until debts are repaid.

We will discuss this plan in detail later. As you review your plan on a regular basis, you will be able to see if you are keeping up with your debts and your daily living expenses. If there is a change in your income, you may need to raise or lower your monthly payments accordingly.

Your future is bright.
You CAN make it! Determine what you owe!

Prioritize Your Debt

*A*s a debtor, you have an obligation to pay your debts to others and to do so without delay. Scripture is very clear on repaying what you have borrowed. Paying a debt *someday* is not good enough. There must be urgency to it. Note the issue of promptness and haste as addressed in the following passage.

Proverbs 3:27, 28

"Do not withhold good from those who deserve it, when it is in your power to act. Do not say to your neighbor, 'Come back later; I'll give it tomorrow'—when you now have it with you."

It is important to pay back all the debts you owe. However, if there is not enough money to make payments on all your loans, consider prioritizing your debts. Set your financial priorities. Just be sure your personal financial priorities match up and are in line with God's priorities for you. What are your financial needs? What are your financial goals? Make an exhaustive list of them. Line them all up in order of priorities. List them in order of importance. Make sure you are considering and seeking the financial path God would have for your life.

Matthew 6:33

"But seek first his kingdom and his righteousness, and all these things will be given to you as well."

Begin now to list your debts and line them up. Debts you will need to pay first include mortgage or rent, utilities, secured loans, and insurance.

Second priorities may include credit cards and unsecured debts to finance companies. Possible examples of third priorities are doctor, dentist and hospital bills. Family members and friends usually are willing to wait.

Your future is bright. You CAN make it!
Prioritize your debt now!

Determine How Much You Can Pay

*N*ow it's time to organize a payment schedule. Writing down your plan will help you achieve it. Use notebook paper and allow enough space to include the number of months to fulfill your plan. For each creditor, list the payment planned, the amount paid, and the new balance due after the payment was made.

Do this with each creditor for each month a payment is due, until the debt with that particular creditor is erased. One way to gain some quick personal satisfaction is to pay off the smallest bill with the highest rate of interest first. Once that debt has been satisfied, take the payment from it, add it to the payment for the second highest interest rate, and apply the money on it. When that loan has been repaid, combine the original payment money from debt #1 and debt #2 and add it to the original money for payment on debt #3. You soon see your cash available for payments increase and your monthly payment going more and more for principle repayment and less for interest expense.

Recording your payments will give you a sense of achievement and satisfaction. Watching the balances diminish will give you an excitement that will help you stick to your goal.

The next step is to decide how much you can pay. Once you have listed everyone you owe, determine how much you can pay each creditor and how long it will take to pay back each debt. Generally it is preferable to limit the amount of credit you owe (excluding your home mortgage) to no more than 10% of your monthly take-home pay. Of course, it's even better to have no debt and be in a position to pay cash for all expenditures. That should be your goal. Following that, your goal should be to own your own home free and clear. A no debt lifestyle is not only good, but also achievable.

If your family has $2,200 a month after taxes and a charitable tithe, keep your credit payments under $220 per month ($2,200 x 0.10 = $220). But if you already have numerous debts, figure out a way to use 25% of your monthly take-home pay for paying back your monthly debts. You usually need 75% of your income to maintain your necessary daily living expenses. Even better, live on 50% of your income and use the other 50% to become debt free.

However, if your living expenses cannot be reduced at this time, a family earning $2,200 a month probably needs to keep $1,650 ($2,200 X 0.75 = $1,650) for basic living expenses. That leaves $ ($2,200 X 0.25 = $550) for debt repayment.

If your minimum monthly payments add up to $696, for example, you must find ways to increase the money available for debt repayment.

Now let's talk about paying back your debts. By now you should have a clear picture of how much money you can manage to pay back and when you will be able to pay it back. The next step is to decide how much you will pay each creditor and how long it will take to pay each creditor. Try to set up your plan so you pay your creditors back within one to three years, or less, of course, depending upon the size of your obligations.

The debt payment plan can be done in several ways.

You may choose to give each creditor an equal amount.

You may choose to pay a larger portion to the creditors you owe the most money—a smaller amount to those you owe the least.

You could choose to pay back a percentage of the total monthly obligation based on the amount of money available for debt payments.

Or you can choose to do a variation of the first three, including repaying the debt obligation with the highest interest expense.

Below are examples using each of the first three methods of debt repayment. Each is based on a situation in which a family has only $500 each month to repay debts.

ALTERNATIVE A

Pay each creditor equal amounts.

Debts	Amount Owed	Amount Required	Amount Can Pay
Auto Loan	$10,000.00	$500.00	$100.00
Credit Card # 1	$5,000.00	$150.00	$100.00
Personal Loan	$7,000.00	$200.00	$100.00
Credit Card # 2	$3,000.00	$90.00	$100.00
Department Store	$2,000.00	$60.00	$100.00
Total	**$27,000.00**	**$1,000.00**	**$500.00**

The amount available from monthly income for debt repayment is $500. The family pays each creditor an equal amount: $500/5 = $100 per month.

ALTERNATIVE B

Pay the percentage of total debt represented by each individual debt.

DEBTS	AMOUNT OWED	PERCENTAGE OF DEBT OWED	AMOUNT REQUIRED	AMOUNT CAN PAY
Auto Loan	$10,000.00	37%	$500.00	$ 185.00
Credit Card # 1	$5,000.00	18%	$150.00	$90.00
Personal Loan	$7,000.00	26%	$200.00	$ 130.00
Credit Card # 2	$3,000.00	11%	$ 90.00	$55.00
Department Store	$2,000.00	8%	$ 60.00	$40.00
Total	**$27,000.00**	**100%**	**$1,000.00**	**$500.00**

To determine the percentage of debt owed, make the following calculation:

Amount owed/total debt = percentage of total debt owed

Example: Auto Loan/total debt = $10,000/$27,000 = 0.37 or 37%

To determine the amount the consumer can pay, make this calculation:

Total amount can pay X percentage of total debt owed = amount can pay

Example: $500 X .37 = $185

ALTERNATIVE C

Pay a percentage of the total monthly obligation based on the amount of money available for debt payments.

DEBTS	AMOUNT OWED	AMOUNT REQUIRED	PRORATED PAYMENT
Auto Loan	$10,000.00	500 x .50	$250.00
Credit Card # 1	$5,000.00	150 x .50	$75.00
Personal Loan	$7,000.00	200 x .50	$100.00
Credit Card # 2	$3,000.00	90 x .50	$45.00
Department Store	$2,000.00	60 x .50	$30.00
Total	**$27,000.00**	**$1,000.00**	**$500.00**

The family has $500 per month available for debt payments. This is 50% of the amount required. Each creditor is offered a prorated payment of 50% of his or her regular monthly payment.

Your future is bright.
You CAN make it! Determine
how much you can pay now!

Create a Payoff Plan

*S*et up your debt-payment plan. The best way to keep your plan simple is to use a spreadsheet (e.g., Excel) or purchase paper with prelined columns. Write the creditor's name in the first column. Figure the percentage of total debt owed each creditor and write it in the second column.

Write the dollar amount you can pay each creditor each month in the next column. If the creditor accepts your plan, write the actual amount you will pay each creditor in the appropriate monthly columns. The key is to know what your income is, and to preplan where your debt repayment spending should be. If you don't know what's coming in, and when and where it should go out, then you will always be caught with not enough cash and creditors screaming for their money.

This might be difficult, but you will have to get this amount out of your monthly income. Divide this figure into the total amount you owe to arrive at the number of months it will take you to become debt free. Interest will add to the time schedule, but the answer you get gives you the approximate amount of time for your debt-repayment plan. The following options may help you repay debts on a monthly basis.

Assess the damage. Make a complete list of all your credit cards and loans (automobile, mortgage, student loans, etc.). Include how much you owe, the monthly payment and the interest rate. If you don't receive a monthly statement for a particular loan, call the lender for all the information.

Pay the most expensive loan first. Make the minimum monthly payments on all your debts except the one with the highest interest rate. Put as much money as you can toward this debt each month until it is paid off. Then apply the payments you were making on that debt toward the loan with the next highest interest rate, and so on. Note: pay credit card bills promptly to reduce the average daily balance on which you're charged.

Transfer your debts to a low-interest-rate credit card. The higher the interest rate, the more money the loan is costing you. Find a card with a low interest rate, and then contact that credit card company to arrange transfer of your other debts to this card.

Cut up the high-rate cards you've paid off so you won't use them again. Also, call or write these credit card companies to cancel the cards. Otherwise you might continue to receive new cards as the old ones expire.

Have a yard sale. What do you own? Which of these can you do without? Notice, I didn't say "want to do without." Most people have no idea of what they can do without until they try. Don't think of how much you will lose on what you paid for the item you are selling. Think of how much you will gain that can be immediately applied to your debt reduction. Your attitude about this will determine your success in working your way out of debt.

Keep a record of your current living expenses for a month. Look for ways to reduce your expenses so you can use the extra money to clear up debts.

Consider selling assets. What assets do you own? Do you have a savings account or stocks and bonds you could cash in to help pay off your debts? Do you have a television, furniture, stereo, car, jewelry or antiques? Could you cash in or borrow against the cash value of your insurance policy?

Increase your income. An extra paycheck will help maintain your present lifestyle while you pay back your debts. However, additional money does NOT cure poor management habits.

- Get a second part-time job.
- Deliver deli sandwiches or pizza.
- Work all available overtime.
- Take in a boarder or a roommate.
- Have a garage sale twice a year. One person's junk is another person's treasure!
- Sell assets (toys, unused household items, CDs and old LPs, clothing, shoes, extra vehicles, boats, property, etc.).
- Ask for a raise.

- Attend school part time to gain new job skills.
- Family jobs in the neighborhood (mowing lawns, trimming hedges, painting, etc.).
- Deliver the paper or local phone books.
- Sell your goods on ebay (They will sell practically anything for you!).

Your future is bright.
You CAN make it!
Create a payoff plan now!

Get Professional Assistance

You may have a heavy load of debt. It is crushing you and getting larger. Its snowball effect is growing every day. You know it, but don't know what to do about it. Debt can be overwhelming because of the large amount and just because of the embarrassment. I know. I've been there. You know you need some help, but you seem to be paralyzed because of it. You know you need to take some sort of action now, but the very thing that can help you turn your debt around seems to keep you from doing so.

You may hope there is a way out, but because you are too close to it, you cannot see the forest for the trees. This is why you need someone disconnected from you emotionally and financially to help give you another perspective on where you are and what you should do. A third party can view your situation from afar and give you the proper subjective counsel you need right now.

When you are caught up in debt, seek help. When there seems to be no way out, seek help. Even before you are at your wit's end, or before you think it is out of control, seek experienced help. Yes, I know how embarrassing it may be to actually tell someone else about your debt problem, especially when you have been careless and irresponsible with your credit. The feeling of shame can keep many people from seeking experienced help, but don't let it stop you! Whatever your hesitation has been, do NOT let it stop you from getting help and learning to become financially responsible.

Contact your creditors. Most creditors will try to help you work it out. The first contact with a collection agency may try to tell you that it must be paid in full immediately. Don't give up. This is what they are trained to tell you. Keep trying. Lenders are not stupid and would rather extend your loan term or reduce your payments than receive nothing at all. I do not mean to suggest that your credit history may not be harmed, because if you are a slow payer, this will be listed in your file. But there is some flexibility between full payment and complete default.

A quick word about seeking credit. Too many inquiries for your credit report can "harm" your credit rating. It may look as though you are applying for credit from too many sources and are overextending yourself. One potential problem for you is that inquiries may be made without your knowledge even when you haven't applied for credit. If you shop around for a new car, every dealer you visit may make an inquiry to see if you are a customer worth pursuing. They get the information they need to make an inquiry from the driver's license you show to take a test drive.

When shopping around for a bank loan, your credit report can be pulled without your knowledge. These inquiries stay on your credit record for up to two years. A bit of timely advice—avoid applying for a lot of credit at one time. Resist giving sellers personal information they need to make a credit check, unless you are serious about buying.

 ## When there seems to be no way out, seek help.

When you have decided to change credit card companies, be sure to notify the company of your intention to cancel. Otherwise it may look as though you have a lot of credit available to you, and you may not get new credit you seek in the future. A credit report will list all your cards and your full credit line, whether you actually use them or not. Better yet, cancel your credit cards in favor of paying cash with a debit card.

Let me tell you now that there is a lot of BAD advice out there. Talk to a consumer creditor counselor. But be very careful! Many are out just to separate you from your money. Beware of those that would suggest a consolidation loan at high interest rates. Beware of those that would take your cash, saying they will make your payments for you, but keep a percentage of what you send to them for yourself. Beware of those that would try to hide under the nonprofit status.

There are many, many phony so called credit-counseling companies across the country. These counterfeit services get nonprofit status from the IRS and then run ads pretending to help you get out of debt. They charge enormous fees that actually put you in deeper debt and take your money from you. They are nothing more than rotten companies that prey upon people in financial trouble like yourself!

The only consumer counselors whose integrity I would trust are the following. This information comes from their Web site.

"Founded in 1951, the National Foundation for Credit Counseling (NFCC)™, Inc., through its Member agencies, sets the national standard for quality credit counseling, debt reduction services and education for financial wellness. NFCC is the nation's largest and longest serving national nonprofit credit counseling network. With more than 1,000 community-based agency offices across the country, NFCC Members help over 1.5 million households annually. NFCC Members, often known as Consumer Credit Counseling Service (CCCS) or other names, can be identified by the NFCC Member seal. This seal signifies high standards for agency accreditation, counselor certification and policies that ensure free or low-cost confidential services. NFCC Member offices can be reached in communities nation-wide, toll-free at 1-800-388-2227, or on-line at: www.nfcc.org NFCC is located in Silver Spring, Maryland."

Your future is bright.
You CAN make it!
Get professional help now!

Communicate
with Your Creditors

Now it is time to communicate with your creditors. Yes, of course, the conversations won't be pleasant, but it's time for you to take control. It is hoped they will be impressed with the fact that you have developed a plan. They will be even more impressed as you send them the regular monthly payments you have promised. Also, tell them that if something happens that would delay one of your payments, you will contact them ahead of the date when the payment is due.

Now that you have worked out a plan, destroy all your credit cards. Do not apply for any more loans except in extreme emergencies. Also, make sure to contact each creditor and explain your plan.

Creditors will generally be more responsive to your proposal if you take the initiative to contact them first and express a sincere desire to pay your obligations. If you cannot visit your creditor, call or write a letter. In your letter be sure to include the following:

- Why you fell behind in your payments (such as loss of job, illness, divorce, death in the family, medical bills or poor money-management skills).
- Your current income.
- Your other obligations.
- How you plan to bring this debt up-to-date and keep it current.
- The exact amount you will be able to pay each month.

Once the creditor has agreed to your repayment plan, make every effort to uphold your end of the bargain. If you fail to follow the plan you and your creditors have agreed upon, you harm your chances of getting future credit. Tell your creditor about any changes that may affect your payment agreement.

Remember, you owe them the money. It is not their fault that you are having difficulty repaying the money you owe. Your attitude, at all times, should be checked with this in mind. Keep a great attitude—one that sincerely desires to repay in full all debts. Be pleasant, upbeat and positive, and let your creditors know you are motivated to pay them all you owe. They will appreciate it.

Your future is bright. You CAN make it!
Communicate with your creditors now!

◈ PRACTICAL APPLICATION 15

Determine and
Reduce Your Time Goal

Write down the number of months it will take to become debt free, based on your initial plan. Now cut the goal in half. Now this may surprise you. Just do it: cut the goal in half. If you have determined it will take four years, or 48 months, to get out of debt, then write down a figure of one-half that time. You may think I'm crazy, but let me give you a formula for cutting your debt repayment in half.

George Fooshee, Jr. gives this illustration in his book, *You Can Be Financially Free* (published in 1976, Fleming H. Revell Company). Assume you have set aside $111.23 monthly to repay your debt of $5,000 with an interest rate of 12%. It will take you five years of monthly payments to pay off this debt. To cut your time schedule in half, it would take a monthly payment of $193.75 for just two-and-a-half years.

Total cost to you, including all debt repayment and interest charges over a 30-month period, would be $5,812.50. Taking five years (60 months) to pay the same $5,000 back at $111.23 a month would cost you a total of $6,673.80. That's $861.30 more in interest and that should give you sufficient motivation to look hard at this plan.

Here's how it works. Subtract the $111.23 monthly payment from the $193.75. Your additional monthly cost to pay off your debt in half the time is not twice the $111.23, but only $82.52. The only way I know of to save money in paying off debts is to pay them off faster. The faster you pay, the less it costs.

"But," you ask, "how can we come up with $82.52 a month above our payment of $111.23? Haven't we cut our budget to a bare minimum?" Perhaps so. The solution to your problem will depend totally upon the creativity of your family.

What is the objective? In this case it is to cut your debt repayment time in half. Expressing this goal in positive terms would be to say you are going to get out of debt twice as fast as you had planned. To do that, you do not have to double your income or cut your expenses in half. In the illustration I used, you need only $82.52 more each month to pay on your debt.

One idea is to find a family in your neighborhood who wants their house cleaned and who would be willing to pay your family to do the job at a family hourly rate. Investing every Saturday to cut your debt-repayment time in half would be a worthwhile family project.

Weekend part-time work is another alternative to earning extra money. Keep your eyes open for lawns that need mowing or shrubs that need trimming, right in your own neighborhood. You'll be surprised how much you're worth if you're willing to invest a few hours a week. Imaginative ways to earn extra money are limited only by a lack of creativity and desire.

Another way to hasten your escape from debt is to agree in advance to add any extra income to debt repayment. This includes raises, bonuses, tax refunds, garage sale income or any other extra income that comes into your family.

Your future is bright.
You CAN make it! Determine
and reduce your time goal now!

Stay Focused on Your Plan

*I*t is important to your future well being to stay focused on your plan. You may be tempted again and again to quit. Don't do it! Each missed payment will set you back in reaching your goal. Starting something is easier than finishing. Many more start the race than finish the race. Life is littered with dropouts who quit when the going gets rough. Tough people are determined not to quit until they reach their goal.

Escaping debt will require persistence. Some new attitudes about your way of living will be essential, but you can do it!

What does it mean to stay focused on your plan? Does it require a lot of effort on your part? Certainly! Daily effort. Wise financial decisions must be made every day.

Here are some descriptive words to make you aware of what is necessary in keeping you focused on your plan:

- Continuance
- Deciding
- Determination
- Doggedness
- Endurance
- Fix on
- Fortitude
- Immovability
- Making up your mind
- Perseverance
- Persistence
- Purpose
- Resolve
- Settle on
- Stamina
- Steadfastness
- Tenacity
- Unchanging
- Unwavering

The Bible has some things to say about being persistent, staying focused and persevering.

Ephesians 6:18

"With all prayer and petition pray at all times in the Spirit, and with this in view, be on the alert with all perseverance and petition for all the saints" (*NASB*).

Hebrews 12:1

"Run with perseverance the race marked out for us."

2 Peter 1:5, 6

"For this very reason, make every effort to add to your faith goodness; and to goodness, knowledge; and to knowledge, self-control; and to self-control, perseverance; and to perseverance, godliness."

James 1:4

"Perseverance must finish its work so that you may be mature and complete, not lacking anything."

Revelation 2:19

"I know your deeds, your love and faith, your service and perseverance, and that you are now doing more than you did at first."

People all want to be successful in whatever they set out to do. The successful people of the world achieve their desired success as the end result of daily, sometimes hourly persistence—staying at the task until it's done. It's amazing how many weaknesses and inadequacies you can overcome if you are persistent. You can change your entire financial picture and change the rest of your life by staying focused on a *get out of debt and get my life back* plan.

Staying the course is not a gift I can give you. It's up to you alone. Persistence is not inherited. It's a state of mind, an attitude. And because it is an attitude, it's something each of us can develop.

The first step to staying on course is knowing exactly what you want. If you have only a vague idea of where you're going, it's easy to give up at the first sign of a problem. You must have a clear goal, an intensive desire to reach it, and a definite plan that shows the path that must be followed.

You must also have faith in yourself. If you believe you can succeed in the task you have set for yourself, setbacks along the way won't cause you to give up. You'll seldom reach a goal without stumbling along the way; faith in yourself enables you to get up and keep going.

When you're developing your plan, spend some time researching so you have confidence your approach will work. Knowing your plan is sound, because it's based on accurate knowledge (whether that knowledge came from books, experience or observations), makes it easier to *persist* and reach your set goal.

Dennis Waitley, one of the most sought-after keynote speakers and productivity consultants in the world today, graphically states, "Most people are like an oak tree in a flower pot; they never grow to their full potential." He states that people tend to remain cramped by poor self-belief and compressed by negative self-talk. These people list reasons why they can't do it.

Few launch into the exhilarating experience of breaking their own expectations with a "Yes, I can" attitude. If you will approach your overwhelming debt with a "Yes, I can become debt free!" attitude, the battle is already half over.

Leonard Ravenhill tells a fascinating story about a group of tourists in a European village. One of them asked an elderly villager, "Have any great people been born in this village?" The old villager paused and then replied, "No! Only babies." Successful people stretch for success—they dig deep into the possibilities of their God-given potential.

With regard to personal finances, successful people are not better than other people; they are ordinary people who have extraordinary attitudes; they are the people who carry the "Yes, I Can" attitude into everything they do.

Faith in yourself enables you to get up and keep going.

Remember Sir Winston Churchill, who said, "If you believe you can, you will. If you believe you can't, you won't. Either way it's your choice."

"Anything less than a conscious commitment to the important is an unconscious commitment to the unimportant."—*Stephen R. Covey,* First Things First, *Simon & Schuster*

Here are two simple rules to keep you focused on your "get out of debt" plan.

Rule 1: Take one more step.

Rule 2: When you don't think you can take one more step, refer to Rule 1.

You can rescue your life and liberate your future if you will:

- Plan Purposefully
- Prepare Prayerfully
- Proceed Positively
- Continue Diligently
- Pursue Persistently

Your future is bright.
You CAN make it!
Stay focused on your plan now!

Keep Your Goal in Mind

*B*ecoming completely debt free is your goal. To get out of debt, you have to stop charging and start taking charge of your spending habits. If you use credit cards without paying the balance monthly, owe money on a loan or are paying off a home mortgage, you're a debtor. Most Americans are in debt; if you're not, some might think you're downright unpatriotic.

Many economists believe that indebtedness keeps our country financially on the move. When was the last time you saw a bank advertisement encouraging you to save? The theme of our consumer-driven economy is *borrow* and *spend*. It's not popular to suggest becoming debt free. However, freedom from debt speaks for itself; in a word, it is freedom.

Financial institutions need money (deposits) to loan to consumers. This money can be borrowed from the federal government or from depositors. Yet you rarely see advertisements trying to convince you and me to deposit our money (a loan to them) in these institutions. Why? Because knowledgeable people already know that it makes good sense to invest their money wisely and not to spend every penny they earn. They don't have to be convinced to make smart investment decisions. Yet, the financial institutions spend millions of dollars appealing to those individuals who do not make wise financial decisions. They become easy targets for credit card companies, debt consolidation advertisements and other consumer loans of all kinds.

Although not a popular theme, and despite the fact that some think they're in debt so deep they can't ever get out, becoming debt free is a worthy, realistic and attainable goal. Getting rid of your debt isn't always easy. The process, however, is actually very simple. Allow no more debt—duh! That means no bank or family loans, and tear up the credit cards.

Develop a balanced budget that allows each creditor to receive as much as possible. Start retiring the debt now. Begin with high-interest debts first. If they're all high-interest, pay the smallest balance first. Once it's paid off, put all the available money on the next, and so on. Most families can be debt free in three or four years. Budgeting is simply telling your money where you want it to go instead of your money telling you where it went after the fact.

I told you it was simple. However, it's not easy. It requires real determination and consistency. If you're having difficulty paying those you owe, keep in mind that it's always better to run toward your creditors than away from them. Creditors who've been ignored don't like to negotiate. However, most creditors will respond positively to a written plan that includes how much you owe and a copy of your budget.

Budgeting is simply telling your money where you want it to go instead of your money telling you where it went after the fact.

Create a detailed repayment schedule that shows exactly how much you are able to pay them each month. Sometimes an objective third party might be necessary to require compliance with the agreements, as I've already stated. Consumer credit counseling organizations around the country can help you do this.

If debt collectors are hounding you, you can do something about it. The Fair Debt Collection Practices Act, passed by Congress in 1977, prohibits certain methods of debt collection. Also, you could report your problem to your state attorney general's office. Many states have their own debt collection laws, and the attorney general can help define your rights.

Remember that nothing positive will happen with your financial problems until you start taking charge of your debts.

Your future is bright.
You CAN make it!
Keep your goal in mind now!

Decrease Your Expenses
and Build Cash

*I*f your spending is out of control, it is time for a little austerity. This will probably mean changing your lifestyle, decreasing your expenses and paying with cash. Ask for help and seek advice about your situation. Consumer Credit Counseling Services is a good place to start.

Other than for purchasing a home, don't borrow money at all. But if you insist on doing so, an important rule for borrowing is: Never borrow to buy depreciating items. Such things as new cars, furniture, clothes, appliances, boats and luxury items should not be purchased until money is available to pay for them. Don't borrow to go on vacation, to invest in the stock market, to get married, to keep up with the Joneses, to gamble, to give the kids a head start, to bail someone else out of a jam, to buy wants, because you want some extra cash, etc.

Consider the many ways you can cut expenses, gain lots of cash, and use the newly found cash to pay down debt.

As you pay off smaller debts, don't start paying less each month on your overall debt. Put that money toward another bill.

Assess the damage. Make a complete list of all your credit cards and loans (automobile, mortgage, student loans, etc.). Include how much you owe, the monthly payment and the interest rate. If you don't receive a monthly statement for a particular loan, call the lender for all the information.

Avoid cosigning or guaranteeing a loan for someone. Your signature obligates you as if you were the primary borrower. You can't be sure that the other person will pay. Proverbs 17:18 speaks clearly to this situation: "A man lacking in judgment strikes hands in pledge and puts up security for his neighbor."

Avoid further credit and debt while you are paying off your bills.

Avoid joint obligations with people who have questionable spending habits, even a spouse. If you incur a joint debt, you're probably liable for it all if the other person defaults.

Avoid large rent or house payments. Obligate yourself only for what you can now afford and increase your mortgage payments only as your income increases. Consider refinancing your house if your payments are unmanageable.

Avoid sales. Buying a $500 item on sale for $400 isn't a $100 savings if you didn't need the item to begin with. It's spending $400 unnecessarily.

Barter your skills for someone else's skills.

Be aware of your spending habits. Stick to the lessons you have learned about how you got into debt and how you're living to get out of it. You will probably discover along the way the things that are really important to you, and what is not so important anymore.

Be patient. You probably didn't get yourself into this situation overnight, so you won't get out of it that quickly either.

Before you purchase that "must have" item, wait six months and think it through again.

Bring your lunch to work.

Buy from thrift bakery outlets.

Buy used rather than new. Cars, furniture, computers, stereo equipment, televisions and appliances can all be found at substantial discounts in the want ads and at garage sales and swap meets.

Charge items only if you can afford to pay for them now. If you don't currently have the cash, don't charge based on future income—sometimes future income doesn't materialize. An alternative is to toss all your credit cards in a drawer (or in the garbage) and to commit to living without credit for a while.

Control impulse buying.

Coupon clipping: Some coupons are worth the clipping effort and others aren't. The most valuable coupons can be identified by one of the following: biggest percentage, largest dollar value, or items used at least once a week.

Create a realistic budget and spending plan and stick to it. This means periodically checking it and readjusting your figures and spending habits.

Credit cards: Don't fall into the minimum trap. If you just pay the minimum on credit card bills, it will take you 20 years or more to pay them off. That means you'll pay more than five times the actual debt in interest.

Credit cards: Before you spend one nickel, make sure it was preplanned in your budget.

Credit cards: Dump the highest rate debts first. The key to getting out of debt is to methodically pay down the bills with the highest interest rates first.

Credit cards: Never use your credit cards to buy anything that is not in your budget for the month. You should, of course, have a budget first.

Credit cards: pay off the balance in full each month.

Credit cards: The first month you're unable to pay the credit cards, destroy them. If you take these vows, you'll never have a problem with credit cards.

Cut up all charge cards (department stores, gas cards, etc.).

Cut up the high-rate cards you've paid off so you won't use them again. Also, call or write these credit card companies to cancel the cards. Otherwise you might continue to receive new cards as the old ones expire.

Cut your cost of transportation. Most people own "more car" than they really need, and the money usually goes out faster than the car anyway. Save a bundle by buying used, and maybe making public transportation a regular part of your routine, which will save you even more.

Cut expensive entertainment costs by renting videos rather than going to movies, eating at cheaper restaurants, eating out less frequently, and brown-bagging it to work. Take food out rather than eating at the restaurant to save on tips and drinks.

Cut your housing costs. You can do it by renting a place with fewer amenities (are you really using that weight lifting room anyway?). And in terms of buying, you're looking at greater expense initially, but home ownership can be a good investment that grows with time.

Deposit money into a savings account regularly and declare it off limits for withdrawals.

Develop a balanced budget that allows each creditor to receive as much as possible.

Develop a strategy. Without a strategic plan for getting there, reaching your goal of financial freedom will remain a dream. A plan turns a dream into a goal. Having a plan liberates you from depending on willpower. Don't depend upon your newfound willpower to curb your spending. Willpower is unreliable emotional fuel. When you have it, it can get you going at breakneck speed, but once the emotion is gone, you fizzle. Willpower is not something on which you should rely.

Develop an awareness of the difference between *wants* and *needs*.

Ditch the car and take the bus.

Do a spending record and a spending plan. Paying attention to your spending patterns will help you in the process of paying your bills with greater control and adherence to your goals.

Do your own chores and repairs instead of hiring them out.

Don't be so quick to pay down your mortgage. If you pour all your cash into your mortgage, you'll have no cushion to fall back on. Better to borrow as much as you can afford when you are buying a house. And with today's low interest rates you can probably get a better return on your money with other investments.

Don't expect instant miracles. Getting out of debt will take discipline and time. Be patient and stay focused on your goals.

Don't impulse buy. When you see something you hadn't planned to buy, don't purchase it on the spot. Go home and think it over. It's unlikely you'll return to the store and buy it.

Don't make high-risk investments, such as investments in speculative real estate, penny stocks and junk bonds. Invest conservatively, opting for certificates of deposit, money market funds and government bonds.

Drive your car an extra year or two before you replace it with a new or used one.

Eat oatmeal instead of expensive prepackaged cereal. It's both healthy and filling.

Eat out less and at home more. The cost of food at restaurants, especially when you add in the cost of service, really adds up. Plus, both the food *and* the service are usually better at home anyway.

Eating in: Use or freeze everything you buy. When you buy the ten-pound bag of potatoes and three pounds go bad, did you really get a bargain? With the exception of using those sprouting spuds for science projects, the extra three pounds you paid for is only going to make your garbage heavier.

Eating at restaurants: Drink water. I know this sounds boring, but did you know that the mark-up on drinks is significantly higher than the rest of the menu? And I don't mean to be a killjoy, but do you remember those grade school projects where you would put your lost teeth in a glass of Coke? Let's face it, water is a great deal all around.

Extra income: Peddle your skills. Whether you have a full-time job or you're not working, you always have a little bit of extra time. You can earn a pretty high per-hour wage if you hone and market one of your skills, such as carpentry, baby-sitting (you can even combine it with looking after your own children), handyman tasks, painting or housekeeping. You would be surprised at how many people would rather pay you than a professional (no offense) who will inevitably charge more.

Evaluate your monthly income sources. Record any money you've earned (paycheck, bonuses, freelance income, tips, etc.). Calculate anything you might have received from investments. Also check to see how much you have in your savings and investments (money not available to spend).

Expect the unexpected. Build a cash cushion you can get to quickly in case of an emergency. If you don't have such a cushion, a broken furnace or other calamity will wreck your budget and push you into a seat on the ship of credit card slaves.

Fast food: Don't order value meals. This applies especially to those people who would have ordered the burger and a drink, but then see that for only a few cents more, they get the fries, too. That timeless truth prevails: there's no such thing as a free fry. So you end up paying more than you intended and digesting the fries, which for some of us, can be construed as a definite liability.

Find alternatives to spending money. For a friend's birthday, take him or her on a picnic rather than to an expensive restaurant. When someone suggests you meet for lunch, propose meeting at the museum on its free day or going for a walk in the park. Instead of buying books and CDs or renting videos from a video store, borrow them free at your local library.

Forget about "buying now, paying later." Save now and buy when you have the cash and it's on sale for half price! It will end up costing you twice as much because it was not on sale and the interest expense ends up doubling the original price!

Get a handle on your spending. If you are like most people, you squander away thousands of dollars without much thought to what you are buying. By making a budget, you can find out where the money goes—and start directing more of the wasted dollars to savings.

Get at least three prices for the same item from different sources.

Get in shape: Ride your bicycle to work.

Get medical insurance. Even a stopgap policy with a large deductible can help in a medical crisis. You can't avoid medical emergencies, but living without medical insurance is an invitation to financial ruin.

Get the most for your money. Shop for value whenever you can. Go to warehouse-type stores, buy items (ones you actually need) in bulk, wait to buy stuff on sale (especially furniture and clothing), get last year's model (car, appliance) this year. It's probably just as good, and the price will be better.

Go shopping with a list and buy only those items.

Gifts: Buy them all year long and keep a gift box. Last-minute gift purchases are usually more expensive because you can't shop around for a better deal. So institute a gift box that allows you to collect good buys as you go, then give them when an occasion arises, such as children's birthday parties, hostess gifts, anniversaries or weddings.

Grow your own garden.

If you finish paying a car loan, keep writing that check every month and invest it in mutual funds.

Improve your gas mileage. Buy an energy-efficient car, check the air in your tires frequently and slow down on the highway.

Incorporate a "get rid of it" box. How often do you put something away and say to yourself, "I wonder if I'll ever use this?" What if, instead of putting those things back, you toss them into a box that gets emptied once or twice a year. That way, you have several months to retrieve the item if you change your mind. But if it stays in the box, then you either sell it or donate it and take the write-off. This technique helps in at least three ways: it's financially smart, it reduces the amount of clutter in your house and it facilitates a happier marriage.

Increase you insurance deductibles.

Inform your kids and or your spouse, if you have a family. Everyone in the family will have to participate—no one person can do all the work alone. So make sure your spouse, and the kids, understand that the family is having financial difficulties and agree together to take the steps that will lead to recovery.

Keep a written account of your progress. Set financial goals. This will help increase your savings and give you peace of mind and less stress about money issues. Progress may seem slow at first, especially if the debt load is large, but it's a great feeling to whittle away at that list of creditors!

Keep track of all expenses for at least a month. You may discover some holes in your budget that can be plugged up.

Know how to avoid good buys. The only way to conquer impulse buying is through self-discipline. Without discipline, no budget will help. *"By what a man is overcome, by this he is enslaved"* (2 Peter 2:19; *NASB*).

Impulse buying is another form of a get rich quick mentality. Scripture says, *"The plans of the diligent lead surely to advantage, but everyone who is hasty comes surely to poverty"* (Proverbs 21:5).

Lottery tickets—stop wasting your money.

Live within your means. Just look at all the people who earn less than you. See how financially secure and happy they are? You can do it with just a few new habits plugged into your routine, such as a spending plan.

Look around for better insurance rates.

Magic rules do not solve financial troubles.

Maintain an impulse list. Write down what you want, and get at least two additional prices. Never have more than one item on your list. Do you know why? Because long before you will have found two prices on the first item, you will probably find two more items you would rather have.

Make a plan to pay off your debts and write it down. If it isn't in writing, it doesn't exist. If you put your plans in writing, you are more likely to follow through on your debt management.

Make a resolution that you will NOT overspend ever again.

Make all gifts: birthday, Christmas, wedding, etc.

Make long-distance calls on weekends, early in the morning and late at night. Or better yet, e-mail or write letters.

Make one trip to the grocery store each week.

Make plans for life after debt. Don't go crazy and run up charge cards as soon as everything is paid off. The last thing you want to do is get yourself into deep debt again. You will probably find that you need to do some things that had to be deferred while you were paying off debts—for us it was catching up on dental work and replacing some appliances.

Make your own coffee instead of stopping by for a latte on the way to work.

Minimize your debt. It is important to your financial health and it can turn your financial life around.

Move in with your parents (but only if you are single).

Never buy anything unless you have budgeted for it.

Pay less on your grocery bill. Eat rice and beans (you will not starve or die!).

Pay your credit cards off every month, no exceptions.

Pay only cash (but save your receipts).

Pay off the most expensive loan first. Make the minimum monthly payments on all your debts except the one with the highest interest rate. Put as much money as you can toward this debt each month, until it is paid off. Then apply the payments you were making on that debt toward the loan with the next highest interest rate, and so on. Note: Pay credit card bills promptly to reduce the average daily balance on which you're charged.

Pay yourself first (well, actually second). After giving to the Lord, use 10% of your income for investments to build your equity. You can learn to live on less if you take the money out of your paycheck before it even gets into your hand. If cutting your salary creates a problem, then make a commitment to invest any pay increases you receive so you don't have to make cuts.

Plan for the future. Set achievable goals, such as spending less than you earn each month, and making regular deposits into an investment fund.

Practice utility control. Install a water-saving shower head, buy energy-saving light bulbs, turn the temperature dial up on your refrigerator and down on your water heater, and turn off the lights and television when you leave the room. Little economies add up to big savings over the course of a year. Turn down the thermostat in winter, and turn off the air conditioner in summer. Put on a sweater in winter and use a fan in the summer to heat and cool your body inexpensively.

Record your monthly expenses. Fixed expenses: mortgage or rent payments, auto and educational loans and insurance. Variable expenses: utility bills, clothing, transportation, entertainment and dining.

Ride public transportation to work or carpool with coworkers. You'll save on gas and wear and tear on your car.

Retail Stores: Make offers on floor models. Floor models may be discontinued or have dings that could easily by hidden with strategic plant or corner placement.

Save any extra money that comes your way from second jobs, rebates, bonuses, medical-insurance reimbursements and tax refunds.

Save food costs. Buy on sale, clip coupons, buy in bulk, purchase generic brands, eat less expensive cuts of meat and don't frequent convenience stores.

Save on supplies. Use sponges rather than paper towels, use a multipurpose cleaner rather than several specialized ones, and recycle newspapers, bottles and cans.

Save on vacations. Explore local recreational sites, ask your travel agent about special deals and visit vacation spas and resorts off-season.

Seek professional help. Debt Counselors of America assist consumers with their financial problems. Call 1-800-680-3328 to request information or visit their Web site.

Sell the nice vehicle and settle for good, used, reliable transportation.

Shop around for lower auto and home insurance rates.

Shop at thrift clothing stores.

Some debt is bad. Don't borrow for things you consume quickly, such as clothes, meals and vacations. There's no quicker way to fall into debt abyss. Instead, put aside some cash each month for these items so you can pay the bill in full.

Some debt is good. Borrowing for a home, college or a maybe a car (0% financing) makes good sense. Just don't borrow more than you can afford to pay back.

Start and maintain an emergency cash fund. This is one of those payments from your monthly spending plan that you shouldn't skip. Once you've built it up to about three to six times your monthly income, keep it there and use it when, not if, your car needs repair or a medical emergency arises or you have to help out a loved one.

Stay at home. You'll save a ton of fuel expense.

Stay away from the convenience stores. Buy from discount grocery stores and outlets such as WINCO, Costco, Wal-Mart, etc.

Stay healthy. Eat right, exercise more, buy a few pieces of exercise equipment and drop the gym membership.

Stay out of the malls.

Stick to a spending plan. Have a list of needs, so that you don't find yourself buying "wants" and not have money for the things you truly need. Put some of your new-found "extra money" into savings, college or retirement funds. Create an emergency fund of at least three months take-home pay (more if you are self-employed).

Stop all long distance telephone calls.

Stop incurring debt. Cut out unnecessary spending and avoid impulse buying.

Stop spending!

Subtract credit card purchases in your checkbook register so you have money for the bill when it arrives.

Take advantage of free programs for kids at local libraries or community centers.

Track your cash flow. Use a small notebook to record the amount and category (food, clothing, etc.) of each purchase, no matter how small. Include check and credit card purchases. Do this every day for three months. Total each category at the end of the month. The information will be used to help you adjust your spending.

Track your expenses. It's a great way to develop better spending habits.

Transfer your debts to a low-interest-rate credit card. The higher the interest rate, the more money the loan is costing you. Find a card with a low interest rate, and then contact that credit card company to arrange transfer of your other debts to this card.

Use coupons, rebates, special promotions, price matching offers and discount shopper cards.

Vacations: try a home exchange. If you have friends who live in other cities or parts of the country, exchange homes for a week. It costs nothing to stay there and you get a much needed change of perspective.

Visit your local library. Many resources are available to give you the particulars on frugal and simple living. It's a great place to check out magazines, compact discs, cassettes, etc.

Wait at least 10 days to buy nonbudgeted items.

Watch where you borrow. It's convenient to borrow against your 401(k) or your home to pay off high-rate debt. But that can be dangerous. You could lose your home, or fall short of your investing goals at retirement.

Your future is bright.
You CAN make it!
Decrease your expenses
and build new cash now!

Control Your Personal Credit

*C*ontrol your credit intelligently. In the process of building our financial future, there are times when we ask another person or a financial institution to use their money for a limited period of time. This is borrowing or taking out a loan. Usually, the lender allows us to use their money in exchange for a percentage fee called interest. Our generation seems to be caught up in "easy credit" because of the ready money available.

Only a few people (if any) do not worry that money may be going out the door faster than it is coming in. Most Americans have revolving credit balances from credit cards and other retail establishments, and a small group are enslaved to mountainous consumer-debt burdens that eat at large parts of their income. It doesn't make much difference whether you are moderately in hock or in a deep hole—you can break the debt cycle.

At one time (a few years ago), it may have made some sense—on rare occasions—to borrow. You could deduct interest payments from your income taxes. With the cost of living running at 8–12% a year, you could repay your loans with cheaper dollars later, but now tax deductions for interest on consumer purchases have dried up; inflation seems to be under control (meaning that expensive dollars remain expensive) and you can't count on huge raises in personal income.

In spite of some lower interest rates that are available, credit card companies continue to charge extremely high interest on the unpaid balances. At the same time, passbook saving accounts pay so little it's hard to see an advantage to them. Falling behind on repaying lenders will only serve to hurt your credit rating. Late payments can remain on your credit file for seven years. Even if you do pay on time, having too much installment debt compromises your ability to borrow for something important in the future. If the whole country is in a recessionary economy, the last thing you should have is a lot of debt.

To be free from all those creditors, it is important to admit a problem in this area and then stop borrowing. You too, as others, may be a spendaholic. Do you have too many credit cards? Do you like to shop too much? Is it hard for you to resist a so-called bargain?

How much debt is too much? A call to a consumer credit counseling service yielded this advice. Spending more than 15–20% of net income on monthly debt payments, not including your payments on a home mortgage, is too much.

Easy availability of credit is partly to blame for a lot of the problem. Creditors are not the tight-fisted people they were years ago. At least twice each week, I get an offer in the mail for a card with a preapproved credit line. All I need to do is sign the offer and return it for instant credit. Potential creditors insure consumer credit with unparalleled leniency—after all, it's hard for them not to make money with interest rates of 18–19%.

People who use credit cards as a receipt process and then pay their outstanding balance in full each month avoid trouble. Credit card companies disguise potential debt problems. It is tough to spot trouble when the minimum monthly payment required reflects only 3–5% of the total balance. One can be dangerously in debt before any difficulties are noticed.

It is illegal for creditors to send you unsolicited credit cards, but they can increase the limits or lines of credit without asking. For people who have difficulty in controlling their spending habits, more credit means more debt, which means more trouble.

Your future is bright.
You CAN make it!
Control your personal credit now!

Manage Your Credit Record

Even if you have a spotless record, a lender may reject you just because you could borrow into oblivion. Cutting up old cards with the scissors alone just doesn't cut it. A person needs to write or call the issuer of the card, ask them to cancel your account and then ask them to notify the credit bureaus that your account has been "in good standing and closed by the borrower."

If you want advice or need special help, numerous nonprofit consumer credit counseling services are available. Check the telephone book for local chapters.

What Is Credit Scoring? You may not have heard of it, but make no mistake: Your credit score has been affecting your life for years.

You may not even know that you have a credit score, but you do; and it's used by credit card companies, home equity lenders, auto loan lenders and finance companies when you apply for credit or a loan. It is produced with a computer model created, most often, by Fair, Isaac & Co. (or "FICO," leading to the somewhat generic term "FICO score").

A credit score is intended to be a snapshot, or summary, of your credit history. A low score can mean you don't get a credit card or loan, or if you do, you will pay a higher interest rate. Some lenders use what it is called "risk-based pricing at the point of origination," which means the lender instantly approves or denies your application, using your credit score and other information to set the price for your loan.

We don't know exactly how a credit score is determined, but we do know that the following items are always considered important:

PAYMENT HISTORY (35%)

Your score is negatively affected if you have paid bills late, had an account sent to collection or declared bankruptcy. The more recent the problem, the lower the score—a 30-day late payment today hurts more than a bankruptcy five years ago.

OUTSTANDING DEBT (30%)

If the amount you owe is close to your credit limit, it is likely to have a negative effect on your score. A low balance on two cards is better than a high balance on one.

LENGTH OF YOUR CREDIT HISTORY (15%)

The longer your accounts have been open the better.

TYPES OF CREDIT IN USE (10%)

Loans from finance companies generally lower your credit score.

RECENT INQUIRIES ON YOUR REPORT (10%)

If you have recently applied for many new accounts, this will negatively affect your score. Among the items not considered are age, race, gender, education, national origin, marital status and receipt of public assistance.

THE RANGE OF SCORES

Credit scores range from 400 to 900, with the average around 700. According to the model, as your score increases, your risk of default decreases. Industry experience shows a direct correlation between low scores and high default rates.

This means you may have a hard time convincing a creditor to give you an affordable loan (or any loan at all) if your score is far below average. Just as your credit history can vary from credit bureau to credit bureau, so can your credit scores. It is possible to have a high score with one credit bureau and a low credit score with another, just as you might have a clean credit history with one bureau and a muddied record with another.

Wide-ranging credit scores are rare, however, although some lenders admit to seeing borrowers with scores that vary by 100 points or more. To combat this, a lender usually uses the middle score, but that can be of little comfort if you have scores of 550, 570 and 700, and the interest rate for a borrower with a score of 570 is two points higher than the rate for a borrower who scores 700.

Narrow ranges are more typical. For example, a person with good credit might have scores something like 685, 702 and 710.

Your future is bright.
You CAN make it!
Manage your credit record now!

Seek Higher Credit Scores

*C*an you do things to raise your credit score? You certainly can. Creditors are not required to tell you your credit score, nor does your credit report show your score.

1. PAY YOUR BILLS ON TIME

This is the single most important thing you can do. How you've paid your bills in the past is usually the best indicator of how you'll pay in the future. Be sure to pay at least the minimum amount required by the date it is due on your account statement or invoice.

You can always pay more (and should!), but you should never pay less than the minimum. Remember—being late on a payment is a negative mark on your credit record, even if you make up the payments later. If you don't pay your bills on time, you can start today! Credit scores emphasize your most recent payment record.

2. AUTOMATE TO BE ON TIME

There are some months when we all goof. We forget to pay the Visa bill. We forget to write a check to American Express.

One way to stop this from happening is to automate as many payments as possible—you can now authorize everyone from your health club to your mortgage lender to your utilities company to automatically deduct funds electronically from your checking account each month.

Then your only challenge is making sure the funds are there to cover those payments. (In fact, some lenders will give you a break on your interest rate for paying this way.)

3. DON'T ALLOW DELINQUENT PAYMENTS

If there is an instance when you are delinquent and you catch it quickly, don't immediately pay the late fee—first try to fight it to keep it from showing up on your credit report.

Call up and explain: You were out of the country. Your child was in the hospital. Often you can get away with one of these excuses because the lender wants to keep your business. Of course, if the excuses are not valid, you certainly can't use them. Honesty is the only principled way.

4. KEEP CREDIT CARD BALANCES LOW

The smart person will get rid of all but one or two credit cards. And then will only use them for the sake of convenience, paying them in full each month. You certainly do not want to apply for too many loans or too many credit cards. This might be interpreted as a sign that you can easily get in over your head on payments you owe. Don't charge as much as your credit limit allows you to charge. Close accounts you never use and try to keep credit card balances low on your remaining credit lines.

Remember, though, it is good for you to use credit because it demonstrates your ability and willingness to pay your bills. You must have some credit history to have a credit score. If you rarely or never borrow money or use a credit card, consider applying for a few credit cards and using them carefully, paying off the debt each month. But keep your overall debt at a reasonable level relative to your income.

5. KEEP ONLY ONE CREDIT CARD

One credit card should be sufficient for most families. Cancel ALL additional charge cards.

6. CLOSE ACCOUNTS YOU'RE NOT USING

Before you apply for an important mortgage or car loan, you'll want to close these dormant accounts. Be careful though not to do it too quickly. If you close them all at once, your new lender might assume you've hit the financial skids. Close one or two a month (including department store cards) until you've closed them all.

Lenders view charge accounts or home equity lines of credit you're not using as a risk that you could go on a spending jag anytime. If you charge up that already outstanding card, they figure, you may not have enough money to pay their bills.

Of course the best way is to close all but one or two credit accounts.

7. DON'T HIT ALL YOUR CREDIT LIMITS

First, make sure your total credit limit (not including your mortgage, of course) is less than your annual income.

Next, see how much debt you have outstanding. If you're using 80% or more of the credit you have available, it's a sign to lenders that you're stretched. In that case, it pays to sign up for another card or to ask to have your limits raised on your existing ones.

As long as you don't tap that larger reservoir, having the additional credit available should help bring your balance back into the acceptable range.

8. MANAGE INQUIRIES INTO YOUR RECORD

The more often someone asks a credit bureau about you, which happens whenever you apply for a loan or a new car, the lower your credit score will be.

Recent rules for lenders require them to count all inquiries for the same purpose during a one-month period (all inquiries from mortgage lenders, for example) as one inquiry, but it's still not a good idea to apply to more than four or five places for credit in any six-month period.

9. MAKE SURE YOUR CREDIT RECORDS ARE ACCURATE

It's important that you review your credit reports at least once a year to make sure they are right. Your credit record, and therefore your credit report, may vary from one company to the other. You don't want your credit score or mortgage application to be based on incorrect information in any of your reports.

Simply contact all three companies that report on your credit—or national credit repositories as they are often called—listed below. If you've been denied credit, you can get your credit report free by following instructions in the written notice you received when they denied you credit. Otherwise, you can receive a copy for a minimal fee.

TransUnion:
800-888-4213

To report fraud: 800-680-7289
TDD 877-553-7803

Experian:
888-EXPERIAN

To report fraud: 888-397-3742
TDD 800-972-0322

Equifax:
800-685-1111

To report fraud: 800-525-6285

Your future is bright.
You CAN make it!
Seek higher credit scores now!

Rebuild Your Credit Rating

*P*eople who have been through a financial crisis—bankruptcy, repossession, foreclosure, history of late payments, IRS lien or levy or something similar—may think they won't ever get credit again. This is certainly not true. By following some simple steps, you can rebuild your credit in just a couple of years.

To avoid getting into financial problems in the future, you must understand your flow of income and expenses. Some people call this making a budget. Others find the term *budget* too restrictive and use the term *spending plan*. Whatever you call it, spend at least two months writing down every expenditure.

At each month's end, compare your total expenses with your income. If you're overspending, you have to cut back or find more income. The best you can, plan how you'll spend your money each month.

If you have trouble putting together your own budget, consider getting budgeting help from a non-profit group, which is usually free or charges a nominal fee.

Take steps to clean up any inaccuracies in your credit report. Credit reports are compiled by private credit bureaus (for-profit companies) that gather information about your credit history and sell it to banks, mortgage lenders, credit unions, credit card companies, department stores, insurance companies, landlords and even a few employers.

Credit bureaus get most of their data from creditors. They also search court records for lawsuits, judgments and bankruptcy filings. In addition, they search county records to find any recorded liens (legal claims).

To create a credit file for a given person, a credit bureau searches its computer files until it finds entries that match the name, Social Security number and any other available identifying information. All matches are gathered to make the report.

Noncredit data made part of a credit report usually includes names you previously used, past and present addresses, Social Security number, employment history, marriages and divorces.

Your credit history includes the names of your creditors, type and number of each account, when each account was opened, your payment history for the previous 24–36 months, your credit limit or the original amount of a loan and your current balance. The report will show if an account has been turned over to a collection agency or is in dispute.

There is a way for you to see your credit report and obtain a copy of it. The federal Fair Credit Reporting Act (FCRA) entitles you to a copy of your credit report, and you can get one free if:

- You've been denied credit because of information in your credit report and you request a copy within 60 days of being denied credit.
- You're unemployed and looking for work.
- You receive public assistance.
- You believe your file contains errors due to fraud.

In addition, you can get one free copy a year if you live in Colorado, Georgia, Maryland, Massachusetts, New Jersey or Vermont.

You will need to provide the following information:

- Your full name (including generations such as Jr., Sr., III, etc.).
- Your birth date.
- Your Social Security number.
- Your spouse's name (if applicable).
- Your telephone number.
- Your current address and addresses for the previous five years.

Mistakes and inaccuracies can happen and you may find them on your credit report. What should you do if you find mistakes on your credit report? As you read through your report, make a list of everything out-of-date. These may include such things as lawsuits, paid tax liens, accounts sent out for collection, criminal records, late payments and any other adverse information older than seven years or bankruptcies older than ten

years from the discharge or dismissal.

Next, look for incorrect or misleading information, such as:

- incorrect or incomplete name, address or phone number
- incorrect Social Security number or employment information
- bankruptcies not identified by their specific chapter number
- accounts not yours or lawsuits in which you were not involved
- incorrect account histories—such as late payments when you paid on time
- closed accounts listed as open—it may look as if you have too much open credit
- any account you closed that doesn't say "closed by consumer"

After reviewing your report, complete the "request for reinvestigation" form the credit bureau sent you, or send a letter listing each incorrect item and explain exactly what is wrong.

Once the credit bureau receives your request, it must investigate the items you dispute and contact you within 30 days. If you don't hear from them within 30 days, send a follow-up letter. If you let them know you're trying to obtain a mortgage or car loan, they can do a rush investigation.

If you are right, or if the creditor who provided the information can no longer verify it, the credit bureau must remove the information from your report. Often credit bureaus will remove an item on request without an investigation if rechecking the item is more bother than it's worth.

If you don't get anywhere with the credit bureau, directly contact the creditor and ask that the information be removed. Write to the customer service department, vice president of marketing and president or CEO. If the information was reported by a collection agency, send the agency a copy of your letter, too. Creditors are forbidden by law to report information they know to be incorrect.

If you think a credit bureau is wrongfully including information in your report, or you want to explain a particular entry, you have the right to put a 100-word statement in your report. The credit bureau must give a copy of your statement, or a summary, to anyone who requests your report. On your statement, be clear and concise; use the fewest words possible.

You may be asking what you can do to rebuild your credit. After you've cleaned your credit report, the key to rebuilding credit is to get positive information into your record. Here are two suggestions:

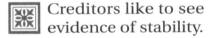
Creditors like to see evidence of stability.

First, if your credit report is missing accounts you pay on time, send the credit bureaus a recent account statement and copies of canceled checks showing your payment history. Ask that these be added to your report. The credit bureau doesn't have to, but often will.

Second, creditors like to see evidence of stability, so if any of the following information is not in your report, send it to the bureaus and ask that it be added: your current employment, your previous employment (especially if you've been at your current job fewer than two years), your current residence, your telephone number

(especially if it's unlisted), your date of birth and your checking account number. Again, the credit bureau doesn't have to add these, but often will.

You can use new credit to rebuild your old credit standing. The one type of positive information creditors like to see in credit reports is credit payment history. If you have a credit card, use it every month. Make small purchases and pay them off to avoid interest charges.

If you don't have a credit card, apply for one. If your application is rejected, try to find a cosigner or apply for a secured card—where you deposit some money into a savings account and then get a credit card with a line of credit around the amount you deposited.

Once you succeed in getting a credit card, you might be hungry to apply for many more cards. But be careful here. Having too much credit may have contributed to your debt problems in the first place. Ideally, you should carry one or two bank credit cards, maybe one department store card and one gasoline card.

Your inclination may be to charge everything on your bank card and not bother using a department store or gasoline card. When creditors look in your credit file, however, they want to see that you can handle more than one credit account at a time. You don't need to build up interest charges on these cards, but use them and pay the bill in full.

Creditors frown on applicants who have a lot of open credit. So keeping many cards may mean that you'll be turned down for other credit—perhaps credit you really need.If your credit applications are turned down, your file will contain inquiries from the companies that rejected you. Your credit file will look as if you were desperately trying to get credit, something creditors never like to see.

If you follow the steps outlined above, it will take about two years to rebuild your credit so you won't be turned down for a major credit card or loan. After around four years, you should be able to qualify for a mortgage.

Your future is bright.
You CAN make it!
Rebuild your credit rating now!

Stay Debt Free

*B*ecoming debt free is only the beginning. The simple truth is that getting out of debt is only the first step. That is how you get to the starting point. Staying out of debt and moving forward to financial independence—that's the bigger challenge, but that's where the big rewards await.

People who have become disciplined and paid off their existing debt have made it to the starting line. Will they continue to progress or did they mistake the starting line for the finish line? How many of them will grab the prize and go back to their old ways of living and thinking?

Many people have repaid a boatload of debt, only to fall back into the temptation and into the old ways of piling up debt. How can we encourage people to not stop, but to move on to the next level and beyond? Is it possible to beat debt for a lifetime?

You have to get to the starting line, establish your long-term goal of reaching financial freedom, define that goal in terms of steps and then change gears from debt recovery to debt prevention. You have to think specifically, not generally, about how you're going to get there and then rejoice because each step from now on will be one of progress, not repair.

In reality, you may not have a clue what you believe about money and its role in your life. Or you might firmly believe things that are not true. No matter what you've done or believed in the past about money and how to take care of it, now is the time to tie yourself to a foundation that will not change, one that will withstand the storms of life.

Let me paint a picture of what it is like to have no debt. What does a debt-free life look like?

- You spend less than you earn.
- You give.
- You save.
- You invest confidently and consistently.
- Your financial decisions are purposeful.
- You turn away from impulsive behavior.
- You shun unsecured debt.
- You borrow cautiously.

- You anticipate the unexpected.
- You scrutinize your purchases
- You reach for your goals by following a specific plan

Some people get out of debt, and after doing so, they toss aside the principles that served them so well in getting out of debt. They handled debt recovery well, but failed to kick into debt-prevention mode. They got to the starting line and then they quit.

⊞ **Living without debt is a lifestyle where you spend less than you earn, give, save and invest confidently and consistently.**

The way I see this whole matter of personal money management is that there are three basic management styles or ways of life. First are those people who needlessly carry heavy financial loads. They carry credit card balances from one month to the next. They owe far more than they can pay and they spend more than they earn. They are forever juggling and trying to keep their heads above water. They are every consumer credit marketing department's dream customer because they fit a predictable profile and contribute to the huge profit margins of the credit card companies.

The next group are those who live paycheck to paycheck and spend every dime they can as they flirt with credit cards, debit cards and ATM cards because it is so much fun living on the edge.

The last group is always the smallest. They fight to maintain their financial freedom by restraining themselves. They embrace the debt-free lifestyle, in that they do not live on credit nor do they mess around with credit cards. They live according to a specific plan. What they do with their money is by design. They give, they save, they invest, and they live beneath their means. They expect the unexpected, they are prepared, and they live with exuberance and confidence because they can smile at the future.

Which person are you? You may be the person who goes the wrong way on an escalator carrying a heavy load. You cannot even see where you are going. You can also get stuck on a treadmill living from paycheck to paycheck.

In contrast, with persistence, you can choose to travel on a moving sidewalk that will take you where you want to go in your financial life. Let me encourage you to make a decision right now to build a strong financial foundation.

I can promise that if you will build a foundation based upon debt-free living principles, it will stand up under all kinds of circumstances. When the financial challenges come, and of course they always do, your foundation will hold and you will come through unharmed.

Living without debt is a lifestyle where you spend less than you earn, give, save and invest confidently and consistently. Your financial decisions are purposeful, by turning away from compulsive behavior, shunning unsecured debt, borrowing cautiously, anticipating the unexpected, scrutinizing your purchases and reaching for your goals by following a specific plan.

Living without debt is about generosity, gratitude and obedience. It is about sound choices and effective decisions. To get your finances in order in your life means to know exactly what to do with your money and having the freedom to earn and spend it when and how you choose. Financial freedom is a way of life—a financially disciplined lifestyle that gets rid of the stress and bondage, exchanging it for a life of peace and joy.

Your future is bright.
You CAN make it!
Stay debt free now and forever!

Understand Financial Goals

I would rather aim at something and miss it than to aim at nothing and hit it. Deciding to get out of debt is the first step. Think for a minute about the benefits. This action will reduce your expenses, delight your creditors, provide financial freedom and so on.

These kinds of benefits provide excellent motivation for you to set a goal of paying off all your debts. A clear goal will put you out in front of 95 people out of every 100, and you will be well on your way to becoming debt free. Just a little side comment, I've never heard of anyone getting out of debt by accident. Determine some worthwhile financial goals. Ask this question, "Is what I want worthwhile?" Your answer to this will determine if your want is a greed or an ambition. Goal setting should bring out the best in a person, allowing him or her to stretch. It should be a sacrificial achievement that is matured with time, effort and service to others. Goals that do not include service to others will eventually hinder, if not destroy, the person who has set them.

Earl Nightingale once said, "Human beings don't have trouble achieving goals: They only have trouble setting them."

In 1872, Calvin Coolidge said this: "Nothing in the world can take the place of persistence. Talent will not; nothing is more common than unsuccessful men with talent. Genius will not; unrewarded genius is almost a proverb. Education alone will not; the world is full of educated derelicts. Persistence and determination alone are omnipotent."

Orison Swett Marden says it this way: "The giants of the race have been men of concentration who have struck sledgehammer blows in one place until they have accomplished their purpose. The successful men of today are men of one overmastering idea, one unwavering aim, men of single and intense purpose."

Goals must be effective and they must be timeless in that they last through the circumstances that come in life. Financial goals that last have the following in common:

- Visualized
- Achievable
- Written
- Measurable
- Manageable
- Progress Reviewed
- Deadline Oriented
- Rewarded

What kind of financial goals are you seeking? Where are you now financially? Where would you like to see yourself? How much time do you have to reach your goals? It's not only a question of whether or not you can reach your goals, but also when you will reach those goals. Your goals and time frame play a big role in your ultimate success.

Enjoying financial security in today's world takes more than simply earning a good living. Some people who have made extraordinary incomes for many years are in terrible financial shape and are not prepared for today, let alone their future. It is essential to make decisions that will help you manage your resources if you are ever going to be financially secure. Many Americans make enough money to become wealthy by the world's standards. The problem is not our income, but our spending. Most Americans waste much of their hard-earned money on the small things, such as a morning appointment with Starbucks for a latte and a bagel. Unfortunately, those little expenditures add up to a large outflow of our cash.

Nothing will improve your performance and your achievements more dramatically and more immediately than a clear picture of where you want to go, a plan to get there, a date of completion and a willingness to overcome obstacles in the way. Just as business and government need strong financial goals to be successful, so families also need to use a systematic approach to managing personal and household financial affairs. Your success depends upon your ability to develop personal and family financial goals and define them in a way that will ultimately achieve your objectives.

Having clear financial goals is a must. The starting point for any financial objective is first setting clear financial goals. You can accomplish just about anything if you set your mind to it and outline the necessary steps to achieve it. But it will be difficult to stay on track if you do not know where you are going. By establishing clear financial goals with specific objectives in mind, you will be well on your way to reaching the financial freedom you are looking to obtain.

We all may be created equally in the sight of God, but we usually end up very unequal. Clearly defined goals focus our vision and channel our energy. Goals are coordinates in time and space you plan to visit in the future. When you set goals, you are making an appointment with yourself to have specific things happen as a result of actions you take today.

Our lives will seldom be any better than our written goals. We make plans and we take action. You just can't hit a target you didn't aim at. Decide where you want to arrive, and begin your journey.

Goal setting works because:

- It focuses the mind.
- It channels energy.
- It gives structure to life.
- It asks for commitment to specific accomplishments.
- It provides motivation.
- Reaching goals becomes habit forming.
- Achieving results spawns new goal setting.

Your future is bright.
You CAN make it! Understand
your financial goals now!

Types of Financial Goals

*U*nderstanding types of financial goals first requires some personal vision. Without vision and without purpose, no financial goals can be met. Having specific financial goals is important because a lack of goals will lead to a lack of planning, leading to inaction.

What is your vision for your finances? What do you want to accomplish? Where are you headed and when will you get there? Fill your thoughts with an image of what can be and what you will accomplish. Set financial goals for yourself to know just where you are going and how you will get there. Then begin to map the process.

Build a financial highway and then get started. What good is the automobile if there are no highways? What good is that power if we are only going to sit around and rev up our engines? Dreams become a reality only if you set financial goals.

Dream big, but be specific. Your financial map will tell you how to get there. By writing down and anticipating in advance the possible bends in the road ahead, your financial goals will give you direction and focus. They break down impossible undertakings into achievable tasks. They will help you keep your vision clear and your footing steady.

SHORT-TERM FINANCIAL GOALS

Short-term financial goals are things that can be accomplished in a relatively short span when compared to your lifetime goals. Maybe you are saving for a newer car or an overseas vacation. These goals should be looked at within a 6–24 month period of time.

Maybe you have incurred $1,000 in debt by purchasing some new stereo equipment. You might want to get rid of this debt by breaking the goal into short little bites by saving $50 a week for the next five months. *Money Magazine* recently did a survey and found that 29% of Americans picked dropping debt as their number one New Year's resolution. How bad is the problem of debt in this country? Outstanding consumer debt stands at $1.7 trillion, and about 40% of it is credit card debt. Paying down debt in small amounts on a regular basis is an affordable and effective way to reach your goals. It doesn't necessarily matter how much. The key is to get into the habit of putting it away.

INTERMEDIATE FINANCIAL GOALS

Intermediate financial goals include those that can be accomplished within a 1–5 year horizon. This might include the purchase of a new vehicle by paying for it in cash. It might be paying off all installment debt. Another example of this might be the children's college education coming your way in five or more years. This might be the new house you have been considering or a remodeling job in your current home.

LONG-RANGE FINANCIAL GOALS

Long-range financial goals generally include things that would take you 5–15 or more years to accomplish. Other possibilities could be a new home or the education of a young child. This category would certainly include your retirement plans. When you set long-range financial goals, you set the stage for making sound investment decisions. Think about your goals and write them down. Then you can put together an investment opportunity aimed at reaching those desired goals.

THE HIERARCHY OF GOALS

- Daily
- Weekly
- Monthly
- Quarterly
- Annual
- Lifetime

1. The accomplishment of daily goals should lead to the achievement of weekly goals.

2. The accomplishment of weekly goals should lead to the achievement of monthly goals.

3. The accomplishment of monthly goals should lead to the achievement of quarterly goals.

4. The accomplishment of quarterly goals should lead to the achievement of annual goals.

5. The accomplishment of annual goals should lead to the achievement of lifetime goals.

Your future is bright.
You CAN make it!
Understand the types of
financial goals now!

Control Your Future
with Financial Goals

SETTING FINANCIAL GOALS

Setting financial goals *gives you control*. As is the case with most successful people, you've probably focused more on making money than bothering with learning how to manage it. Although you have your attorney, your insurance agent, your banker, your CPA and your broker, you may not have given a lot of thought to a sound financial plan. Have you strategized in a way that will enable you to reach your financial goals? You need to. Your financial well being and success will not come by sheer luck and inattention to your goals. In fact, that will guarantee your family economic disaster. Financial goals are reached by knowing what you want, where you are going, making informed choices and using all appropriated strategies to set out on your course.

Setting financial goals *takes the control from others and puts the control of your financial future into your hands*. It becomes your blueprint that will guide you through the financial peaks and valleys of life. Without spending limits and preparations for your financial future by setting current goals, you, your dependents and your assets are not adequately protected against the risks of life. This can lead to needless waste of your current resources. Your daily decision making could be controlled by your current desires, not your future needs. If you do not take control of your financial possessions now, you will likely pay higher income taxes, which may have been avoided with a sound financial plan.

Setting financial goals *points you in the right direction*. It helps point you toward specific family goals and gives you leverage over your financial resources.

What do you need your resources to do for you? Without setting proper financial goals, your long-term needs will not be met. Your children won't have a means to get a good education, your spouse will not be prepared in case of your disability or death and you will be forced to live on a retirement income of much less than you might need.

Setting financial goals *helps you know yourself*. Financial success begins by knowing yourself. This includes knowing your objectives, determining your investment goals, your lifestyle and the type of investment goals that make you comfortable. Because your goals and needs are unique to you, making wise investment choices is very important. You will learn about yourself by taking into account your investment objectives, your tolerance for risk, your time horizon, your financial knowledge and your financial health. Another part of knowing yourself is setting realistic expectations. Are you one who can accept higher risk for higher potential returns?

> **Taking the time to carefully plan for your financial future is the act of accepting personal responsibility for it.**

Conversely, will you be satisfied with lower returns by choosing conservative investments? The best way to get to know yourself, and to start down the path to achieving your financial goals, is to get time on your side. This can only be maximized if you begin at once.

Setting financial goals *keeps you on track.* Living in a busy world with all sorts of demands and opportunities to spend can play havoc with our available financial resources. We all have some sort of money challenges from time to time. It's part of life and living. This is why setting financial goals are so important. How can you possibly think about the future that is 10, 20 and 30 years away when your checkbook is now empty and you won't get paid for another 10 days!

Setting financial goals *helps you make the appropriate decisions* based upon your previously written goals when attempts are made to rob you of your cash. Your money will actually seem to go further if you know where it goes.

Know what you want to accomplish with your income, know what is wise spending and where you are spending foolishly and carefully plan your spending in advance.

Taking the time to carefully plan for your financial future is the act of accepting personal responsibility for it. Certainly, there will be times when you need information and advice from outside sources, but the ultimate decisions are yours. By staying on track with your financial goals, you will increase your ability to get what you want out of life.

Setting financial goals *helps you to build financial assets.* Whatever your choice of an investment vehicle, without a goal, you are likely just to hit and miss. Your last choice for spending available income is going to be putting it away for your retirement. This means that whatever is left at the end of the week is what you will save. Your savings will not grow unless you make it your first choice of what to do with each paycheck. A definite spending goal will help you build assets. You can begin to build assets by first limiting the taxes you are currently paying. The goal of every taxpayer should be to pay your fair share and to pay everything that is legally owed. Tax evasion is both illegal and immoral. Tax avoidance through proper planning, however, is both legal and moral.

Setting financial goals *helps you prepare for retirement.* Many uncertainties surround the subject of retirement. These include the uncertainty of your health, the economy, inflation, your age, the success of your investments and more. Because of this, it is of vital importance that you start when you are young before time becomes your enemy. And even if you are ready to retire, setting financial goals is still important. We are living longer than ever before and the uncertainty of inflation and other expenses should cause us to commit to careful planning and strategic goals. When investing, it is important to take a long-term view, giving your investments time to grow.

Setting financial goals *helps with educational expenses*. In building your overall family asset base, discuss with your family what goals they might have in mind. Of course, for the parents, this includes retirement plans. For the children, it definitely includes their education. One of the greatest gifts parents can give their children is a good education. Instead of funneling large sums of money for furniture or a vehicle, let them earn their own money, but give them a head start in their earning potential by helping them get a solid education. This will cut their umbilical cord to your purse strings, enabling them to gain earning power themselves.

> By staying on track with your financial goals, you will increase your ability to get what you want out of life.

Every family must spend according to its family values. This is how to set financial goals. It is not that values are right or wrong, rather that values vary from family to family. The purchase of a new house or maybe a new business start-up could be planned in your future, as well as an infinite list of other possibilities. Building assets for additional, yet unknown, projects also requires that you continue to set and consider future financial goals, and now is the time to begin.

Setting financial goals *prepares you for the unexpected*. One general goal is to help you protect yourself against a number of risks. These might include the loss of income, the death of a family member, medical expenses, disability, unemployment, property and liability losses, and others. At the very least, goals help you set up an emergency fund to act as a buffer for unplanned expenses. Change is a way of life. Things happen. Life isn't always smooth. Jobs are lost. Health problems confront. Vehicles break down. Emergencies arise. Most experts recommend setting aside anywhere from six months' to a year's salary in liquid assets, such as CDs or money market accounts. In addition, it is important to purchase disability income, life, long-term care, or other types of insurance to help protect you, your family and your assets against the loss of income, illness, disability or other financial circumstances.

When you recognize the possibility of mishaps that will affect your finances, you can plan for their occurrence in advance. You may have to make slight changes or adjustments in your financial goals, but should something unforeseen come your way, the financial burden can be lessened. Your advance planning can lessen your anxiety and reduce the effect of a potentially severe blow to your finances.

Setting financial goals *improves communication within families*. Setting financial goals, launching those goals and staying on track is a family team effort. Setting goals is full of tough choices. People who do not have a lot of extra income will have to prioritize their spending and separate their needs from their wants and desires. They may not get the house of their dreams, a new car every couple of years or the education for their children at the best private colleges available. Families have to be willing to accept trade-offs.

If you have a family, you all must come together to build a sure financial base. If one family member controls spending and promotes saving and the others do not, you will only reach a small portion of the assets you are attempting to build. Each family member should contribute to setting the goals, determining the priorities and considering the various consequences of abandoning the goals. By working together, it becomes a family project that enhances unity, stable relationships and a method to keep each family member on track.

Your future is bright.
You CAN make it!
Control and protect your future
with financial goals now!

Steps to Setting Financial Goals

STEPS TO GOAL SETTING

To be successful at anything necessitates knowledge of goal setting, measuring progress and achieving milestones. In its simplest form, goal setting includes the following steps.

WRITE DOWN YOUR FINANCIAL GOALS

Use paper and pen or your computer to crystallize your thinking. Writing down your goals leads to commitment. You become open to new ideas about what you really want to accomplish. This helps you prepare and ready yourself for the future. Writing down your ideas makes you available to new opportunities. Gather all of the information you have relating to your current financial condition, your assessment of where you are and where you want to be, and begin to gather all the necessary paperwork.

You will need to know exactly where your income is coming from and what your spending habits are. Be very detailed. You must know about your employee benefits, insurance benefits, any insurance policies you have purchased, your living will, a complete and detailed statement of your net worth, a personal income and expense statement, the likely cost of your child's future education, your retirement desires, and in short, a written document of your past, present and future financial situation. This will take some time, but you cannot prepare written financial goals without some intimate knowledge of your financial situation. Have you analyzed your history of spending? Have you examined your spending habits? Have you investigated all future costs? Do you know the source of your financial leaks? Have you found the holes in your budget and identified areas requiring immediate change?

Know your purpose, your objectives and your specific goals. If your objective is to be financially sound, what specific goals will you set for your future? Define clearly what those goals are. Where are you going? Where do you want to be? How will you get there? Which goals are for next month, and which ones are for five years from now? What are your priorities?

GIVE YOURSELF A DEADLINE

Specify a time for achieving your objective. Get started on your financial journey by being deadline motivated. Deadlines help get you started and keep you moving. You become a person on a mission.

You have a target. Goals are worthless without a plan of action and some deadlines. Develop specific deadlines that will keep you on track toward meeting that goal. In the beginning you will need to set up a budget. Consider having automatic payroll deductions for savings or retirement purposes, a plan for contributing to your employer's 401(k) program, contributing to your own IRA account, and so on. Look at those specific deadlines, prioritize them and then put them into action.

Financial goals and objectives should cover all time elements. They should anticipate changing needs as your life changes. It is never too early to understand your purpose, organize those objectives in a clear, concise manner and then set the appropriate goals that will put you on your path to financial freedom.

SET YOUR STANDARDS HIGH

In general, the higher you set your goal, the more effort you will have to expend toward reaching it. The more lofty the goal, the more motivated you will be to reach it. As you reach certain milestones in your blueprint of progress, you'll become inspired to give it all you've got to reach your desired result. It is a strange thing that often it takes just as much effort, energy and hard work to reach small goals that lead to little more than poverty and misery as it does to reach higher goals that lead to success, prosperity and abundance. So aim high! If you shoot for the moon and miss it, at least you'll still be among the stars.

SET REALISTIC, OBTAINABLE GOALS

Be levelheaded and pragmatic when setting your financial goals. Goals that are set too high, so that they become unattainable, will be a source of never-ending frustration for you and possibly your family. While they might look very good on paper, if you cannot reach them, you may eventually abandon all your goals and simply give up.

BE DETAILED AND SPECIFIC

Explicit objectives and precise family financial goals must be set. Goals that are vague might never be met. Don't ballpark your numbers or your goals. Don't say to your family, "Let's buy a small farm in the valley in a few years." Or to your spouse, "Let's set a goal of moving to Mexico when we retire." Though serving in a Third World country might be your purpose and retiring in Mexico might be your objective, when it comes to setting goals, the numbers must be very clear. Numbers include your age, the year, the dollars needed and every other detail that might enter into this picture.

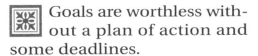 Goals are worthless without a plan of action and some deadlines.

BE FLEXIBLE

Each of your goals must be accommodating to whatever life brings your way. Situations change, people change, desires and wants all change family goals. Be prepared to be elastic with however your family affairs change your course. Every pilot expects that "course corrections" (changes in wind direction and velocity, inclement weather, payload, etc.) will be necessary during flight. If you have a family to consider, within the family unit changes that affect goals and plans might include health, family size or income.

BEGIN WITH THE FIRST STEP

Start now—right now. Ask questions, do research and consult a professional. Get the advice and information you need to create a plan today. It is important to think it all through. It's important to blueprint your strategic plan. It's also important to see the eventual result. One does not always know all the forks in the road when beginning the journey. But if you know where you are now and where you want to be, then you can start with what you know and get moving to where you want to be. You probably already have some ideas about just what kind of goals would be of interest to you or your family members. Setting goals gives you a direction.

The best way to get started is to just start! Don't get caught up in the little things and miss the big picture! By never getting started, you are being defeated by time. If you move ahead and do not get bogged down with the daily problems and challenges of life, you can make time your friend. Time is either your greatest asset or your worst enemy.

> Your future is bright.
> You CAN make it!
> Set financial goals now!

Understand Financial Decisions

*B*efore you begin to think about financial stability or long-term investment strategies, you must understand the decision-making process—or risk losing what it may have taken you years to accumulate.

Decision making is an activity that cannot be avoided. It is a process we must engage in every day to function effectively as individuals. Making decisions about financial affairs demands conscious attention to one's goals as well as to money.

Although decisions call for some kind of action to be completed, not all actions are the result of decisions. For example, when you get up in the morning, you go through a series of activities: you wash your face, brush your teeth, dress, comb your hair and eat breakfast. These actions you perform out of habit. The same can be said about many expenditures of money. Often we spend money not as a result of a decision, but as a kind of daily habit, or even just an impulsive purchase.

HOW A DECISION OCCURS

A decision occurs when a judgment is consciously made after weighing the facts and examining the alternatives and their outcomes. The decision is the choice one makes from a field of alternatives. The decision is complete when it is acted upon—that is, when we do what we have decided to do (or be, or obtain, or change, or begin). Until some action is taken, the decision is not a decision; instead, it is still an idea or notion or unsettled problem in one's mind.

Decisions often must be lived with for some time; many times they have a way of altering lives, even when it is least expected. Therefore, to see how decisions operate, it may be helpful to identify some of their characteristics.

CHARACTERISTICS OF DECISIONS

1. DECISIONS ARE INTERRELATED

A decision has a history; that is, it is related to a past and to a future. Something has occurred prior to the decision that related to it, and events will occur in the future as a result. Think of a row of dominoes standing on end. When the first domino is knocked over, the entire row falls in orderly succession.

Decisions work in a similar way—once a decision is made, it sets in motion a chain reaction of further decisions.

2. Making a choice involves risk

There is no way of knowing for sure, in advance, the result of a decision. Although we may base the decision on all the facts available and obtain the best advice, there is still the possibility that the results will not be what we anticipated. That's how most of our decisions are made—the outcome cannot always be predicted. The risks involved are often the reasons people find it difficult to make decisions, particularly big ones.

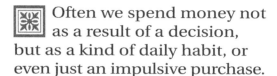 **Often we spend money not as a result of a decision, but as a kind of daily habit, or even just an impulsive purchase.**

3. Decisions cause change

Although it is true that some decisions may not involve change, decisions that require the use of resources call for change.

Decisions often require one to do things differently. If one wants to lose weight, it means a change in eating habits and regular exercise. A change in attitude usually precedes the actual decision.

Often the decision cannot be made until a change in attitude occurs that will permit one to accept the results of the decision. Many people who have stopped smoking will testify to this. The decision to stop had to be preceded by a change in attitude regarding the habit, a change that finally permitted the smoker to say, "Yes, I want to stop."

4. Decisions require commitment

A commitment is a pledge we make to another person or to ourselves. This means we agree to do something or to take some course of action. It further implies that we will accept the results of what we do as well as the conditions under which we must act. Commitment, therefore, is necessary.

When the whole notion of commitment is related to decision making, two commitments are involved:

a) The primary commitment to a goal
b) The commitment to follow through on the decision and accept the results

Consider first the matter of goals. Without a serious and determined commitment, one often lacks the incentive and courage to make major decisions related to the goal and to follow through on them. Without resolve to one's goal, the drastic attitude and behavior changes, that are sometimes needed will hinder you at every turn.

Consider the commitment involved in fulfilling the decision and accepting the results. More often than not, a decision, to be acted upon, calls for a course of action that means work of some kind, or that alters habits, or that limits the use of certain resources (like your money).

In other words, a decision demands self-discipline. Unless there is a firm commitment to the decision, you might be tempted to throw in the towel—to give up rather than follow through. If you are involved in a self-improvement program, you must accept the pattern of change necessary to achieve your goal; you must be committed to your course of action.

5. DECISIONS INVOLVE COST

The cost of a decision may be measured in terms of money, but not necessarily. The cost may also be measured by what has to be given up as a result of making the decision, sometimes referred to as its "opportunity cost." For some people, the cost of the decision to lose weight can be measured in terms of what they can no longer eat. If one needs a second job, the cost may mean less free time for social activities.

With financial decisions, the cost in dollars and cents can be easily recognized. Sometimes children need dental work and braces. When making the decision to finance the dental work, families face the prospect of having to live on thousands of dollars less over the next three or four years. Orthodontia is usually worth the cost, however.

For the family hoping to buy their dream house, the decision is more complex and the cost far greater because it will be felt for many years to come. After all, there is just so much money, and when some of it is used for one thing, there will be less to use for other things. This cost of the financial decision is often overlooked, and yet it can make the decision a difficult one to live with and to accept.

Your future is bright.
You CAN make it! Understand
financial decisions now!

The Decision-Making Process

*T*he decision-making process basically consists of three simple steps.

1. SEEK ALTERNATIVE SOLUTIONS

"There's more than one way to skin a cat" is an old saying that means there's more than one way of doing things. To make a decision with some confidence, it is helpful to look at all the possible ways of solving the problem. Thus, one can better measure the resources against the alternatives and examine more clearly the possible solutions in terms of the particular circumstances.

2. WEIGH THE ALTERNATIVES

Information must be gathered about costs and materials in order to make most decisions. The facts and information gathered are necessary so that one can weigh the alternatives. Compare the possible solutions, know what resources would be used in each case, and have an understanding of the outcomes of each solution.

All too often the alternatives cannot be judged very accurately unless more is known about them. It is impossible to decide from among several methods if one does not know what each method involves. Take the matter of financing a car.

The alternatives may include financing through the dealer, borrowing from the credit union, or using savings to pay cash for the car. What, for example, will it cost to finance the car through the dealer? What will it cost to borrow from the credit union? What will be lost in interest earnings if one uses savings? How does interest lost compare to the charges required to pay for the loan? Unless the car buyer knows what is involved in each method, it will be difficult to weigh the choices and come to a decision best suited to his or her financial and individual needs.

3. MAKE A CHOICE

After studying the alternatives, one is ready to make a choice. The choice is the decision one makes after carefully examining the several possible courses of action. What one chooses will be based on personal goals and the availability of resources.

Three things that go into making most decisions—seeking the alternatives, weighing the alternatives, and making a choice. Each is important. But until the decision is implemented, it doesn't really help solve anything. It now becomes a matter of management—managing the resources and activities necessary to put the decision into action.

Having made a decision, one must assume responsibility for it and follow through with it. Even though there may be some risk involved in whatever is chosen, a person must be ready to accept and live with the consequences of a decision. People often spend time worrying about their choice and wondering if another decision would have been better or more to their liking. Make a habit of not worrying whether you made the right decision. Commit to a choice and accept the result of that choice, right or wrong. To spend time second-guessing your decision only hinders your effectiveness in living with a decision. The mature individual can make decisions and put them into effect without worrying about what might have been.

The effectiveness of a decision is measured by whether or not it helps accomplish whatever one sets out to do. If the course of action chosen turns out to impede progress toward a goal, probably that choice will not be made again.

It may be necessary to stop and find out what is hindering the desired outcome. When the course of action requires more money than anticipated, another way may have to be found. Otherwise, the expense incurred may adversely affect other areas of concern.

Financial decisions require specific knowledge and information. Any decision that involves the use of financial resources requires careful thought, particularly a decision that may affect one's life for a long period of time. To buy Brand A or Brand B is not a very serious problem, since the expenditure probably involves just a few dollars. If the decision is a poor one, the loss will not seriously affect our day-to-day living.

Your future is bright.
You CAN make it!
Understand your
decision-making process now!

Steps to Making Great
Financial Decisions

A decision to finance a car, purchase a home or plan an investment program will have consequences that extend far into the future. Because of the long-range effects of many of these decisions, you need all the advice and factual help you can get. To help make the best financial decisions, try these five steps.

1. RECALL PAST EXPERIENCE

One's own experience is not foolproof, but if it is true that "experience is the best teacher," then at least you can apply what has been learned and avoid making the same mistakes.

2. KEEP FINANCIAL RECORDS

Financial records may not provide answers to new problems, but they can shed light on how much money is available. Even the most elementary records can reveal a great deal about one's financial situation. In considering a venture that requires a financial commitment of some kind, it is necessary to know how it may affect commitments that have already been made. From one's records it is possible to determine how much income has already been committed, how much is required for daily living expenses and how much will be available for new expenses.

3. BORROW EXPERIENCE FROM PEOPLE YOU KNOW

Often our own experience and our own records do not relate to the financial problem we must solve. For example, if one wants to go about setting up a personal investment program, nothing from past experience may help in this area. Perhaps you are planning to buy your first home. It will be important to find a friend who has already done so and ask about closet space, traffic areas, kitchen sizes, acquiring a down payment, and working with realtors. Other people's experience may not always suit your needs or situation, but it can suggest some possibilities and serve as a starting point.

4. LOOK UP SPECIFIC INFORMATION

To find the information and knowledge you need on investment in real estate, mutual funds or stocks, it might require several trips to the local public library or to the Internet. This kind of background information and understanding is essential in choosing a course of action.

5. CONSULT PROFESSIONALS AND EXPERTS

Sometimes experts are not in the same professional field, but have a lot of personal experience. Other professionals are far from being experts! There finally comes a time when one must consult a professional or an expert, especially when considering financial matters. Specialists in each field can give sound advice. Accountants, for example, are in the business of helping people solve critical and perplexing financial and tax problems. But seek several references before taking the advice of any professional!

Just because a problem has been solved once and the solution seems to be functioning as planned does not mean the problem will never have to be solved later on.

Decisions need to be reviewed. They seldom remain fixed for all time. Just because a problem has been solved once and the solution seems to be functioning as planned does not mean the problem will never have to be solved later on.

Nothing about life remains static. Things are constantly changing. It is impossible to predict accurately what we will face next week or next year and to forecast what financial problems will confront us five and ten years down the road. To keep up with the changes in our lives, financial decisions, as well as a multitude of others, must be reviewed regularly. They must be kept in line with one's goals and circumstances.

Your future is bright.
You CAN make it! Take steps
toward making great
financial decisions now!

Plan for the Future

hat is involved in the planning process? Planning is outlining a course of action to achieve a goal, thus fulfilling a desired objective. It is predetermining today a course of action for tomorrow. It is throwing a net over tomorrow and making something happen. It is being tomorrow-minded rather than yesterday-minded.

The only way to reach a financial goal is to work at it. The most important step in reaching the goal is to develop a plan to achieve it. That's why it is so important to plan ahead for your retirement and your financial future. While the idea of planning ahead and building a solid financial strategy for success can sometimes be intimidating and overwhelming, once you get started, it will become easier.

With a little planning and a better understanding of what your investment options are, you too can successfully manage your money and pursue your financial goals.

Why plan? Here's why: to achieve your financial goals, to put ideas to work, to make things happen, to be prepared, to cope with change, to be in control, to decide what you want to do with your money and to decide how your money should work for you. It is essential to plan for every area of your financial future and to make sure you are on track to meet those financial goals. Your needs will change throughout your lifetime. Review your plan every year or so to make sure your financial goals are the same. If they have changed, your planning strategies will have to change.

Take time to plan. Good planning is an essential step toward meeting your financial goals. Planning can be top down and bottom up. It involves communication with those concerned. Plans must be evaluated and revised from time to time.

PLANNING CHECKLIST

1. SET SPECIFIC MEASUREMENTS OF PROGRESS

Answer questions of how much, where, when and at what cost. The progress points must be obtainable. You must consider obstacles and priorities.

2. OUTLINE PROCEDURES

What has to be done? How will it be done? Consider equipment and materials, money and people. When will this thing be done? Set a tentative schedule. Where will it be done?

3. ASSIGN ACTIVITIES

Involve people. Involve their skills, knowledge and experience. Stimulate motivation and interest. The planning process is no better than the goal, the goal is no better than the objective and the objective is no better than the purpose or reason for existing.

4. IDENTIFY FINANCIAL GOALS

Like any other success in life, quality output comes from a quality plan of action. It is impossible to reach any goal without such a road map to your success. Nothing worthwhile happens by accident. It's difficult to accomplish anything important without a detailed, specific plan.

Financial planning offers you a coordinated and comprehensive approach to achieving your personal, family and financial goals. With proper planning, you will take specific steps to reach your financial goals and manage your current and future assets.

A clear, solid plan, like the blueprint for the construction of a house, can show you which steps to take. The steps, one by one, will guide you so you will not have to stop and think about each step before taking it. You'll have the benefit of systematically following ideas you have carefully considered in advance.

To begin, take time to think through your plan completely. Engage others to help you with your plan. There is no such thing as too much input. Don't neglect the details, either. If, for example, your plan is to improve a specific part of your financial future, be sure to give some specific thought about how exactly you plan to do it. Let's say that one of your goals is to spend less money. One of your plans must direct you in specific ways to achieve that goal.

Constructing this plan might include tracking actual cash. Now, of course, it is relatively easy to track the big purchases, but how about the little ones? What about the pocket change that disappears so easily, the $20-dollar bill here and the $5-dollar bill there? Why not gather the family (if you have one) and track for one week, or seven days, exactly where every dime was spent. For the kids, you might want to track each penny.

> A clear, solid plan, like the blueprint for the construction of a house, can show you which steps to take.

The small stuff might not seem like a lot, but multiply it by six family members and you might be very surprised how much it adds up in one month's time. This newly "found" money may just help you start saving toward that short-term goal. Long-term, it could probably fund your retirement! Actually, it takes very little money saved weekly over a lifetime, along with compounded interest, to amount to up to hundreds of thousands of dollars. It just takes commitment, patience and time.

The ability to carry the plan with you and physically consult with it on a regular basis necessitates that it be written down and mobile. Not only will you remind yourself of tasks you should be addressing, but you will be able to regularly monitor the work you are doing according to your plan. Everyone has unique aspirations, hopes, dreams and motivations that serve as a guide for daily life.

Those who are able to clearly identify their financial goals early in life have a very distinct advantage in achieving those goals and maintaining a commitment to their own personal values and principles they have set out to follow. In following the financial plans you have outlined to reach your goals, be sure you continue to unearth new facts that could necessitate any course corrections.

If your results don't happen according to your plan or fulfill your expectations, it may be time to reconsider your plan. Was it realistic? Was it flexible? Did it take into account unforeseeable events or circumstances? Did you follow it to the letter? Does it need some revision? Financial planning is simply drawing up a blueprint that outlines the specific steps to take that will lead you to meaningful personal and financial goals.

Some questions you will need to consider again and again. Are your financial goals clear and realistic? Do you know exactly what you are trying to accomplish and why? If these are not perfectly clear, your chances of succeeding will be hindered. In the planning stage, you must be aware of some of the obstacles that may prevent you from reaching your goals. Above all, do not see your shortcoming as a permanent failure. Instead, learn from your experiences.

Revisions—due to unexpected changes that affect your work, or reconsideration about your objectives—may be needed. As you progress through the months and years, your financial plans will certainly evolve to account for changes in your personal life as well as fluctuations in our economic climate.

If any of the following change, the plan must change: purpose, objectives, goals, net worth, asset allocation, liquidity, cash flow, debt, investment vehicles, risk tolerance, retirement goals, insurance needs, earnings ability, family size, tax liability, etc.

Updates in your planning will be necessary as goals and objectives change. There might be changes in your income or lifestyle. Job changes might cause a change in your financial planning. The bottom line is to stay flexible.

Your future is bright.
You CAN make it!
Plan for your future now!

Save Money on Mortgage Interest

Y ou can save by paying off your home mortgage faster! Across America, homeowners are taking 15-year mortgages or making extra payments on long-term mortgages, which has the effect of shortening the term. Any homeowner who has looked at an amortization schedule realizes that a large part of the monthly payment merely covers the interest charges on the outstanding debt, instead of paying down on the original loan.

Faster payments lower interest costs and allow you to own your home free and clear sooner. A paid-up home is the cheapest way to live in retirement. By making slightly larger monthly payments than your loan requires, you'll significantly reduce your total interest cost and pay off your mortgage years early. For example, send in $50 extra in advance every month on a $150,000, 30-year, 10% mortgage, and you'll save $68,325 and reduce the term of your loan by more than five years.

While it is true that mortgage interest can offset your taxable income, this has limited value. The offset does not reduce the tax itself; rather it reduces taxable income. If you are in the 28% tax bracket, a $100 mortgage-interest deduction will save $28 in federal taxes, $31 if you are in the 31% tax bracket, and so on. The remaining part of that $100 mortgage ($72 or $69) interest payment is lost. Additionally, people with adjusted incomes well over $125,000 may not be allowed to deduct all their mortgage interest.

Instead of making only the minimum payment required by a lender, many people today are repaying their loans more quickly than necessary. One way to do this is to use a 15-year rather than a 30-year amortization schedule. Another way is to prepay the mortgage either by making extra payments or by increasing the size of the regularly scheduled payments and specifying that the surplus should be applied to principal. According to *Spirit Magazine*, adding a mere $10 a month to each payment, beginning in the third year of a $100,000, 30-year mortgage at 8%, can save $8,515 in interest charges and will pay off the debt 16 months early.

David Ginsbury, president of Loantech, says, "Making just one prepayment of principal a year can make a tremendous difference over time." He goes on to note that starting with the same $100,000 loan at 8% for 30 years, a prepayment of $500 each December will cause the mortgage to be paid off 29 months early, while one-time annual prepayments of $1,000 and $2,000 will retire debt in 22 years 7 months and 18 years 8 months respectively. These results are so dramatic that it might seem as if every homeowner should begin prepaying immediately. But don't forget to first have about six months of income set aside as an emergency fund.

Your future is bright.
You CAN make it!
Save money on your
mortgage interest now!

Save with Good Spending Habits

You can save by developing good spending habits! Spending money to get the most out of it is something you will have to work at, just as you will work to earn it in the first place. You will have to carefully plan expenditures in advance that fit your budget. Stay on budget. Spend time analyzing just where you are in your monthly cash flow. Having a budget with specific goals and monthly prespending set allocations will help you build in restraints on your impulse buying—guaranteed!

Instead of buying now and paying later, it's time for you to reverse the order. Save now and pay later. When it comes to celebrating birthdays and anniversaries, participating in baby showers and graduations, attending weddings and other special events, stick to your budget! If you know a lot of people, you could easily spend hundreds of dollars you do not have on cards, gifts and other budget busters! Participate in these events with great restraint. If long-distance telephone calls and travel are involved, be wise and prudent.

Have you developed good personal spending habits and buying restraints? With your limited income, you will need some financial magic. Most of the magic will come from you by putting roadblocks and obstacles into your spending path. Do you put first things first when you make purchases? Do you buy what you need most or what you want? Do you shop in more than one store to compare the price and quality of a particular item you want? Do you resist the temptation to buy something just because it's on sale or it appeals to you at the moment, rather than buying something you might need more?

What about the discretionary money you spend on pets, pet supplies, pet toys and pet food? How much do you need to indulge your pets? Basic food and water makes all pets more than happy. Do you care for too many pets? Would a friend who has none appreciate the gift of a loving pet?

What about your hobbies? How much do you spend on doing the things that are purely for sport or leisure? Is every pursuit necessary? How many thousands of dollars have you spent just to pursue your hobby?

What items do you collect because you are interested in them? Do you really need every piece of that collection? How many sets of dishes can you really use? How many kinds of toys can you store? How many books do you have room to store?

What about your out-of-town trips and vacation expenditures? How many weekends do you need to spend on the road? Think of all the extra costs you will incur by leaving home. Your travel costs will include: automobile gas, maintenance and more miles on the car; restaurant food, motels and hotels, entertainment, amusement park fees; or museum entrance fees, snacks, shopping, and on and on.

You can save by pausing before purchasing! Before spending your hard-earned resources, pause a while to ask yourself three simple questions:

1. Can I really afford it?
2. Do I really need it?
3. Is it worth what I'm paying for it?

Whether or not you can afford it may be a simple matter of addition and subtraction—you either have enough money or you don't. But more often it will be a matter of deciding how important this particular purchase is compared to other purchases you may want to make.

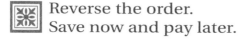 **Reverse the order.
Save now and pay later.**

Many of us get pulled into great so-called discounts and bargains. So what if you participate in an advertised sale that gets you 50% off the regular retail price? In some industries, 50% off is the norm. In others, 50% is still marked up several hundred percent. Besides, even if you buy at 50% off, you could save 100% of the total purchase price if you didn't buy it at all! We would like to have many things that would make life easier and more fun. Don't think you must always deny yourself all of these; after all, life is supposed to be fun as well as work. Many things that would have been considered luxuries in past years are now considered necessities. But you are going to have to pick and choose according to your particular desires. The more limited your budget, the more picking and choosing you are going to have to do. This is one of the hard facts of life.

Your future is bright.
You CAN make it! Save with
good spending habits now!

Save Money by Doing It Yourself

*S*ome costs are beyond our personal ability to control. Included in this category are healthcare costs, the price of a gallon of gas and dental work. Of course you can prevent some cost altogether by not driving as much and keeping your consumption of sweets to a minimum. Other costs can be controlled in time, but because of various conditions and circumstances, they cannot be controlled immediately. Included in this category is the ongoing expense of interest charged on the balance of your debt.

But one category of expenses you can control is the personal choice group. Some things you can do yourself today, right now, that will result in saving some of your hard-earned cash.

You can save by doing these things yourself!

- Always switch off the lights when you leave a room.
- Borrow books from your local public library instead of buying them.
- Buy a used car rather than a new one.
- Buy holiday cards and decorations after Christmas at half price or less, and save them for next year.
- Eat out at lunchtime rather than at dinner—it is usually at least 40% cheaper.
- Give yourself haircuts and experiment cutting your family's hair.
- Look for a special discount package when planning a trip or don't go at all
- Practice the art of trading down: a layer or two down in your favorite gourmet coffee store, one step down in suits, in travel arrangements, in size of rental cars, etc.
- Put aside gifts that can't be used or returned with the name of the giver, and later on give them to someone else as a gift. Important: Catalog each gift to be sure not to give it to the person who gave it to you! (But don't save unused fruitcakes until next year!)
- Return empty bottles to the supermarket and get a refund on your deposit.
- Review insurance policies to avoid overlapping coverage.

- Save the plastic or paper bags from the supermarket to use as garbage bags.

- Take advantage of free or low-cost offers: snacks at the supermarket, free visits to try out a health club, two-for-one meals at a restaurant, etc.

- Start walking or jogging in the park or the street, and avoid the cost of joining a health club. Use free city parks and tennis courts instead of paid recreational areas.

- Wash your car yourself instead of taking it to the car wash.

- Wear a sweater at home during cool months so you can keep the thermostat turned down.

- When eating out, take advantage of the special fixed-price early dinners.

- When you become tired of some article of clothing, instead of disposing of it, put it aside for a season or two, then take it out again and it will look new.

- With relatives or friends, arrange for children's hand-me-downs to be saved and passed on from child to child.

How can you save some real money if you are a homeowner? If you are a homeowner and your house needs some reworking and updating, but you have a very limited budget available, should you open an equity line of credit or take on a second home mortgage? Certainly not! What can you do to spruce up your home without mortgaging it to the hilt?

For starters, instead of buying new kitchen cabinets to replace the existing ones, you can save yourself the expense and simply reface the current ones. This will also save you the cost of new flooring, countertops and other things related to new cabinets.

Your bathtub can be reglazed instead of replaced. Fixtures can be replaced with very expensive ones, or inexpensive ones that look just as good and last just as long. Instead of changing window locations and appliance outlets, keep them where they are. Moving things around causes huge cash outlays to plumbers, electricians and other professionals.

If your rooms look small and crowded, instead of adding a room to your house or moving a wall or two, try changing their look by painting the ceilings and walls. This will save you some big dollars. Additionally, rearranging the furniture or simply getting rid of some will enlarge the look and feel of the room. By adding a skylight or two, your living comforts will increase and it will seem lighter, brighter and roomier.

It is easy to pick up the telephone and make a phone call to get someone else to do the dirty work, but give it a try yourself. Not only will you receive great personal rewards from accomplishing a job well done, but it will also save your budget from potential disaster. So get off the couch, turn off the television, stay at home and do the work yourself.

Your future is bright.
You CAN make it!
Save lots of money by
doing it yourself...now!

Money-Saving Solutions

HOW TO SAVE MONEY

You can save by developing new habits! Become a skillful shopper. Regional retail centers are exciting places. In supermarkets, thousands of goods line the shelves and invite attention. It takes skill and determination to walk down the aisles and resist temptation. The skillful shopper prepares a shopping list before going to market and buys only those items needed.

Learn to read labels and interpret them. Make substitutions for the higher-priced items, judge the value of the week's bargain offerings and decide whether the "best buys" are best for the family. Careful shopping can save many dollars a week in the budget.

You can save by *not buying on impulse*! Don't be an impulse buyer. Everyone is tempted now and then to go on a shopping spree and buy something on impulse. The temptation for many families is to suggest going window-shopping. That very innocent suggestion soon turns into impulse buying. To give in to these impulses once in a while may be a healthy response to one's mood or to a special occasion. But when impulse buying becomes a personal habit, when it takes place on every trip to the supermarket or to the department store, then it can do real damage to even the best of budgets and financial plans. It is even worse if something bought on impulse has no use after it is taken home.

You can save by *getting rid of credit card debt*! Get rid of credit card debt. Here is a good way to save some big money fast. That is one great investment sure to pay off, yet we fail to recognize it even though it's right in front of us every month. Pay off your credit cards! Let's say for example that you owe $2,000 on a Visa card. Many charge cards still have an interest rate in the neighborhood of 19%.

PAYING CREDIT CARD DEBTS

Instead of taking that $2,000 bonus check and investing it into some low-interest-paying bank account, pay off that credit card and get a great return on your money! Paying off the outstanding balance is the same as getting a check for $570, tax-free! And one more thing, be a real friend to yourself: Cut up the card and cancel your credit. You'll be glad you did! It's the best financial investment you can make.

You can save by *using installment credit sparingly*! Recognize that any installment purchase or loan means one more fixed expense in the budget. Although credit is readily available, and most anything can be obtained, be wary of the "low-down, low-monthly-payment" offers. There may be times when installment purchases are unavoidable, but this kind of spending, if excessive, can become a costly way of providing for family needs or for achieving family goals.

You can save by *choosing quality over price*! Do you look for quality rather than only cost or appearance when you buy something you want to last a long time? Do you save sales slips, guarantees, and other records of purchases where you know you can find them? Do you buy at reliable stores that stand behind their merchandise? Read the labels on boxes, packages or other purchases to determine the real quantity or quality you are getting for your money. Instead of purchasing your wants immediately, put money aside to save for something you want but can't afford at the moment.

You can save by *taking good care of your assets*! Take care of the assets you already possess. Clothes last longer and remain better looking if they are kept clean and pressed. Food lasts longer when it is properly stored. Equipment lasts longer and gives better service when used according to the manufacturer's instructions. It makes sense to prolong the use of one's possessions by taking care of them. The longer we can use an article, the more we are getting for our money.

You can save by *updating your homeowner's policy*! Update your homeowner's insurance. As a rule, you need to be covered for at least 80% of the cost of rebuilding your house. Otherwise you won't get full reimbursement, even if a fire destroys only one room. Ask your insurance agent how to estimate the cost. If you rent, get tenant's insurance to cover furniture and other valuables. Many renters fail to do this, thinking losses will be covered by the landlord. Not so!

You can save by *updating your life insurance policy*! Recalculate your life insurance. You need only enough to take care of your dependents if you die. If there is a non-breadwinner in the family, generally stick with low-cost term insurance, then cut it back or cancel it when the children grow up. Primary breadwinners, by contrast, often have to provide for an aging spouse, so they may need some cash value insurance whose premiums won't rise as they get older. If you have no dependents, you don't need life insurance. Put cash into retirement funds or disability insurance instead. Disability is overlooked by many people.

You can save by *starting a retirement fund*! Start a retirement fund. If you work for a corporation that has one, use the 401(k) plan. If employed by a firm with no pension plan, open an Individual Retirement Account. As a rule, both the contributions to these plans and the earnings are untaxed until you withdraw the money, so tax savings help pay the cost. If you leave your job, you can take 401(k) savings with you. Do not fail to use these plans! They're the best route to independence in old age.

You can save by *getting the best health insurance possible*! Get the best health insurance you can get. If you aren't covered at work, try to participate in a group plan through an organization you belong to or can join. Alternatively, call Blue Cross/Blue Shield or a Health Maintenance Organization (check the Yellow Pages). If you can't afford what they offer, talk to an insurance agent about a high deductible policy that covers only major medical costs. (You pay the small bills, but the huge ones are covered.) Today's buyers often take deductibles of $1,000 to $5,000, which greatly lowers costs. Whatever you do, never buy insurance advertised by celebrities on TV; it's not worth the cost.

You can save by *using non-monetary resources*! Learn to use other resources besides money. It is very easy to rely entirely on financial resources for all the goods one wants and needs. But this kind of thinking and living places a very heavy burden on the individual and family income and often postpones the day when a goal can be achieved. However, by developing skills among family members, and by substituting one's time, energy and skill in place of money, many services can be provided at home without dipping into the family funds. This kind of planning and achieving often provides far greater satisfaction than does the routine of shopping and buying.

GETTING YOUR MONEY'S WORTH

Is it worth what I'm paying for it? This is where spending money becomes a real skill. Worth or value is often hard to determine. Value in this case means the quality of the product itself; it also means the usefulness of the product for your particular purposes. You have to think about both. In determining value, price alone can be misleading. The lowest price may be the best value for your money, but then again it may not be. The highest price doesn't necessarily mean the best value either. Usually, you will find the best value somewhere in between.

CONSIDERING QUALITY

Generally, when you are buying a product where length of service and performance are important, quality—how well it is made, how well it functions, how long it will last—is first consideration. Price is, within budget limits, a second consideration. Appearance may or may not be a consideration. If it's a suit or dress, yes; if it's an electric drill, probably not. If you are buying a product where length of service is not so important—soap or paper napkins, for instance—the lower price is usually the better value for your purposes. Quality is not as important, as long as what you buy does the job to your satisfaction. A lot of hard work and a little luck will stretch your dollars.

Your future is bright.
You CAN make it!
Begin to save lots
of your money now!

SPENDING/BUDGETING WORKSHEET

My Spending	Monthly	Yearly	Budget	Actual	Diff (+ or -)
ALLOWANCES					
Parents					
Children					
CHARITY					
My Local Home Church (10-15%)					
Local Church Special Project #1					
Local Church Special Project #2					
Charity #3					
Charity #4					
Other					
DEBT REPAYMENT					
Student Loan					
Home Equity Loan					
Credit Card #1					
Credit Card #2					
Personal Line of Credit					
ENTERTAINMENT					
Movies/Videos/Sporting Events					
Recreation/Parks					
Weekend Trips					
Vacations					
Other #1					
FOOD					
Groceries					
Restaurants					
School Lunches					
Work Lunches					
HOUSING					
Mortgage or Rent					
Real Estate Taxes					
Gas					
Electric					
Water					
Sewer					
Phone - Landline					
Phone - Internet					
Phone - Cell/Pager					
Cable/Satellite					
Garbage/Sanitation					
Home Repairs					
Home/Appliance Maintenance					
Yard Upkeep					
Other #1					

My Spending	Monthly	Yearly	Budget	Actual	Diff (+ or -)
KIDS' SPECIAL EXPENSES					
School					
Lessons #1					
Lessons #2					
Camp					
Sports #1					
INSURANCE					
Vehicle #1					
Vehicle #2					
Vehicle #3					
Life #1					
Life #2					
Life #3					
Life #4					
House #1					
House #2					
Disability #1					
Disability #2					
Long Term Care					
MEDICAL/DENTAL					
Premiums					
Co-payments					
Prescriptions					
Vitamins					
PERSONAL					
Haircut/Beauty					
Dry Cleaning/Laundry					
Clothes					
Gifts					
Subscriptions					
SAVINGS PROGRAM					
Emergency Fund					
401(k)/Retirement					
College Fund					
Investment Fund					
Christmas/Birthday					
Other #1					
TRANSPORTATION					
Car Loan/Lease Payment					
Gasoline					
License Plates					
Maintenance					
Repairs					
Other #1					
OTHER					
Misc. #1					
Misc. #2					

APPENDIX 2

Biblical References to Finances

Accounting
Daniel 6:1-3
Matthew 18:23
Matthew 25:14-30
Romans 14:12

Against the Unfortunate
Deuteronomy 24:14
Psalm 10:2
Psalm 12:5
Proverbs 14:20-21, 31
Proverbs 21:13
Proverbs 22:16
Proverbs 24:23
Proverbs 28:8
Matthew 18:23, 34
Luke 11:42
Luke 16:19-25

Attitudes, Viewpoints and Actions
Psalm 112
Proverbs 10:4
Proverbs 13:4, 11
Proverbs 24:10
Proverbs 28:27
Ecclesiastes 5:12
Malachi 3:5
Luke 6:35a
Romans 12:11
Ephesians 4:28
Blamelessness
Psalm 1:1, 2
Psalm 37:37
Psalm 112:6
Proverbs 10:16
Proverbs 11:4
Proverbs 12:12
Proverbs 16:8, 11
Proverbs 19:1
Proverbs 21:3
Proverbs 22:1
Proverbs 28:6, 13
Matthew 7:20

Luke 3:12-14
Luke 8:15
Luke 12:57, 58
Luke 20:22-25
Romans 13:7
Galatians 6:9

Borrowing
Exodus 22:14
Deuteronomy 15:1-11
Psalm 37:25
Proverbs 3:27, 28
Proverbs 22:7
Matthew 5:25, 26, 40
Matthew 18:23-35
Luke 12:58, 59

Budgeting
Proverbs 16:9
Proverbs 19:21
Proverbs 22:3
Proverbs 24:3, 4
Proverbs 27:12
Luke 12:16-21
Luke 14:28-30
Luke 16:1-8
1 Corinthians 16:1, 2

Caution
Proverbs 8:12
Proverbs 12:16, 23
Proverbs 13:16
Proverbs 14:8, 15, 18
Proverbs 15:5
Proverbs 16:21
Proverbs 18:15
Proverbs 22:3
Proverbs 27:12
Hosea 14:9
Amos 5:13

Contentment
Joshua 7:7
Proverbs 30:7-9
Matthew 20:1-16
Luke 3:14

Luke 12:15-21
2 Corinthians 6:10
Philippians 4:11, 12
Colossians 3:2
1 Thessalonians 5:16-18
1 Timothy 6:6-10
Hebrews 13:5

Counsel
Proverbs 3:13
Proverbs 12:5, 15
Proverbs 13:20
Proverbs 14:7
Proverbs 15:22
Proverbs 19:20
Proverbs 24:3, 6
Proverbs 27:9

Cosigning Notes
Proverbs 6:1-5
Proverbs 11:15
Proverbs 17:18
Proverbs 20:16
Proverbs 22:26
Proverbs 27:13

Debt
Deuteronomy 15:6
Deuteronomy 28:12, 13
2 Kings 4:1-7
Psalm 37:21
Proverbs 3:27, 28
Proverbs 6:1-3
Proverbs 11:15
Proverbs 17:18
Proverbs 22:7
Proverbs 27:13
Matthew 5:25, 26
Matthew 18:23
Luke 12:58, 59
Romans 13:8

Diligence
Proverbs 6:4
Proverbs 12:11, 24
Proverbs 13:11

297

Proverbs 14:4
Proverbs 16:3
Proverbs 21:5
Proverbs 24:3, 4, 7
Matthew 20:13
Romans 12:11
2 Timothy 2:6
1 Thessalonians 4:11

Dishonesty
Psalm 37:37
Psalm 15:5
Psalm 62:10-12
Proverbs 10:15, 16
Proverbs 11:1, 16, 18
Proverbs 12:3, 12
Proverbs 13:7, 11
Proverbs 15:6, 27
Proverbs 16:2, 11
Proverbs 17:2
Proverbs 20:21
Proverbs 22:28
Proverbs 24:16, 19, 20
Proverbs 28:6, 18
Jeremiah 9:4
Matthew 18:7
Matthew 27:5
Luke 9:25
Luke 11:42
Luke 16:1, 10-14
Luke 19:8
Luke 20:46, 47
Romans 2:21, 22

Ego
Psalm 75:4
Psalm 107:40
Proverbs 11:2
Proverbs 12:9
Proverbs 15:25
Proverbs 16:18, 19
Proverbs 18:12, 23
Proverbs 19:1
Proverbs 28:11
Proverbs 29:23
Jeremiah 9:23
Jeremiah 22:21
Matthew 23:12
Luke 14:11
Philippians 2:3
1 Timothy 6:17

Envy
Psalm 73:2
Proverbs 23:17
Proverbs 24:19

Excellence
Proverbs 18:9
Proverbs 22:29
Colossians 3:17, 23
1 Peter 4:11

Getting the Facts
Proverbs 14:8, 15
Proverbs 18:13
Proverbs 19:2
Proverbs 23:23
Proverbs 27:23, 24
Luke 14:28-32
James 1:5

Giving
Isaiah 66:20
Psalm 96:7, 8
Psalm 112:5
Proverbs 3:9, 10
Proverbs 11:24-26
Proverbs 28:22
Mark 4:24
Mark 12:41-44
Luke 6:38
Acts 2:45
1 Corinthians 16:1, 2

Greed
Psalm 73:2, 3, 17, 20
Proverbs 23:4, 5
Proverbs 28:25
Luke 12:15
Luke 18:24
Ephesians 5:5

Helping the Unfortunate
Psalm 69:33
Psalm 72:1, 4-15, 17
Psalm 109:31
Proverbs 14:21
Proverbs 14:31
Matthew 5:42
Matthew 6:19, 20
Matthew 10:42
Luke 3:11
Luke 9:48
Luke 10:35
Luke 12:33

Luke 19:8, 9
1 Timothy 5:3, 8, 15, 16
1 John 3:17

Hoarding
Psalm 49:11, 16, 17
Proverbs 13:22
Proverbs 28:22
Malachi 1:7, 9
Malachi 3:8
Matthew 6:24
Matthew 19:23
Luke 12:16-20
Luke 12:21, 33

Honesty
Deuteronomy 25:14, 15
Psalm 112:1-3, 5
Proverbs 10:3, 9
Proverbs 13:5, 11, 21
Proverbs 16:8
Proverbs 20:7
Proverbs 24:27
Proverbs 27:1
Proverbs 28:18
Proverbs 30:7, 8

Honesty versus Unmerited Gain
Deuteronomy 25:15
Proverbs 11:1
Proverbs 16:8
Proverbs 22:16
Proverbs 28:8
Jeremiah 22:13
Luke 16:10
Romans 12:17

Humility
Proverbs 22:4
Jeremiah 9:24
Matthew 6:1-3
Luke 17:3
Luke 19:8
1 Corinthians 1:26-31

Inheritance
Proverbs 13:22
Proverbs 17:2
Proverbs 20:21
Ecclesiastes 2:18, 19, 21
Ezekiel 46:16-18
Luke 15:11-31

Investing
Psalm 62:10
Proverbs 11:24, 28
Proverbs 16:1-9
Proverbs 21:5
Proverbs 23:4, 5
Investments
Proverbs 21:20
Proverbs 24:27
Ecclesiastes 6:3
Matthew 6:19-21
Matthew 13:22
Matthew 25:14-30, 45
Luke 14:28, 29
Luke 19:13-26
2 Peter 2:20
2 Peter 3:10

Laziness
Proverbs 6:6-11
Proverbs 12:24
Proverbs 13:11
Proverbs 14:4
Proverbs 19:15
Proverbs 21:17
Proverbs 22:13
Proverbs 26:13
2 Thessalonians 3:6, 10

Lending
Exodus 22:25, 26
Deuteronomy 23:19, 20
Deuteronomy 24:10, 11
Nehemiah 5:7, 10
Psalm 15:5
Psalm 37:26
Proverbs 28:8
Ezekiel 18:8
Luke 6:34, 35
Luke 7:41

Needs
Psalm 37:25
Matthew 6:8, 25-33
Philippians 4:19
Planning
Proverbs 16:1
Prosperity
Genesis 39:3
Deuteronomy 28:11
Deuteronomy 29:9
2 Chronicles 31:21

Psalm 1:3
Psalm 35:27
Luke 15:13
John 6:12

Retirement
Psalms 37:25
Proverbs 16:31
Proverbs 20:29
Saving
Proverbs 6:6-8
Proverbs 21:20
Proverbs 30:24, 25

Sharing
Exodus 16:18-20
Acts 4:32
Romans 12:13
1 Corinthians 9:7-11, 14
2 Corinthians 8:8-15
2 Corinthians 9:6-13
Galatians 6:6

Self-control
Matthew 7:13, 14
2 Corinthians 8:11
2 Thessalonians 3:11
Hebrews 12:11
Slothfulness
Proverbs 18:9
Proverbs 24:30, 31
Ecclesiastes 10:18
2 Thessalonians 3:11
Hebrews 6:12

Suing
Matthew 5:42
Matthew 6:3
Matthew 10:42
Matthew 13:12
Luke 6:30-36
Luke 12:57, 58
1 Corinthians 6:1-7

Supporting the Wealthy
Deuteronomy 1:17
Deuteronomy 16:19
Proverbs 14:20
Proverbs 28:21

Taxes
Matthew 17:24-27
Mark 12:14-17
Luke 20:22-25
Romans 13:6, 7

Tithing
Genesis 14:20, 22, 28
Malachi 3:10
Matthew 23:23
Luke 11:42
Hebrews 7:1-10
Waste
Genesis 41:36

Trust
Jeremiah 17:7, 8
Mark 6:9
Mark 8:34
Philippians 4:19
Wealth
Deuteronomy 8
Proverbs 10:22
Proverbs 28:13
Jeremiah 17:8-10
Luke 6:38
John 10:10
2 Corinthians 8:9
Philippians 4:19
3 John 2

Wives
Proverbs 31:10-31

Work
Deuteronomy 24:14, 15
Proverbs 6:6-10
Proverbs 10:4, 5
Proverbs 12:11, 24
Proverbs 14:23
Proverbs 16:26
Proverbs 28:19
Ephesians 4:28

Worry
Psalm 50:14, 15
Proverbs 12:25
Matthew 6:27-34
Philippians 4:6
1 John 4:18

Topical Index

Scriptures Used Index

STATEMENT OF FINANCIAL CONDITION

(Personal Balance Sheet)

Prepared by the _____ Family as of (mm/dd/yy)

ASSETS (What You Own)		
CURRENT ASSETS		
Cash – (checking accounts)		
Cash – (savings accounts, money markets, CDs)		
Personal Property – Market Value (auto, jewelry, etc)		
Other Assets (itemize)		
TOTAL CURRENT ASSETS		$
LONG-TERM ASSETS		
Certificates of deposit		
Debt Owed to You (notes, contracts)		
Life Insurance (cash values)		
Partial Interest in Real Estate		
Real Estate (net market value)		
Retirement Accounts (IRAs, SEPs, 401(k)s, etc.)		
Securities (stocks, bonds, mutual funds, etc.)		
Vehicles (market value)		
Other Long-Term Assets (itemize)		
TOTAL LONG-TERM ASSETS		$
TOTAL ASSETS		$
LIABILITIES (What You Owe)		
CURRENT LIABILITIES		
Charge Accounts (itemize)		
Credit Cards (itemize)		
Current Monthly Unpaid Bills		
Personal Debts (short-term)		
Unpaid Taxes and Interest		
Unsecured Loans (short-term)		
Other Short-Term Debts (itemize)		
TOTAL CURRENT LIABILITIES		$
LONG-TERM LIABILITIES		
Home Equity Loans		
Loans – (You Owe)		
Mortgages on Real Estate $		
Notes Cosigned, etc.		
Student Loans		
Taxes – (You Owe)		
Other Long-Term Liabilities		
TOTAL LONG-TERM LIABILITIES		$
TOTAL LIABILITIES		$
NET WORTH (owner's equity)		
(Total Assets – Total Liabilities)		$

Bibliography

BOOK RESOURCES

10 Minute Guide to Beating Debt, Susan Abentrod, Howell Book House; (January 1, 1980)

101 Real Money Questions, Jesse B. Brown, John Wiley & Sons; 1 edition (January 3, 2003)

21 Unbreakable Laws of Success, Max Anders, Thomas Nelson, 1996

25 Day Financial Makeover, Francine L. Huff, Fleming H Revell Co; (February 2004)

8 Critical Lifetime Decisions, Ralph Palmen, Beacon Hill Press; (February 2002)

A Christian Guide to Prosperity, Fries & Taylor, Communications Research; (February 1984)

A Look at Stewardship, Word Aflame Publications, 2001

Anointed for Business, Ed Silvoso, Regal, 2002

Answers to Your Family's Financial Questions, Burkett, Tyndale House Publishers; (June 1991)

Answers Your Questions about Biblical Economics, Avanzini, Harrison House, Incorporated; (November 1992)

Avoiding Common Financial Mistakes, Ron Blue, Navpress, 1991

Baker Encyclopedia of the Bible; Walter Elwell, Michigan: Baker Book House, 1988

Becoming the Best, Barry Popplewell, England: Gower Publishing Company Limited, 1988

Biblical Roads to Financial Freedom, Katz, Destiny Image; (November 2003)

Business Buy The Bible, Cook, Lighthouse Publishing, Inc.; (September 1, 1997)

Business Proverbs, Steve Marr, Fleming H. Revell, 2001

Cheapskate Monthly, Mary Hunt

Commentary on the Old Testament; Keil-Delitzsch, Michigan: Eerdmans Publishing, 1986

Conquering Debt God's Way, Ammons, Abilene Christian University Press; (October 2003)

Creating Your Personal Money Map, Pope, Tyndale House Publishers; (January 1, 2004)

Crown Financial Ministries, various publications

Customers as Partners, Chip Bell, Texas: Berrett-Koehler Publishers, 1994

Cut Your Bills in Half; Pennsylvania: Rodale Press, Inc., 1989

Debt-Free Living, Larry Burkett, Dimensions, 2001

Debt-Proof Your Marriage, Hunt, Fleming H Revell Co; Workbook edition (August 2003)

Die Broke, Stephen M. Pollan & Mark Levine, HarperBusiness, 1997

Doing Business by the Good Book, Steward, Hyperion Press; 1st edition (January 2, 2004)

Eerdmans' Handbook to the Bible, Michigan: William B. Eerdmans Publishing Company, 1987

Eight Steps to Seven Figures, Charles B. Carlson, Double Day, 2000

Everyday Life in Bible Times, Washington DC: National Geographic Society, 1967

Faithful Finances 101, Moore, Templeton Foundation Pr; (July 2003)

Fasting For Financial Breakthrough, Towns, Regal Books; (July 2002)

Financial Dominion, Norvel Hayes, Harrison House, 1986

Financial Freedom, Larry Burkett, Moody Press, 1991

Financial Freedom, Patrick Clements, VMI Publishers, 2003

Financial Peace Planner, Ramsey, Penguin USA (Paper); (January 1998)

Financial Peace, Dave Ramsey, Viking Press, 2003

Financial Self-Defense, Charles Givens, New York: Simon And Schuster, 1990

Flood Stage, Oral Roberts, 1981

Generous Living, Ron Blue, Zondervan, 1997

Get a Financial Life, Kobliner, Fireside; Revised & Expanded edition (June 6, 2000)

Get It All Done, Tony and Robbie Fanning, New York: Pennsylvania: Chilton Book, 1979

Getting Out of Debt, Howard Dayton, Tyndale House, 1986

Getting Out of Debt, Mary Stephenson, Fact Sheet 436, University of Maryland Cooperative
    Extension Service, 1988

Getting Your Financial House in Order, Bragonier, Broadman & Holman Publishers; (October 2003)

Giving and Tithing, Larry Burkett, Moody Press, 1991

God's Plan for Giving, John MacArthur, Jr., Moody Press, 1985

God's Will Is Prosperity, Gloria Copeland, Harrison House, 1978

God's Plans for your Finances, Nichols, Whitaker House; (December 1997)

Great People of the Bible and How They Lived; New York: Reader's Digest, 1974

How Can I Ever Afford Children?, Hetzer, John Wiley & Sons; 1 edition (August 24, 1998)

How Much is Enough - Harness the Power of Your Money Story, Klainer, Basic Books; 1st edition
    (December 24, 2001)

How Others Can Help You Get Out of Debt; Esther M. Maddux, Circular 759-3,

How to Have More Than Enough, Ramsey, Penguin USA (Paper); (April 2000)

How to Manage Your Money, Burkett, Moody Publishers; (February 2002)

How to Manage Your Money, Larry Burkett, Moody Press, 1999

How to Personally Profit From the Laws of Success, Sterling Sill, NIFP, Inc., 1978

How to Plan for Your Retirement; New York: Corrigan & Kaufman, Longmeadow Press, 1985

Is God Your Source?, Oral Roberts, 1992

Jesus CEO, Laurie Beth Jones, Hyperion, 1995

Keys to Financial Freedom, Leonard, Legacy Publishers International; (June 2003)

Life Matters, Merrill, McGraw-Hill Trade; (May 16, 2003)

Living Beyond the Possible, Myers, Evangeline Press; (September 2003)

Living on Less and Liking It More, Maxine Hancock, Chicago, Illinois: Moody Press, 1976

Making It Happen, Charles Conn, New Jersey: Fleming H. Revell Company, 1981

Master Your Money or It Will Master You, Arlo E. Moehlenpah, Doing Good Ministries, 1999

Master Your Money, Ron Blue, Tennessee: Thomas Nelson, Inc. 1986

Miracle of Seed Faith, Oral Roberts, 1970

Mississippi State University Extension Service

Money Management for Those Who Don't Have Any, Paris, Harvest House; 1st edition (1997)

Money Talks, Temple, Zondervan; Book and CD-ROM edition (January 1, 2003)

Money, Possessions, and Eternity, Randy Alcorn, Tyndale House, 2003

More Than Enough, David Ramsey, Penguin Putnam Inc, 2002

More Than Enough, Ramsey, Penguin Putnam Inc.; 1st edition (February 15, 2002)

Moving the Hand of God, John Avanzini, Harrison House, 1990

Multiplication, Tommy Barnett, Creation House, 1997

NebFacts, Nebraska Cooperative Extension, NF91-6

Personal Finances, Larry Burkett, Moody Press, 1991

Portable MBA in Finance and Accounting; Livingstone, Canada: John Wiley & Sons, Inc., 1992

Pray and Grow Rich, Briley, Pub in the Glen; (June 1, 1998)

Priceless, Ramsey, J Countryman Books; (July 25, 2002)

Principle-Centered Leadership, Stephen R. Covey, New York: Summit Books, 1991

Principles of Financial Management, Kolb & DeMong, Texas: Business Publications, Inc., 1988

Put Your Money Where Your Morals Are, Scott Fehrenbacher, Broadman & Holman Publishers; (October 2001)

Rapid Debt Reduction Strategies, John Avanzini, HIS Publishing, 1990

Real Wealth, Wade Cook, Arizona: Regency Books, 1985

Rich Dad Poor Dad - What the Rich Teach Their Kids about Money, Kiyosaki, Warner Business; Abridged edition (January 1, 2000)

Rich God Poor God, Avanzini, Abel Press; (April 2001)

See You at the Top, Zig Ziglar, Louisianna: Pelican Publishing Company, 1977

Seed-Faith Commentary on the Holy Bible, Oral Roberts, Pinoak Publications, 1975

Shop, Save, and Share, Kay, Bethany House; (January 2004)

Smart Money, Ken and Daria Dolan, New York: Random House, Inc., 1988

Sound Mind Investing, Pryor, Sound Mind Investings; Revised edition (December 2000)

Speak the Word Over Your Family for Finances, Salem, Harrison House, Incorporated; (May 2003)

Storm Shelter, Blue, Thomas Nelson Inc Publishers;

Strong's Concordance, Tennessee: Crusade Bible Publishers, Inc.,

Success by Design, Peter Hirsch, Bethany House, 2002

Success Is the Quality of Your Journey, Jennifer James, New York: Newmarket Press, 1983

Supernatural Business, Floyd, Creation House; (February 2003)

The 10-Day Financial Breakthrough, Paris, RiverOak Publishing; (April 2002)

The Almighty and the Dollar; Jim McKeever, Oregon: Omega Publications, 1981

The Automatic Millionaire, Bach, Broadway; 1st edition (December 30, 2003)

The Challenge, Robert Allen, New York: Simon And Schuster, 1987

The Family Financial Workbook, Larry Burkett, Moody Press, 2002

The Finish Rich Workbook, Bach, Broadway; Workbook edition (January 1, 2003)

The Great Investment, TD Jakes, Putnam Pub Group; (November 2, 2000)

The Joy of Success, Collins, Quill; (January 6, 2004)

The Law of Rewards, Alcorn, Tyndale House Publishers; (July 2003)

The Management Methods of Jesus, Bob Briner, Thomas Nelson, 1996

The Millionaire Mind, Stanley, Andrews McMeel Publishing; (August 2, 2001)

The Millionaire Next Door, Stanley, Pocket Books; Reprint edition (October 1998)

The Millionaire Next Door, Thomas Stanley & William Danko, Pocket Books, 1996

The Money Book for Kids, Nancy Burgeson, Troll Associates,1992

The Money Book for King's Kids; Harold E. Hill, New Jersey: Fleming H. Revell Company, 1984

The Money Trap, Gallen, HarperResource; 1st edition (February 4, 2003)

The Seven Habits of Highly Effective People, Stephen Covey, New York: Simon And Schuster, 1989

The Shrewd Christian, Atkinson, WaterBrook Press; (February 17, 2004)

The Total Money Makeover, Ramsey, Thomas Nelson; (January 21, 2004)

The Treasure Principle, Alcorn, Multnomah Publishers Inc.; (October 4, 2001)

Theological Wordbook of the Old Testament, Chicago, Illinois: Moody Press, 1981

Treasury of Courage and Confidence, Norman Vincent Peale, New York: Doubleday & Co., 1970

True Prosperity, Dick Iverson, Bible Temple Publishing, 1993

Trust God for Your Finances, Jack Hartman, Lamplight Publications, 1983

University of Georgia Cooperative Extension Service, 1985

Virginia Cooperative Extension

Webster's Unabridged Dictionary, Dorset & Baber, 1983

Woman's Guide to Family Finances, Kay, Bethany House; (January 2004)

Word Meanings in the New Testament, Ralph Earle, Michigan: Baker Book House, 1986

Word Pictures in the New Testament; Robertson, Michigan: Baker Book House, 1930

Word Studies in the New Testament; Vincent, New York: Charles Scribner's Sons, 1914

Worry-Free Family Finances, Staton, McGraw-Hill; (October 28, 2003)

You Can Be Financially Free, George Fooshee, Jr., 1976, Fleming H. Revell Company.

Your Key to God's Bank, Rex Humbard, 1977

Your Money Counts, Howard, Dayton, Tyndale House, 1997

Your Money Management, MaryAnn Paynter, Circular 1271, University of Illinois Cooperative Extension Service, 1987.

Your Money Matters, Malcolm MacGregor, Bethany Fellowship, Inc., 1977

Your Road to Recovery, Oral Roberts, Oliver Nelson, 1986

ONLINE RESOURCES

American Savings Education Council (http://www.asec.org)

Bloomberg.com (http://www.bloomberg.com)

Bureau of the Public Debt Online (http://www.publicdebt.treas.gov)

BusinessWeek (http://www.businessweek.com)

Charles Schwab & Co., Inc. (http://www.schwab.com)

Consumer Federation of America (http://www.consumerfed.org)

Debt Advice.org (http://www.debtadvice.org)

Federal Reserve System (http://www.federalreserve.gov)

Fidelity Investments (http://www.fidelity.com)

Financial Planning Association (http://www.fpanet.org)

Forbes (www.forbes.com)

Fortune Magazine (http://www.fortune.com)

Investing for Your Future (http://www.investing.rutgers.edu)

Kiplinger Magazine (http://www.kiplinger.com/)

Money Magazine (http://money.cnn.com)

MorningStar (http://www.morningstar.com)

MSN Money (http://moneycentral.msn.com)

Muriel Siebert (http://www.siebertnet.com)

National Center on Education and the Economy (http://www.ncee.org)

National Foundation for Credit Counseling (http://www.nfcc.org)

Quicken (http://www.quicken.com)

Smart Money (http://www.smartmoney.com)

Social Security Online (http://www.ssa.gov)

Standard & Poor's (http://www2.standardandpoors.com)

The Dollar Stretcher, Gary Foreman, (http://www.stretcher.com)

The Vanguard Group (http://flagship.vanguard.com)

U.S. Securities and Exchange Commission (http://www.sec.gov)

Yahoo! Finance (http://finance.yahoo.com)

Magazine Resources

Business Week

Consumer Reports

Forbes

Kiplinger's Personal Finance

Money

Smart Money

US News and World Report

Worth

Newspaper Resources

Barrons

USA Today

Wall Street Journal

Washington Times

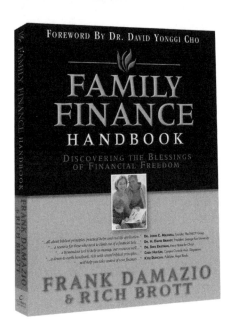

" The *Family Finance Handbook* from Rich Brott and Frank Damazio provides a well-informed financial and stewardship guide for the individual, classroom, small group, and church stewardship presentation. It's all about biblical principles, practical helps and real life application."

DR. JOHN C. MAXWELL
Founder, The INJOY Group

"I pray that our Heavenly Father will abundantly bless your family with financial health through the reading of this book, so that you may also bless others for His glory."

DR. DAVID YONGGI CHO
Senior Pastor, Yoido Full Gospel Church, Seoul, Korea

"Although it is true that the joy of the Lord is our strength, nothing can rob us of that joy more than financial difficulty. The *Family Finance Handbook* is a tremendous tool to help us manage our resources well and thus stay joyfully strong in Jesus. "

DR. DICK EASTMAN
International President, Every Home for Christ

FAMILY FINANCE HANDBOOK

Discovering the Blessings of Financial Freedom

FRANK DAMAZIO & RICH BROTT

With insights gained from twenty-five years in business and ministry, the authors impart to the reader biblical principles of stewardship and financial management. Readers learn how to get out of debt and are carefully guided through the investment process in this comprehensive and well-crafted resource.

Family Life / Finance / Christian Living

Softcover, 288 pages, 7 ½" X 10"
0-914936-60-3

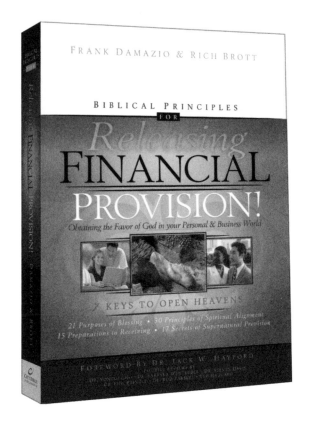